DISCUSSING
AND DECIDING

DISCUSSING AND DECIDING

A Desk Book for Group Leaders and Members

THOMAS M. SCHEIDEL

LAURA CROWELL

University of Washington, Seattle

Macmillan Publishing Co., Inc.
New York
Collier Macmillan Publishers
London

Macmillan Publishing Co., Inc.
866 Third Avenue, New York, New York 10022

Collier Macmillan Canada, Ltd.

Library of Congress Cataloging in Publication Data

Scheidel, Thomas Maynard
   Discussing and deciding.

   Bibliography: p.
   Includes index.
   1. Decision-making, Group. 2. Discussion.
3. Leadership. 4. Small groups. I. Crowell, Laura,
joint author. II. Title.
HD30.23.S34   658.4'03   78-7382
ISBN 0-02-406750-4

Printing 1 2 3 4 5 6 7 8   Year 9 0 1 2 3 4 5

PREFACE

Discussing and Deciding: A Desk Book for Group Leaders and Members is designed for continuing use by anyone whose daily life includes leading or participating in deliberative discussions of small groups. The book should be useful for any person who is concerned with improving the effectiveness of such groups, whether they take place in a school, church, community, business, or other setting.

We see this desk book as part of a person's professional equipment, a tool to be used regularly. The book should therefore be kept handy—on the desk—as a ready aid to help the reader assess a particular group situation he or she may face and to bring to mind quickly some available alternative courses of action for meeting the special conditions of that situation.

It is our hope that this book will do for the participant in a small deliberative group what a book on parliamentary procedure can do for the participant in a large decision-making body. These two settings—small group and parliamentary body—are very different, yet both need structure and some agreed-upon procedures if their goals are to be achieved.

This book can be used with the *Instructor's Manual* in a classroom or workshop setting, or can stand by itself as a ready desk reference for any active citizen or community leader, business or professional person.

Discussing and Deciding is divided into three major parts. The first part gives an overview of the group discussion process, and then develops the significant discussion concepts of task work, team work, and leadership work. The chronological pattern in the second part shows these work activities in interaction and gives a detailed, step-by-step analysis of the group process from premeeting preparation to the handling of the closing minutes themselves. The third part describes a number of special techniques and useful procedures for discussion groups and suggests additional sources for each. In addition, a selected list of shelf books is included that would make good complementary reading for this desk book.

We wish we were able to thank personally the many students in our classes and workshops who, while studying with us, helped to develop these ideas for improving the use of the discussion process. And we want to thank Lloyd Chilton, executive editor of Macmillan's college and professional division, for the support, encouragement, and assistance he has provided throughout our efforts on this book.

T.M.S.
L.C.

TO THE READER

This book is for the desk of any person who leads or takes part in discussion groups.

Shelf
Books

All serious students of group leadership (and of discussion procedures in general) will have carefully chosen books on these subjects on their shelves. These shelf books explain basic psychological and sociological concepts, and give details of myriads of research studies. Such books are valuable resources.

A
Desk
Book

We believe that discussion leaders and members need, in addition, a desk book on discussion procedures, one that distills the most valuable insights on leadership and membership from the rich materials in a dozen fields and from the personal experience and research of its authors. We believe that these highly useful ideas should be presented in clear-cut, relatively brief form for use by intelligent men and women everywhere who use group discussion as a method in community organizations, business and professional work, church, and home.

Flexi-
bility

Although this book can join *Robert's Rules of Order* on a leader's desk, it is not a *Rules of Discussion*. Flexibility, not regularity, is essential in the discussion process. Consequently, this desk book will not present a list of prescriptions, but instead presents a rich variety of possible procedures as alternatives from which an individual LEADER or TEAM MEMBER can draw ideas for ways to meet particular situations and purposes appropriately.

Depth   Pertinent aspects of research studies in sociology, interpersonal relations, communication, conflict-resolution, business management, and the like, and examples from the life about us as well as timeless experiences of our culture are presented to give depth on the points being made. And throughout the desk book, careful footnotes make the path to the shelf books easy for those who want more expanded treatment.

CONTENTS

Part Two The Chronology

Chapter 5

Preparation for the Meeting   111

Chapter 6

The First Few Minutes   137

PART ONE

The Components

CHAPTER 1
THE GROUP
DISCUSSION PROCESS

People often talk together in groups—because they want to, or because they need to, or both. In addition to those business or professional assignments that call for us to join with others in policy-making and decision-making discussions, much of our time outside the family setting involves our work in small groups. We meet in community and service club committees to decide on ways of gathering and handling recyclable materials, in school and church committees to plan creative programs for our children, and in small social groups to share ideas on the higher property assessments just announced, developments in Washington, D.C., or the new boating regulations.

Our personal experiences in these groups vary a great deal. Work with others can be stimulating and enjoyable. We have all felt the exhilaration at the close of a successful group meeting, when we are sorry to leave at the end of the session and we say a few extra good-byes. We have known times when the group product was remarkably good and clearly better than what we could have accomplished if we were each working alone. On the other hand, there are times when we wish we were working alone, when working in a group seems to hinder rather than facilitate effective work on the problem.

What makes the difference between a successful and an unsuccessful meeting? At too many meetings the goal is not understood the same by all members and no plan for reaching the goal is agreed upon and carried out. Some persons habitually come to the meeting unprepared; some can see only their own way, whereas others refuse to get involved deeply at all. In some groups the leader dominates; in others the leader is weak. Success or failure for many groups can be attributed to matters of (1) *procedure* and/or (2) *participation* and/or (3) *leadership*.

1.1 DIFFICULTIES EXPERIENCED IN GROUP WORK

Many task groups fall victim to certain common difficulties. For example, when working in discussion workshops we have begun by presenting a hypothetical problem (written out on one or two pages) to persons in a group we have formed and, without detailed instructions, asked them to reach a decision about the problem. Some interesting observations can be made about the discussions that resulted. With no special tutoring and guidance, these groups, almost without exception, drift into the same set of problems.

1.11 Procedure

Several of the usual difficulties noted in these groups relate to procedures of the group. Examples are as follows:

1. *No procedure established.* These workshop groups rarely begin by considering and agreeing upon a procedure to be followed. They begin without any talk of where they are going (goal) or how they will get there (procedure).

2. *Solution before problem.* The very first comment made is usually a solution—an answer to the discussion question, such as "I think the best solution would be. . . ." —before the group has fully described and clarified the nature of the problem.

3. *Few alternatives considered.* The group rarely considers many of the *feasible* alternative solutions to the problem. Rather, the members settle their discussion on one or two solutions that happen to be offered initially and move rapidly to an ill-founded consensus.

4. *Criteria for solution not developed.* The criteria or standards to be applied to the alternative solutions are seldom listed and elaborated. One or two standards will be mentioned as someone argues for one position, as "I believe this would be a good solution because . . ." but the group members will likely not discuss and settle on a set of standards to be applied to a list of possible solutions.

5. *No uniform application of criteria.* Partly because of these difficulties, the standards for selecting a workable solution are rarely applied uniformly to the various suggested answers to the problem. Thus, one alternative may be rejected for one reason whereas another, somewhat lacking in the same respect, is accepted; the test that brings rejection of one alternative may never be applied to the others.

6. *Consequences of alternatives not considered.* The group members will rarely follow the alternatives through to their consequences. Furthermore, every solution, if adopted, would bring changes to the total system other than the specific ones sought, and these unintended changes are not often contemplated and evaluated. The implications of a proposed course of action are not probed.

But one might say—"Well, what can be expected from groups

meeting to have a brief, impromptu discussion of a topic? And how could a group coming together for the first time, and without any special instructions, be expected to do better? The situation is not typical."

How, then, do "typical" groups proceed? It seems that such groups also experience common difficulties. Irving Janis[1] studied group work and decision making at the highest governmental levels. He listed, and explained in detail in his *Victims of GROUPTHINK*, several major defects in the decision-making groups he studied. Some difficulties he found were as follows:

1. A full range of *alternatives* was not considered.
2. There was a failure to assess fully the *risks and drawbacks* of a course of action.
3. If a possible course of action was initially labeled as unsatisfactory, it never received *full consideration and evaluation*.
4. Little or no attempt was made to get *information from outside experts*.
5. There was a *selective bias* shown in reaction to information and judgments from persons outside the group.
6. Members failed to plan implementation fully and to develop *contingency plans*.

Groups working at the highest national levels probably experience many of the same procedural difficulties observed so often in the workshop groups. Fundamentally, groups— temporary and casual, or extended and crucial—often lack a clear and sound structure for proceeding.

For larger working groups (with, for example, twenty or more members) very specialized rules for proceeding have been developed to control some of the potentially disruptive influences mentioned. The system of "parliamentary procedure" has developed over the past two hundred years to facilitate the transaction of business in accordance with democratic principles in larger groups, such as the British Parliament and the United States Congress. These procedures have been widely applied by groups and organizations to ensure free and full expression of ideas, the rule of the majority, and the protection of the rights of the minority. These procedures have done much to provide order and structure to large group meetings, and when they fail, it is usually because they have been misunderstood or misapplied.

But our concern is with smaller groups, for whom explicit parliamentary procedures are really not appropriate; such rules are too rigid and formal for the fluidity, the give-and-take that is the essence of the small group discussion process. Nevertheless, such basic parliamentary principles as the right of all members to be heard, respect for minority opinions, and the right of all to know what is transpiring, need application in all groups, small as well as large. One set of difficulties frequently noted in decision-making groups is the need for appropriate structures and procedures to facilitate effective group effort.

1.12 Participation

A second type of difficulty noted in the workshop groups relates to the participation of the members.

1. *Poor listening habits*. Members often fail to listen carefully and actively to the others. They seem not to have developed the habits necessary to permit them to think about the problem and, *at the same time*, listen to, understand, and consider the contributions of others.

2. *Failure to develop ideas as a group*. Partly because of their inability to listen, the members of groups often do not seem to be *thinking together* and to be building a line of thought together. Too frequently they engage in a collective monologue in which each person gives his or her own ideas and keeps repeating them without adapting to and taking into consideration the ideas of others. Comments are presented without being related to what has just been said by others.

Janis also found problems of member participation in the groups he investigated. He suggested that *groupthink*, the "deterioration of mental efficiency, reality testing, and moral judgment," can occur in groups with high "cohesiveness" and "concurrence-seeking" tendencies. Janis's reservations are a contemporary echo of earlier views. Nearly a century ago the concept of "group mind" was proposed and discussed by writers such as Gustave Le Bon. Le Bon[2] asserted that in a group the intellectual powers of the individual are diminished whereas the emotions become heightened and take on a more prominent role. Fifty years ago Sigmund Freud[3] made this same observation in writing about group efforts and the ego. The reservations about group deliberation are thus not new.

In the face of these reservations one might well ask whether the work of a group will ever be preferable to that of an individual. By sheer numbers alone a group should be able to bring to a task more mental energy, more accumulated experiences, and more available time for gathering information and time for reflecting on the problem than could any single individual working alone. Yet we know that these resources potentially available to the group are not often fully used.

Many studies by social scientists point to certain conditions that are necessary if the potential advantages of the group setting are to be realized. Marvin Shaw[4] reviewed much of this research and suggests that groups can come up with a greater accuracy and quality of solution than an individual when the group (1) can have a division of labor and a uniting of contributions from individuals, (2) is dealing with a topic demanding creation of ideas or remembering a mass of information, (3) is operating so that some members can recognize and correct the individual errors of others, and (4) has its interest in the topic and a sense of rapport aroused by interaction in the group activity.

Problems of participation are common in all groups. Members need coordination and cohesiveness; they need to be able to work together at the height of their individual capabilities if they are to achieve the most effective group product.

1.13 Leadership

The following problems with leadership were found to be common in the workshop groups.

1. *Leaderless drift.* Without having a leader appointed beforehand, the group tends to drift until someone finally takes over. Many of the difficulties listed in the preceding sections begin during this drifting. Once begun, these problems seem to gain a momentum that makes them very difficult to correct.

2. *The wrong person takes over.* The person who emerges as leader during this drifting later often seems to have been the wrong choice. Robert Bales supports the likelihood of this occurring early in a group that discusses without an appointed leader:

> A work-acceptant person who likes to analyze and give his opinion is generally more active than one who is cautious and

likes to confine his contributions, so far as possible, to giving information only. And the one who likes to give suggestions is more dominant still. Dominant members not only have a high total rate of participation, but they are likely to want to participate as early as possible in the meeting, and to get ahead with the action immediately.[5]

Thus, the person who emerges as leader early in these workshop groups tends to be solution-minded rather than problem-minded, and will tend to advocate a personal position instead of seeking full group participation.

3. *Others attempt to dislodge the person dominating.* Since the person now dominating the group came to the front by self-assertion rather than by a clear and agreed-upon way, others see the same path continually open to them. This constant jockeying for power means that the group without an appointed leader may never have a chance to enjoy the benefits of stable organization.

Janis has noted that the leaders in the groups he studied tended to (1) state personally preferred solutions too early in the group meeting and (2) stifle thereby free and full contributions from others in the group.

Many studies have compared leadership styles,[6] ranging from a dictatorial (that is, rigid control and dominance) to a laissez-faire (no control and withdrawal) approach. The middle ground, in which an appointed leader provides procedural direction, emotional support, and some substantive comments—when and to the extent that these contributions are appropriate and needed—appears to maximize the group potential and overcomes as much as possible the group difficulties that concern leadership.

1.2   **RATIONALE OF THIS BOOK**

Our concern is with interaction as it takes place in small groups assembled to discuss a common problem. How small are "small groups?" We see such groups as having five, seven, ten or so members, one of whom acts as leader. Each group of this type will vary from others over a number of dimensions:

1. *Number of meetings.* Members may meet just once or a number of times.

2. *Whom represented.* Members may represent no one but themselves, or each member may be a delegate appointed to serve the interests of a particular organization or group.

3. *Solution for whom.* The group's decision may be derived for the personal enlightenment of the decision makers, as the basis of action by this group or others, or as a recommendation to some official or group.

4. *Significance.* The decision may be urgent or casual.

5. *Informed.* Members may be well informed or with little knowledge, specific or general.

6. *Group skills.* Members may have a high degree of group skills (of interaction, of communication, of problem solving) or they may be inexperienced and reticent.

7. *Acceptance of leader.* Members may expect the leader to run the show, from providing the information to providing the solution, or they may balk at his suggestions and try to handle the problem themselves.

There may be several points between the extremes in many of these items, and within the group the individual members may range from one end of the continuum to the other. Clearly, no one set of suggestions to members and leaders could cover all the possible combinations of factors that make each group unique. Nevertheless, many strategies, approaches, and practices can be suggested that should help those working in small groups. Our intention is to present and illustrate several of these approaches. The reader can then choose, modify, and integrate whichever suggestions seem appropriate and useful for a given, admittedly unique, situation.

There is a common disparagement of "how to do it" books; perhaps this is a general reaction against the practical, or, indeed, the overly practical. It is assuredly also a reaction against the flood of guidebooks that now threatens to inundate us, each declaring that it contains all the answers needed to lead us to fame, fortune, a better personality, greater physical beauty, and a happier life.

It is nevertheless our intention to attempt a "how to do it," one, however, *with a difference.* We believe that the small discussion group is the atom of our social order, and we mean to present practical suggestions for improving the quality of the interaction and the output of those groups. Research results and theoretical formulations underscore what we know from

our everyday experiences in group meetings: that exact prescriptions and detailed rules cannot be given. Realizing that
individuals and situations differ and that each is unique, we
believe that it is yet possible to suggest alternatives, formats,
and strategies that have worked better than others. Our aim is
to present several possible courses of action and to suggest
standards by which to choose one over another in a given case.
As with any art, training and practice can lead to improvement.

1.3   **BASIC ASSUMPTIONS OF THIS BOOK**

The analyses and suggestions presented in this book arc
guided by four basic assumptions.

1.31   Every Discussion Group Has a Task and Can Be Viewed As a TASK Group

An individual may go to work in the morning and be asked
to sit in on a meeting aimed at devising an advertising campaign
for a new company product. Later in the day he or she may
meet with a small group to hear reports about a number of
proposed new products and decide on the priorities for their
production—which of these new products should go into production? with what resources and on what schedule? Still later
this person may meet with members of other divisions in the
company to organize the United Fund campaign; the aim here
would be to develop a smoothly operating and efficient campaign. After work he or she could attend a League of Women
Voters meeting to exchange ideas and information on political
issues of concern or attend a church fellowship meeting or a
Parents Without Partners meeting in which mutual support and
social interaction would be the major goal. He or she may also
attend a group therapy session with the hope of finding help
to stop smoking or to lose weight, or to improve self-abilities
in coping with any number of personal problems.

In each of these groups there is a task to be accomplished, a
goal sought, work to be done. Even when a meeting has a
largely *social* aim, we can consider the means to that social end
as the task or work to be done. It is the underlying task that
prevents a group meeting with a social goal from becoming

merely a party. A personal growth group or assertiveness training group may have no goal outside the personal development
of the group members, but that development is a task.[7] In this
sense we believe that every group that meets with an end-to-
be-accomplished can be viewed as a TASK group and can be
evaluated in terms of its TASK performance.

1.32   Every Discussion Group Can Be Viewed As a TEAM

Consider a baseball team as a model of a small working group.
The Giants clearly have a goal or task to accomplish. We can
describe and evaluate their efforts in terms of that task—how
many games did they win? Did they come home with the
division title? These questions relate to the ultimate task, the
final goal. It is also possible to evaluate how they went about
accomplishing the task, how they *played the game*. It is possible
to say that a certain player is an excellent pitcher, has a 21–8
record, and has contributed much to the team's success. Or we
might say that another player, an outfielder, batted .325 and
hit 35 home runs, and was largely responsible for the season
record. The contributions of both the pitcher and the outfielder
have been helpful in the group task. If we were to analyze the
abilities and skills needed and the work done by these players
we would see great differences, yet they have been working
together toward a common goal. The ball team is truly a small
group with a task.

If ball players are to be successful in achieving their goal of
winning the pennant they will need good TEAMwork. It is
difficult to specify what makes a successful team, but some
answers are possible. To be successful in any given season the
group first needs able personnel for the various jobs that must
be done. But the club needs more than personnel. The members
will not be successful without effective teamWORK. The individual efforts must be coordinated and integrated: the pitcher
and catcher must work together; the outfielder and infielder
must work together. As the outfielder catches a ball the infielder
must move into position for the throw that will be coming.
The outfielder must be able to catch the ball and throw, knowing where the infielder will be. Knowing what you must do,
and doing it, and knowing what the others must do, and being
able to count on its being done—this is TEAM WORK.

The task and team work evidenced by a sports team is familiar to us all. To consider a small discussion group in similar terms may at first seem unusual. But we would like to suggest just that; to emphasize the parallels between sports teams and discussion groups. We have asserted that every discussion group is a TASK group and has TASK WORK to be done. We have now suggested that every effective discussion group must also demonstrate TEAM WORK. Discussion groups are potentially TEAMS and their progress can be described and evaluated in terms of TEAM WORK as well as in terms of TASK WORK.

1.33   The Discussion TEAM Is Focused on Its TASK by Its LEADER

Every sporting team has a manager who is primarily and mainly responsible for integrating the work of the individual players. The manager assumes the responsibility for coordinating their efforts, and he keeps their attention on their goal. Again, the sports team parallels the discussion group: the small discussion group also requires a leader who can coordinate the work of the group members, who will focus the attention of the group members on the goal. The leader can keep the larger view and context in mind while the members concentrate on the immediate aspect. Some group members provide spirit and enthusiasm as well as ideas; others are quieter but may be depended upon for valid information at every meeting. But the group needs *one person* whose primary and most essential duty is to coordinate the efforts of the members and to focus them on the TASK.

For a time it was unfashionable to write about designated leaders in groups. The argument was that groups would not need assigned leaders because the leadership duties could be shared by all, or a single "true" leader would emerge during the meetings. Some behavioral scientists of the 1950s and 1960s took up the issue, holding that *shared* leadership was more "democratic." Practical men such as Douglas McGregor, an eminent industrial philosopher who applied theories of social psychology to practical problems of management, stood against this displacement of the leader. Most real discussion groups, such as school boards, divisions of a business, and community study groups, have a person who is designated to serve as the leader. Most task discussion groups, as most sporting teams, have leaders and work efficiently when their leaders take over these duties of coordination and focusing. John Adair, who as adviser on leadership training at Sandhurst between 1963 and 1968 developed a course that was used widely in the British armed forces and in industrial programs in Britain as well, described his concept of a leader as:

> a person with certain qualities of personality and character, which are appropriate to the general *situation* and supported by a degree of relevant technical knowledge and experience, who is able to provide the necessary *functions* to guide a group towards the further realization of its purpose, while maintaining and building its unity as a team; doing all this in the right ratio or proportion with the contributions of the other members of the team.[8]

This is the leader of whom we speak in this book. This leader is not inherently different from the other group members except in specific duties and responsibilities. Some of these specific tasks may at times be performed spontaneously by members, but how much the leader shares these coordinating and focusing duties with members will depend upon the situation. It is the duty of the leader, however, to make certain that all such acts needed by the group are performed.

A group with an important TASK that can work as a TEAM under the guidance of an able LEADER is a situation heartily to be desired. It is a goal toward which we hope to make some contribution.

1.34 Any Discussion Group TEAM (Members and Leader) Can Improve Its Work Significantly by Careful Study and Application of Sound Group Discussion Methods

We have said that this will be a "how to do it" book—but *with a difference*. We cannot give absolute and certain prescriptions. But we can and will present detailed suggestions of possible patterns and procedures for incorporation into the planning and progress of the group. Concepts and strategies that are useful for members and for leaders are considered.

In speech communication education, which has been a topic of scholarly concern for over two thousand years, there has always been the question of nature or nurture. Can a person's basic abilities and aptitudes be improved? The answer from the ancient Greek and Roman speech teachers onward has been Yes. They have counseled us to take basic abilities as givens and build upon them. For thousands of years this training has helped in communication. All of our own educational practice is built on the Yes answer to that question. And we know from our combined fifty years of experience in teaching group discussion courses, workshops, and seminars that such training, if undertaken seriously and with active involvement, can lead to significant improvement in discussion abilities.

1.4   PLAN OF THIS BOOK

This book is divided into three parts. In the first part we examine the basic components of discussion groups meeting for a variety of purposes, such as sharing information, probing ideas, evaluating alternatives, and making decisions. The second part is concerned with the interaction of these components in chronological order and in detail, moving from the preparation necessary before the group meeting to follow-up evaluations of group productivity. In the third part we present details of special techniques, approaches, and methods as resources applicable to particular situations. Also we offer a list of shelf books with annotations to help in the reader's selection and use.

But this book is a desk book, one to be kept within reach of your hand, ready for easy and frequent use.

FOOTNOTES—CHAPTER 1

1. Irving Janis, *Victims of GROUPTHINK* (Boston: Houghton Mifflin Company, 1972). See especially Chapters 1, 8, and 9.
2. Gustave Le Bon, *The Crowd: A Study of the Popular Mind* (New York: The Viking Press, 1960). Originally published in 1895.
3. Sigmund Freud, *Group Psychology and the Analysts of the Ego* (New York: Bantam Books, Inc., 1960). Originally published in 1921.
4. Marvin E. Shaw, *Group Dynamics: The Psychology of Small Group Behavior*, 2d ed. (New York: McGraw-Hill Book Company, 1976), pp. 58–80.
5. Robert F. Bales, "Communication in Small Groups," in George A. Miller, *Communication, Language, and Meaning* (New York: Basic Books, Inc., 1973), p. 215.
6. Shaw, *Group Dynamics*, pp. 275–279.
7. Speaking of psychotherapy, W. R. Bion asserted: "Every group, however casual, meets to 'do' something . . . . When patients meet for a group-therapy session it can always be seen that some mental activity is directed to the solution of the problems for which the individuals seek help." *Experiences in Groups* (New York: Basic Books, Inc., 1959), pp. 143–144.
8. John Adair, *Action-Centred Leadership* (London: McGraw-Hill Book Company, Ld., 1973), p. 15.

CHAPTER 2
THE TASK WORK

2.1 Sound Thinking

    2.11 Need for Information

    2.12 Need for Idea-Development

    2.13 Need for Management of Differences in Information and Idea-Development

2.2 Systematic Thinking

    2.21 Problem Management Sequence

2.3 Conclusion

"Eureka!" shouted Archimedes as he leaped from his bath and ran naked through the streets. He had been trying for some time to find a way to determine whether any silver had been mixed with gold in a crown that had been made for the king of Syracuse. When he stepped into his tub and it overflowed, the principle of displacement flashed to his mind, and he ran out shouting "Eureka! Eureka!" ("I have found it! I have found it!"). Similar stories of sudden scientific insights have been told involving Galileo, Newton, Watt, and many others.

But problem solving and decision making in groups is a different matter. The essence of the work of a task group is *thinking together*. Even if one group member were to have a sudden insight, it would not be wise for that person to run out shouting "Eureka!" The idea should first be presented clearly and understandably to the others in the group, who can all consider and evaluate it; they can think together about it. An individual will often accept a faulty idea, one that may be caught and rejected by other members of a group. One of the great advantages of group thinking is that it keeps many people from running about shouting "Eureka."

One major requirement for group thinking is effective communication. Group thinking must be overt (observable and observed), capable of being communicated, and communicated. Individual thinking can be internal and implicit, but group thinking must be open and explicit, communicated and considered by all the group members. To be maximally effective, group thinking must reveal two qualities that are more easily named and explained than performed: *sound thinking* and *systematic thinking*. [1]

2.1   SOUND THINKING

Evidence and the *inferences* based upon that evidence are the stepping-stones of thought. Evidence is the basic data with which we work, and inference is the process by which we move from the known data to claims, relationships, and speculations beyond that data. We may have the facts or evidence on the sales of a certain product and on the current market situation, but inference is needed to estimate what the sales will be in the coming quarter. In inferences we move beyond the known to the unknown. Group thinking requires careful assessment and agreement both on matters of evidence and inference. These two elements make up the "ideas" that are developed by the group process.

Group members should face three important needs in developing ideas.

2.11   Need for Information

Throughout the thinking process group members must ask whether they have accurate facts and sufficient facts: *accurate* in what they tell us and *sufficient* in covering all aspects that need to be covered. Evidence comes in many forms: specific examples and instances, historical cases, graphic illustrations, accounting data, summary reports, predictions of trends, analogies with similar situations, experiences of individuals, and experts' judgments and opinions. These forms of evidence differ from each other in the sturdiness of the grounding they offer us, not only on the basis of their appropriateness to a particular problem but also intrinsically, that is, on the basis of their internal validity, whatever the problem. A group must spare no effort to see that "facts" are correct in detail, true to the reality they represent, and not slanted in the telling. When we use someone's expert opinion as grounding, that opinion should be examined for its essential reasonableness and the giver of the opinion should be examined for his or her expertise and freedom from vested interest.

The following are some of the tests of evidence and of the sources of evidence that group members can apply:

TESTS OF EVIDENCE AND SOURCES

Evidence

1. *Accurate*? Is the evidence as presented accurate, correct, and true?
2. *Appropriate*? Is the evidence appropriate? Does it fit exactly what the group is discussing? Are the cases presented typical and representative, or are they atypical and unusual examples?
3. *Recent*? Is the evidence the most recent available? Or is it dated? Is it collected at an appropriate time for the specific question being considered?
4. *Consistent*? Are all the items of evidence consistent with each other? Do they fit together in a meaningful pattern?

Source

1. *Accurately cited*? Is the source quoted correctly? Or could the statement be taken out of context?
2. *Competent*? Is the source truly an expert on this matter? An expert in one field may not be an expert in another.
3. *Reliable*? Is the source reliable? Is the source known to be dependable for providing sound evidence?
4. *Biased*? Is the source known to have any special bias or prejudice on this topic?
5. *Vested interest*? Will the source profit personally if his or her testimony is accepted? The most convincing expert is one who testifies counter to his or her own special interests.

The group members need information, gathered personally or gained from testimony by authorities, on which to ground their thinking and idea-development. The questions just listed may be usefully applied to test the dependability of the group's facts and information.

2.12 Need for Idea-Development

Additional tests are appropriate when the group members move beyond the basic evidence in their development of ideas. In the cooperative development of ideas a thought comes before the group like a piece of modeling clay, tentatively shaped for group consideration by one member; in the hands of the group it is changed, added to, and reshaped as the members work collectively toward their goal. This piecemeal task is accomplished by suggestions from the entire group, each contributing his or her best insights to the matter at hand. Attempts to determine which participant is contributing most are irrelevant; the *group-developed* thought-line is the important thing. One member carries the thought-line onward until another takes over its development momentarily and then another. The members are pursuing a line of thinking together; each helps wherever and however possible.

Two kinds of contributions that assist in *idea-production* should be distinguished, those concerning the substance of the discussion itself and those concerning matters of group procedure. Contributions relating directly to the content of the discussion topic—adding facts, raising an exception, requesting an example, and so forth—may be termed *substantive* contributions. Those relating to the mechanics—schedule for accomplishing the mutual task, matters of participation or use of time, the "policing" and managing functions, and so forth—may be termed *procedural* contributions. Substantive contributions will far outnumber procedural comments in a successful discussion group, but procedural contributions will be necessary to assure the optimum flow of substantive comments.

Group members should be alert to these two different types of comment and the needs they fill in developing group ideas. A group may work with several substantive thoughts at a time in developing an idea, but it is better not to carry on with unresolved substantive *and* procedural thoughts at the same time. Generally it is better to stick with and resolve a procedural question before moving to the next substantive matter, and vice versa.

Group members will also be working for *idea-correction*. All members should be checking every contribution for *clarity*, *relevance*, *soundness*, and *significance*, and providing any needed corrections.

The group must work to make ideas *clear*. Is the thought understandable and interpreted similarly by the group members? Once an idea has been presented it can be helpful for others to rephrase it in their own words and check to see if they have clearly understood what the other person had in mind. "Is the point, then, that . . . ?" "Are you saying . . . ?"

Is the idea *relevant* to the topic under discussion and to the specific point under discussion? Irrelevancies and tangents are major pitfalls for group work. A comment may be appropriate to the topic, but be out of phase with the particular point being discussed, and therefore be irrelevant at the moment.

TESTS OF INFERENCE AND IDEA-DEVELOPMENT

Making Generalizations

1. *Abundant instances*? Is the generalization based upon a sufficient number of instances? Is the size of the sample tested large enough?
2. *Typical instances*? Are the conclusions reasoned from typical cases?
3. *Negative instances*? Are only positive instances and examples offered? Are there any negative (counter) cases?

Using Analogies

1. *Figurative analogies used for proof*? Are the two cases compared from similar domains (as if comparing two cities and thereby using a *literal* analogy) or from different domains (as if comparing a city to a heart and thereby using a *figurative* analogy)? Are figurative analogies used appropriately for clarity and illustration or are they used to establish proof for the idea-development?

2. *Literal analogy adequate*? If a literal analogy is drawn, do the *significant* items of similarity far outweigh any differences?

Inferring Causation

1. *Confusing correlation for causation*? If two events occur together care must be taken in labeling one the cause of the other (A causes B). The reverse could be true (B causes A). Or both could be effects of a different unspecified cause (C causes both A and B).
2. *Cause or effect*? Most events can be viewed both as effects and causes; that is, effects of what led to them and causes of what follows from them. In reasoning about causation, attention must be given to considering the appropriate levels.

Is the idea contributed a *sound* idea, that is, one to be relied upon? All forward movements of the group's thought-line should be tested out with much the same procedure as that of a climber making progress up a steep rock face. The choice of the next possible footing is guided by the general notion that it will support the weight to be put upon it, but the consequent use of that ledge is dependent upon how well it holds up to tentative testing. And it is the same with a group; the group reaches forward with information and inference toward new segments of the thought-line and gives especially careful, tentative testing to important or questionable segments as it goes. A member should question openly any idea he or she considers to be unsound.

To test the soundness of thinking, members should learn to differentiate between the *evidence* used by the group and the *inferences* or thought-line development based upon that evidence. Just as tests of evidence and sources were listed earlier, it is also possible to list some tests for inference and idea-development. These questions should assist group members in assessing the soundness of their thinking.

Finally, group members should assess the *significance* of the ideas under consideration. Is this idea being given too little importance? Or too much? The idea's relationship to the larger framework of the total discussion should be examined. If the significance attributed to an idea is inappropriate, the correction should be made by the group.

2.13 **Need for Management of Differences in Information and Idea-Development**

Differences in ideas occur in discussion groups at several identifiable levels. The following scheme for analysis, adapted from suggestions by Barnlund and Haiman,[2] should be helpful for the group participant who is aiming to improve the validity of the group thinking.

Drawing upon their extensive research in small group discussion, Barnlund and Haiman list five different levels at which group conflict may develop. They suggest that group members should understand at which level the difficulty is occurring; they then can attempt to resolve it at that level but, if unsuccessful, they can move to another level.

Levels of Potential Conflict and Conflict Management

1. assertion
2. reasons
3. evidence
4. values
5. group goal

Differences often appear at the level of *assertion*: "The public schools are failing." "Criminal rehabilitation just doesn't work." Assertions such as these may well be the starting points of conflict; they need to be examined by the group. The tests of idea-correction listed can be applied: Is the meaning clear? Is the point relevant, sound, and significant? The assertion may be discounted as failing to meet these standards. If not, the work of the group in fleshing out the idea for judgment by use of these criteria should help to prepare it for further assessment. If resolution cannot be achieved at this level, the group should try at a different level.

Group members could suggest movement to another level by asking, "What are the *reasons* behind this assertion?" Members can work together on this thinking and they may come up with reasons for the assertions mentioned, such as "Standardized test scores are dropping" and "There is a very high rate of recidivism." The connections between these suggested reasons and the assertions previously made can be probed by the group. Do the reasons support the assertions? Is the inference sound? At this level some errors in reasoning may become clear and the substantive problem can be resolved. But perhaps not.

If not, the group members may then ask "What is the *evidence* we can find to back up these reasons?" They might investigate "What test scores are dropping? How much drop is there? How appropriate are the tests themselves?" Such questions ask for evidence and move the conflict toward resolution. At this point the tests of evidence listed earlier could be applied.

If all of these attempts still do not resolve the problem, the group should consider the level of *values*. The substantive conflict may not be found to be based on differences or misunderstandings about evidence or assertions, or reasons. The difference may be found to lie at the level of values, with members working from essentially different value systems. One may believe firmly that "prisons are for punishment," whereas another may be convinced that "prisons exist for rehabilitation." Such basic differences in values can sometimes bring group progress to a halt, but it is hoped that they need not. If the conflict is centered at this level, the group should discuss the values and try to draw out the differences clearly. It may be possible then to assess the evidence and reasons supporting those competing values. But our values are usually developed over a long period and are firmly set; we cannot expect significant shifts in values to result from group meetings. Nevertheless, if the difficulty exists at the level of values it is best that the group members know this to be the case; then they can attempt mutual modification or suspend judgment.

In the end, one basic value is shared by all group members who agree to come together to discuss problems and policies— and that is a common desire to reach the *group goal*. The group goal may, in the last resort, suffice to provide the motivation needed for group members to resolve substantive differences or to make the accommodations necessary to permit continuation of the development of the thought-line.

It is not necessary, of course, that every substantive conflict occurring in a group be worked out. But such differences should be analyzed and evaluated as a part of sound group thinking. The five levels presented here may be useful for such analysis, and the notion of moving from one level to another may serve as a useful strategy for managing these differences.

The consideration of these various needs and the application of the recommended tests should help to ensure that group thought will be *sound*. It should be obvious that, although all of these tests are applicable and can be considered, not every one could be or need be fully developed in the group meetings. We have attempted to be complete in our listing but, clearly, only *significant points at issue* require careful, explicit group discussion. Appropriate checks for soundness should be made throughout the discussion.

2.2   **SYSTEMATIC THINKING**

Group thinking will be most effective if it is systematic. But what the "system" should be is perhaps the most difficult of all questions for task groups. It requires some detailed examination.

A wide range of procedures has been proposed for use by decision-making and policy-making groups. At one extreme, for example, is the system proposed by the Dutch economist Jan Tinbergen,[3] who advocates a complete and very comprehensive analysis. His system requires thorough work especially on three crucial steps: (1) a clear set of values and long-range goals should be agreed upon initially, (2) a comprehensive search for alternative plans should be pursued, and (3) the potential consequences of alternative courses of action should be considered prior to any final selection of a plan to be adopted. Systems such as this, considered as ideal by Tinbergen, have orderly procedure, sequential development, and completeness and comprehensiveness as their hallmarks. Some persons have labeled such systems as the "rational" approach.

On the other extreme are "incrementalist" systems such as that presented by David Braybrooke and Charles E. Lindblom in *A Strategy of Decision*.[4] These scholars argue that the "rationalist" system is too demanding. They suggest that we have neither the time nor the intellectual resources to make comprehensive investigations of most of our genuine social problems. Their system asks that we remain problem oriented rather than become goal oriented, and that we seek merely to get away from the problem without defining a distant goal toward which to strive. As a second requirement the incrementalist system asks that we move away from the problem with a course of action only slightly (a small step) different from the status quo. It holds that if we take only a small step with our new action the risk is limited and we can usually return to the present system if the new approach fails. The incrementalist approach is orderly, exploratory, and conservative. It has been described as a process of "muddling through." It seeks piecemeal reform rather than radical transformation.

But there is also a middle ground. Sociologist Amitai Etzioni,[5] one exponent of this position, has proposed a "mixed-scanning" approach that attempts to combine some of the most useful elements from the rationalist and the incrementalist approaches. We draw on mixed-scanning, the rational system, and the incremental system in presenting what we believe to be the most useful comprehensive system—the Problem Management Sequence. We present a basic outline for that system, a description of its elements, and then illustrate its application to one social problem.

2.21 Problem Management Sequence

The Problem Management Sequence is important for several reasons. First, it is the classic pattern for problem solving with the longest theoretical roots. In 1910 the distinguished American philosopher and educator John Dewey described his five "Steps to Reflective Thinking."[6]

1. *A felt difficulty.* Something perplexing and puzzling occurs in our experience. A new situation occurs for which we have no answer, or perhaps an older "tried and true" solution breaks down and no longer fits the needs. We have a problem.

2. *Location and definition of the difficulty.* Observations are made and data are gathered to make clear just where the difficulty lies and what it is. The attempt is made to discover fully the nature of the problem.

3. *Suggestions of possible solutions.* Alternative hypotheses and potential solutions to the problem are advanced at this stage. The suggested alternatives grow out of the careful analysis made as a result of the second step.

4. *Mental exploration and elaboration of alternative hypothesized solutions.* The meaning and implications of the various possible solutions are probed. The consequences are investigated. We reason: "If this hypothesis is true, then it follows that. . . ."

5. *Further observation and experimentation.* Here we test by specific and planned observation the proposed hypotheses and their implications in order to accept or reject them. We make a decision.

Dewey's steps were intended to describe the process by which an individual solves problems. In our view, group decision making is a somewhat different matter. The group members must communicate and make their ideas explicit and understandable. The individual need not do this. The group members must give some consideration as to *how* they will "think together," that is, to procedural matters. Group members must articulate and agree upon standards of judgment to be applied. Despite these differences, the Dewey steps have played a significant role in the evolution of the Problem Management Sequence.

The Problem Management Sequence is also important because it is potentially one of the most comprehensive patterns. At least the leader, if not *all* group members, should be familiar with this sequence. One can always omit the subordinate aspects of a complex system to fit a specific situation, and if one understands a complex pattern it is easier to comprehend and use a simpler pattern. One who can play bridge or chess can pick up hearts or checkers fairly easily. It does not, however, work the other way. Knowing the simpler does not equip a person to be able immediately to work with the more complicated. For most social problems the pressure of time, resources, and abilities of the group participants would require some limiting of the full PMS approach. Nevertheless, group members would do well to know and start with the full sequence in mind.

Groups meet for many purposes that are less demanding than the need for comprehensive problem management and decision making, as we have emphasized. A reading group, for example, may meet with the limited goal of exchanging information and opinions about a book or report the members all have read. The task requirements of this group are contained within the larger task requirements of the Problem Management Sequence; indeed, presentation of information occurs at many points in the sequence. So there is no need to consider information-sharing group functions as being separate and unique. Group participants who are in command of the more comprehensive PMS should have all the skills required for sharing information. The same would be true for groups meeting to set up standards or to make a choice between alternatives, and even the somewhat different purpose of developing interpersonal relationships and group rapport.

Our own experience with teaching the sequence has resulted in considerable support for it. One former student, as a new employee in Washington State government, was assigned to set up a working conference with representatives from four adjacent states. Recalling the Problem Management Sequence he had been taught ten years before in a Principles of Group Discussion course at the University of Washington, he arranged morning sessions to examine the nature and causes of the problem and afternoon sessions to suggest standards for solutions, to list alternative solutions, and to reason to a choice among solutions. Before the meeting he sent out an agenda sheet that included relevant questions to be taken up in each of the four sessions. Later that week, jubilant over the success of the conference in its task and in the members' response to the procedures used, he wrote to his former professor: "Keep teaching that outline in your classes! *It works*." Repeated testimonials of this type convince us of the value of knowing the PMS thoroughly.

But effort, ability, and experience with the sequence are needed if the Problem Management Sequence is to have optimum usefulness. Just as "common sense is not really very common," there is no certainty that a group adopting the PMS will be successful. The special needs and constraints of the particular situation must be assessed and adaptations of the sequence must be planned. As any other tool, the Problem Management Sequence can be misused.

Our adaptation of the Problem Management Sequence may be outlined as follows:

STEP I.   Describing the problem
  A. Clarifying "problem" terms in the discussion question
  B. Specifying symptoms (signs) of the problem
  C. Appraising size and scope of the problem
   1. Extent, trends, and seriousness
   2. Implications
   3. Inadequacies of present programs
  D. Synthesizing nature and urgency of the problem

STEP II.   Analyzing the problem
  A. Searching out causes and underlying conditions
  B. Planning the approach
   1. Choosing DIRECTION of attack
   2. Clarifying CRITERIA for judging plans of attack
    a. Utility (quantity and quality)
    b. Feasibility (availability of resources— men, money, and materials)
    c. Promptness (of installation and of effect)
    d. Congruency with BOUNDARIES (values that must not be harmed too much)

STEP III.   Proposing plans for managing the problem
  A. Listing and describing proposals
  B. Pruning to an active list (preliminary assessment)

STEP IV.   Selecting "best" plan for managing the problem
  A. Comparing alternatives (on criteria) to select "best" plan
  B. Comparing "best" plan with untouched symptoms to determine worthwhileness

This outline is now fleshed out by detailing and explaining the steps of the Problem Management Sequence.

Table 2-1.

STEPS	EXPLANATION
STEP I. DESCRIBING THE PROBLEM	A problem is present when there is (1) a hurtful situation, one that actually brings injury, or (2) a distressing gap between *what is* and *what could be* or *ought to be.*[7] It is this undesired state of affairs that the group proposes to describe, analyze, and plan a remedy for.
A. Clarifying "problem" terms in the discussion question	To focus their efforts effectively the group needs to agree on definitions of any key terms that may be construed differently by various members. On the question, How can we best increase voter turnout in our municipal elections?, the group would need to clarify the key words *voter turnout* (are absentee voters included or not?) and *municipal elections* (the immediate ones only or all the ones to come?); the other words—framework words—probably need no attention. Someone might want to define *increase* in order to clarify the size of the problem ahead, but the definition could be better answered in the third part of this first step where the group will have worked out its description of the problem's "nature and urgency."
B. Specifying symptoms (signs) of the problem	Here the group's search begins— of how the problem has manifested itself, what "hurts" it has introduced and to whom. The members not only need to assure themselves that the problem truly *exists* but to come to know what forms its hurtful results are taking: not only *that* the problem *is*, but *what* it *is*.

Data on specific instances as well as statistics on occurrences, increases, decreases, and the like, of injuries, injustices, hardships, and all gaps between *what is* and *what could be* or *ought to be* need examination.

This examination must include *all* the relevant symptoms (data must, of course, be current and accurate) or all the subsequent work of the group will be distorted and undependable from this point on. Were important symptoms overlooked, they would be analyzing and trying to remedy a problem that *does not exist* in the form that they are talking about.

C. Appraising size and scope of the problem

Whereas the work of specifying the symptoms and signs was to look at each manifestation of the problem separately, the *appraising* step turns back to look at the problem *as a whole*— How widespread is it? What trends can be seen in the way it shows itself? How frequent and how harmful have the "hurts" been in comparison with what they might have been? Actually, how large do they loom in their challenge to our well-being? Thus, the group reasons from its survey of the present situation to a judgment of how serious the problem really is.

1. Extent, trends, and seriousness

The reporting on the extent and trends is quantitative, but judging the degree of seriousness is qualitative in nature: *extent* asks *How much*? *trends* asks *What changes*? and *seriousness* asks *How bad*?

2. Implications

But the harmful effects occurring now are not the only ones to be considered. Harmful effects that seem likely to occur in the somewhat distant future—if nothing is done to handle the problem beyond what is being done at the present time—must also be examined.

Certain present symptoms may be greatly intensified in the future, or entirely new injuries to individual or public welfare may result from this problem. The group's concept of the size and scope of the problem must include an appraisal of any likely widespread, far-distant bad results, any cloud on the future it creates.

3. Inadequacies of present programs

In most situations some programs are already in effect to try to manage the problem but these programs are not, for various reasons, fully successful (otherwise the symptoms that have been discovered would not exist). The size and scope, as examined by the group, must include consideration of these programs and their primary flaws.

Furthermore, this look at inadequate present programs will give information that may be useful in later steps of the PMS. Sometimes one or more of these presently failing plans can be improved sufficiently to stand as one of the alternatives listed in Step III and, perhaps, compared with others in Step IV. Also, knowing flaws that have made these plans unsuccessful can at times reveal factors in the mood of the general public, and thus give warning of what to avoid or handle differently in the plans considered in Steps III and IV.

D. Synthesizing nature and urgency of the problem

From the detailing of the symptoms and signs a brief, clear pictorial statement of the *nature* of the problem can be drawn.

This vivid statement not only serves as synthesized description of the problem but may be helpful in working out the list of causes in Step II.

From the examination of the size and scope of the problem, inferences can be drawn on *how urgent* the need for improvement in managing the problem truly is. Such a decision is basic to later thought on how much time, energy, and money can be spent on it, for whatever resources are used in managing the problem under consideration are thereby removed from other serious problems.

STEP II.   ANALYZING THE PROBLEM

A. Searching out causes and underlying conditions

From suggestions of various analysts as well as from members' experiences and knowledge, a listing of all significant *causes* should be produced. This listing can also include any *conditions* in the problem situation that allow, invite, or precipitate the operation of the causes without themselves actually producing the problem.

For example, if a group were studying the causes of devastating forest fires in a certain area, it would be necessary for the members to list campers' cigarettes and the unpredictable occurrence of lightning strikes (both *active* CAUSES), but it would also be helpful for the group to consider the amount and nature of dry, accumulated underbrush in the forested areas (a potential *contributing* CONDITION).

Causes are like slippery eels. As you grab one it slips away. Since a group can always find a deeper cause springing from a still deeper one, it must ask where to stop and at which level it should work. For example, what about the causes of the headache, fever, and generally weak feeling that let you know you have a cold? The immediate cause is an unseen and not directly felt virus. And the virus may require special conditions to cause the cold—a general physical weakness brought about by going without adequate sleep for several nights, or getting caught in the rain, and so on. When your question is—How can I best prevent having another—you will have to move down the chain of causes and conditions *to the level at which you can do something about it*.

It is important for groups not to name attitudes as causes; the social, economic, political, and personal causes that produce these attitudes should be uncovered. For instance, a group might initially think of listing *racism* as a cause. But this term serves mainly to name an attitude and is too abstract and general to be very useful for groups truly seeking the causes underlying significant social problems. It would be far better to specify the *particular* actions referred to when discussing causes rather than to fall back on the more ambiguous term *racism*.[8]

In social problems, causes are not absolute and invariable; we are dealing with *probabilities* and *generalizations*. Knowing that we are hazarding guesses, we can but make our lines of reasoning the best possible.

B. Planning the approach

   1. Choosing DIRECTION
      of attack

Planning the approach for managing the problem begins with the choice of a *major cause* of the symptoms discovered—a highly important and somewhat lengthy task. Deciding which of the important causes to strike at is important because here is determined *which* of the symptoms will—it is to be hoped—be reduced or eliminated; in the meantime, all other symptoms (though perhaps weakened in their effect by successes in the attack upon these) will continue their harm as before.

In some situations, however, the symptoms are so intolerable or are increasing so rapidly or the opportunities for their correction are diminishing so rapidly that the first attack must be launched directly at the most harmful symptoms rather than at the underlying causes. If the forest is on fire, the first aim must be to extinguish the blaze and prevent all damage possible. Only later would we try to discover and remedy the causes of the disaster to prevent further occurrences.

A detailed examination of the causes (and conditions) on the basis of the symptoms for which they are largely responsible should reveal the most central of the causes, and thus the appropriate DIRECTION for attack, an attack to be made by means of the plan chosen in subsequent steps.

Since causes may exist in such different realms as social, political, or psychological, it may be appropriate for certain groups to restrict their attention to causes operating in one particular realm. If the group must report its recommendation or decision to a sponsoring organization, the group will be guided in its choice of a direction of attack by the scope of that organization's authority, ability, and interest. The group would ask itself these guiding questions: What is this group being asked to accomplish? and What types of approach (that is, attacks upon causes in what realm or realms) could feasibly be adopted by the agency to whom it reports?

It is granted that in most problems even a highly effective attack launched upon only *one* key cause will leave many symptoms untouched. Yet the rifle-shot technique is better than the scattered attack of a shotgun. With the more centered attack, the lines of causation and probability are clearer.

2. Clarifying CRITERIA for judging plans of attack

A group needs standards on which to judge its proposed course of action. The following general criteria are inherent in the thoughtful consideration of any problem. They may need to be restated in more specific terms to apply to the particular problem being studied.

a. Utility

The utility of a plan for managing the problem derives from two factors: *quality*—How well will the plan accomplish the task asked of it? and *quantity*—How fully will the plan cover the hurts produced by the chosen cause, that is, have the scope desired?

The group needs to agree on a threshold of utility: what degree of effectiveness must a plan promise to be worthy of consideration?

b. Feasibility

How available are the resources— the men, money, and materials— which the plan would require? In other words, how practical and realistic is it?

A general awareness of available

resources will enable the group to judge whether a specific plan is feasible enough to be considered among the alternatives (Step III), but more specific analysis of resources will be necessary in deciding which alternative is "best" (Step IV).

c. Promptness

Relevant on this criterion would be the time it will take to get a plan installed and the time for the claimed results to occur.

The group members must also have some sense of how soon they must be able to see substantial positive effects from the plan.

d. Congruency with
   BOUNDARIES

Although it is in the nature of any action that it sacrifices certain values to some extent while it seeks to preserve others, yet that sacrifice must not be too great.[9] We must not spend too much for the whistle, Ben Franklin said. Although we want to reduce forest fires, we would surely not want to limit the freedom of the public to enjoy the forest areas too much.

Customs, beliefs, or rights of individuals, institutions, or the public must not be harmed *too much*, either directly in the action of the plan upon the major cause (chosen as the DIRECTION) or by its inadvertent effect upon other values.

That a plan is likely to be *expensive* is not in itself a blow to some boundary (although it usually would constitute a weakness as far as the *feasibility* criterion is concerned). But if, being expensive, the plan was likely to harm individuals or the public severely (for example, cutting down their nutritional intake too much), it would be damaging the welfare boundary.

The group needs to think out what damage to private or public welfare might be likely to come through this attack on the selected cause and to build a general notion of what the upper limit of such damage that could be tolerated would be.

The members need to alert themselves to any relevant government regulations so that violation of these standards would be noted in assessing plans of action.

Furthermore, the group members need to consider such expressions of public tolerance as are implied in these questions: What are the views of the larger public that may eventually have to accept or confirm the group's recommendations? Would that group adopt the proposed plan? There is little need to recommend changes that are so unpopular that they will not be followed or enforced.

As the members build these notions of BOUNDARIES, they would do well to state them in the negative and as matters of degree; for example, a plan must not harm the welfare of the residents nearby too much.

Furthermore, some sense of which one (or two) of the criteria will rightly play the largest role in managing this particular problem will need to be developed.

The most dynamic of the criteria is *utility* (How much will the plan *do*?), but matters of *promptness* (soon enough?) and *feasibility* (Can the plan really be carried out?) and *congruency* (Can we afford its damaging effect on our other values?) will always have some importance and, at times, primary importance. The relative importance of the four criteria differs from one problem to another, and the group members must think out the relationships appropriate for the problem they are discussing.

STEP III. PROPOSING PLANS FOR MANAGING THE PROBLEM

A. Listing proposals

How does the group assemble its list of alternative plans?[10] There are many sources, including proposed plans now being given public attention, plans composed by remodeling or extending present programs, plans in use for similar problems elsewhere, and plans created by the group members in their "search work." It is important that (1) widely different plans are included in the list, certainly all those that have any reasonable chance of striking effectively at the key cause while staying more or less well in line with the boundaries; and (2), although as little time as possible should be devoted to the details of the proposals at this point, yet the basic purpose and structure of each proposal is clearly identified, for only thus can the group avoid duplication and fruitless overlapping in its list.

Specific approaches can be used on occasion to enhance the group's productivity in assembling the list of plans. The following techniques are described more fully in Chapter 10, *Resources and Other Sources.*

1. *Brainstorming*

Osborn's plan: a freewheeling group suggests items for a listing with all criticism held back and with strong support for the production of *many* ideas and *different* ideas. Another panel (or the same one) later evaluates the list for the most promising; these few selected ideas are sharpened and heightened by modification and combination.[11]

Gary Davis's modification: a group engages in "stop and go" brainstorming. Short periods (about ten minutes) of unrestrained freewheeling are interrupted by periods of evaluation, the latter serving mainly to keep the group on target by selecting the apparently most profitable directions.[12]

2. *Nominal Group Technique*

The first two steps of the Nominal Group Technique can be useful for list making in groups. These steps include (1) a silent generation of ideas in writing by each group member, and (2) a round-robin recording of members' ideas on a flip chart or chalkboard.[13]

3. *Lateral Thinking*

Edward de Bono[14] suggests lateral thinking as an alternative to the usual "vertical" thinking used in problem solving. He suggests the usefulness of looking at problems in new and different ways.

A group may attempt "metaphorical" thinking to achieve imaginative solutions. The members may use (1) *direct analogies* and look at parallel relationships in nature, (2) *personal analogies* and imagine themselves directly involved in the problem, or (3) *fantasy analogies* and think of excellent but "farfetched" solutions.[15]

The group may strive for innovation (improvement) in contrast to creation (invention) in listing possible solution plans.[16]

Proposals that are listed should be considered, at least for a brief time, before being dropped.

4. *Synectics*

William J. J. Gordon[17] suggests ways of promoting creativity in developing solutions by thinking in analogies *to make the strange familiar* and, by looking at things from new viewpoints, *to make the familiar strange*.

B. Pruning to an active list

The criteria listed (in Step II B 2) can be applied briefly (and only to the depth necessary) to eliminate obviously weak proposals from the listing. Duplications that have slipped in can also be removed.

Etzioni[18] suggests that the alternatives be examined and those that reveal a "crippling objection" be rejected. Crippling objections would include

(a) *practical objections* because the alternative requires means that simply are not available.

(b) *normative objections* because the alternative would violate the basic values of the decision makers, and

(c) *political objections* because the alternative would be opposed by persons whose support would be essential for making the decision and/or for implementing it.

The group would hope to have no more than perhaps a half dozen proposals remaining on its *active* list.

STEP IV. SELECTING "BEST" PLAN
FOR MANAGING THE
PROBLEM

A. Comparing alternatives
(on criteria) to select
"best" plan

Two plans on the list—probably the first two—should be compared carefully on each of the criteria in turn. This means that plan I faces plan II on *utility* (quality and quantity), and after facts are presented inferences are drawn in order to determine which plan is superior on this criterion and how much so.

Where one plan is found to be superior on *utility*, for example, and the other on *feasibility*, *promptness*, and *congruency*, the group's decision must take into account not only the degrees of superiority but also the relative importance of the various criteria.

The winning plan in this first set of comparisons is then pitted against the next plan in similar fashion, and the better of the two is determined; the process is repeated as often as is necessary to select the "best" of the alternatives suggested.

If the process of comparison seems to suggest that adding an element to, or altering some feature of, this "best" plan would bring still greater improvement in reducing the symptoms, the suggested modification must be contrasted with alternative modifications rather than adopted without such testing. Furthermore, such a modified plan would have to be scrutinized to decide whether the modification might really diminish the *utility* of the unamended plan or weaken its claims on *feasibility*, *promptness*, or *congruency*. If the modified plan survives these tests, it should be carried forward in the inquiry as the "best" plan. It may actually have become a plan with both a long-range component and a short-range component.

When the group has chosen a "best" plan, it may be wise to try to choose a second "best" plan. Often the second solution will be superior to the first.[19]

One fact of group work is that a final consensus is not always possible. In such cases, all need not be considered lost. If a group can go only so far as to reduce the number of feasible alternatives, it will have made a worthwhile contribution. Sometimes merely presenting a few promising alternatives, the reasons a choice could not be reached, and the values involved may help others to choose one or another of the alternatives.

B. Comparing "best" plan
with untouched symptoms

At this point in the discussion the group should, as it were, come up for air. Now that the plan is selected and its likely results (great or small) agreed upon, it can be helpful to ask—what will it NOT do? The group should be aware that the chosen plan will not remove such symptoms as result from causes at which it was NOT designed to strike—those symptoms will continue to exist. The question is: Is the reduction of symptoms that will be achieved by the plan—in contrast to the other symptoms that will remain—acceptable to the group? The group would here give brief attention to symptoms (discovered in Step I) that result primarily from *other causes than* the one toward which the chosen plan is striking (the cause chosen as the DIRECTION).

This is a planned "scanning"[20]

that can help to assure the right-ness of the DIRECTION and of the *selected plan* or can set those choices aside tentatively and re-turn to take a quick look at other casual factors in the situation (in Step II).

The members weigh these two—their chosen "best" plan on the one hand and the symptoms that the plan will NOT cover on the other—and ask themselves frank-ly: is the selected plan *worth-while*?

If the plan is judged worthwhile, the group can feel more secure in its choice. If the plan cannot truly be considered *worthwhile* (in the light of what it will *not* do), the group may (1) seek a second solution for this same cause; the plan it now decides upon may be a substitute for or a supplement to (with adjust-ments between the two worked out) its earlier "best" plan. Or (2) select a new DIRECTION from among the causes or under-lying conditions and work through the steps of listing plans and selecting the "best" again.[21]

The Problem Management Sequence can be illustrated with a genuine social problem that a group of community leaders might well meet to discuss. We consider the problem of *juvenile crime* and *juvenile justice*, a societal problem of considerable importance at this time and one that will doubtless continue to be crucial to the welfare of the country.

Suppose a group of urban residents was meeting over a period of weeks to discuss the question: How can we best reduce the incidence of juvenile crime in our city? In the first place we should note that this would be a well-phrased question for group consideration. It gets to the point of the problem, it delimits the scope of the problem to one city, it calls for con-sideration of a range of alternatives, and it is clear and concise. It does not ask for a simple listing, as would What are the causes of juvenile crime? And it does not prematurely focus on a single alternative, as would Should all juvenile offenders be required to receive psychiatric counseling? Rather, it calls for full consideration and a carefully drawn solution to a limited and clearly stated problem.

The discussion question, then, is How can we best reduce the incidence of juvenile crime in our city? We are sketching here an application of the PMS to this problem. We do not present the detailed and documented information that a group would have to have to make its judgments in each of the steps. We try to show how group members would work with whatever the facts were at the time of their discussion.

Table 2-2.

STEPS	COMMENT
STEP I. DESCRIBING THE PROBLEM	
A. Clarifying "problem" terms in the discussion question	For the topic considered the word *juvenile* would require defining. Suppose that a child of six was caught shoplifting. Should that child be treated with the same procedures as a sixteen-year-old who stole a similar item? English law held that children under the age of seven were incapable of crime. And, at one time in the United States, children fourteen and over were treated as adult offenders. So, should *juvenile* be defined as a person seven to thirteen, sixteen, eighteen, twenty-one? The choice of the upper limit could well affect any final decision because the age chosen would influence the number of offenses, types of offenses, and appropriate solutions to be considered. The group members must reason to the definition they will use.
B. Specifying symptoms	Symptoms are the observables— incidents, specific cases, numbers, dollars of damage. For example, there were ____ cases of vandalism, ____ incidents of tire slashing, ____ cases of car theft last

month. The loss from vandalism totaled ____ dollars.

Symptoms (signs) can be labeled, classified, and counted. These facts make the members aware (or more aware) that *a problem exists* and *of what it consists*.

C. Appraising size and scope of the problem

   1. Extent, trends, and seriousness

The members begin to work with their data about the incidence of juvenile crime. Are the numbers significant in size? To what shall they compare them? In one study in Michigan it was revealed that only about 3 percent of the teenagers reported as involved in delinquent acts were apprehended and had their cases fully recorded. How easily can the members generalize from such a small sample to the larger group? And if the rates of apprehension for different acts vary (which is likely), then the profile of juvenile crime recorded for the 3 percent may distort the profile for the full 100 percent.

Another problem occurs when the standards for reporting juvenile crimes change periodically, making comparisons over time very difficult and potentially misleading. As an example, in a certain city, only thefts over $50 in value were reported before 1973. Since that time all thefts have been reported. If one did not know about the change in standards and merely compared the incidence of reported crime, there would seem to have been a dramatic increase in thefts in that city. Such comparisons from time to time and from place to place can be misleading if taken on face value only.

After seeing the size of the problem in their own city and looking at the trends (in numbers and types of crimes, for instance), the group members turn to the matter of seriousness. What do these facts mean in terms of safety on the streets, even in the halls of school buildings? By such considerations they decide *how bad* they think the situation is.

---

2. Implications

The members have no doubt that the overall social and political character of the general public in the city and state will be weakened by the continued involvement of teenagers in crime. No valid estimate of the size and scope could overlook this threat from juvenile criminals becoming adult criminals.

If juvenile crime continues unchecked, the members reason that taxes may be increased, property values harmed, and so on.

The *size* of the problem includes this loss of human potential and these harmful results on other citizens.

---

3. Inadequacies of present programs

The members list the programs that have been established in their city—in churches, by civic groups, and concerned citizens. Looking at each program briefly, in turn, they point out why it has not handled the problem of juvenile crime in their city effectively. One has been successful among the juveniles reached, but has reached only a few. Another has failed because it lacked trained personnel, and so on. And these judgments they render are not off-the-cuff charges but inferences from facts.

The members will remember

these efforts later when they build a list of possible proposals of their own—avoiding mistakes of similar nature, utilizing good ideas that need only a change or two to make a present program work, and so on.

D. Synthesizing the nature and urgency of the problem

The group members need here—not more facts—but reasoning from the inferences they have drawn up to this point. If they have found that the crimes brought harm to property and lives of others as well as danger and degradation to the youths themselves, that all these evils were increasing and measured high against those in cities of comparable size, that they feared for the future well-being of their citizens as well as lamented the loss of the human potential, they are indeed ready to picture the juvenile crime situation in their city as an increasing threat to the juveniles and others as well, and to agree that the need for better handling of the problem is urgent indeed.

STEP II.   ANALYZING THE PROBLEM

A. Searching out causes and underlying conditions

The members turn to the task of listing the *causes* of this problem as they have found it to be, and the *conditions* that allow (and even at times, encourage) the operation of the causes. They can easily produce a lengthy list, but they extend themselves to see that it contains *all* the *important* factors; they list such factors as:

    broken homes
    neglectful families
    rejecting families
    parents who are inadequate
        role models
    biological inheritance

"natural" rebelliousness of youth
insufficient affection received
feeling unwanted
inadequate job opportunities
poor facilities for leisure time
failure to learn discipline
undesirable peer models
addiction to TV crime shows
low self-esteem
few experiences of success
severe mental disturbances

They realize that every one of these factors has been associated with some instances of juvenile crime, but no factor is related to every instance. They also realize that some juveniles in these situations are not involved in any criminal behavior at all.

B. Planning the approach

  1. Choosing DIRECTION of attack

The members reason that, as a citizen group, they are free to plan or recommend (in STEP IV) a solution requiring action by other groups as well as themselves.

They begin to process their list of causes. Considering that the situation will allow them to plan their attack upon causes and conditions rather than symptoms, they examine the list to eliminate ones that could not be attacked, such as *biological inheritance* and *severe mental disturbances*. Causes that concern the home seem important to them, and these are considered in turn. The *natural rebelliousness of youth* is viewed as important but they decide to seek a factor that would trigger such a feeling into delinquent acts. They consider *addiction to TV crime shows* significant but their study of the work of researchers indicates that this factor does not itself *cause* acts of delinquency but rather stirs up these acts in children already possessing a predisposition toward delinquency.

Continuing their work on the list of causes—bringing data to bear, and reasoning from their own experience—the members finally agree that the key cause of delinquency in their city is *inadequate job opportunities*. They realize that attacking this cause will not manage the whole problem but they believe that a real dent in the problem can be made by choosing this DIRECTION.

2. Clarifying CRITERIA for judging plans of attack

   a. Utility

They agree that the plans they are willing to consider must get sizable numbers of youths into wage-earning positions rather than simply provide training for them. Their plans must reach all ethnic groups, they decide.

   b. Feasibility

All plans to be considered must be capable of being staffed, housed, and paid for.

   c. Promptness

They will consider plans that will go into effect by the beginning of the following year, and can be expected to show substantial results by the second year after that.

   d. Congruency with BOUNDARIES

The members agree that the private rights of the juveniles in these programs must not be infringed upon too much. They also hold that having the youths in these jobs must not endanger the public safety nor put too much of a drain upon the public purse.

STEP III. PROPOSING PLANS FOR MANAGING THE PROBLEM

   A. Listing proposals

Once the group chose its approach—to strike at *inadequate*

job opportunities—the members have worked at assembling a list of plans that would have some chance of managing their city's problem; they have tried to include plans of many kinds, plans that involve the business community, ones that spring from city government, others related to voluntary associations. They range from an expanded City Peace Corps to local school jobs. Each is known by a characterizing title but the purpose and structure of each are understood. Some are plans used in other cities; some are modifications of plans used locally; some are the creation of this group itself.

B. Pruning to an active list

Here the group works to reduce its list to a manageable number. The members eliminate the overly costly ones, the ones requiring too much time to set in motion, the ones that duplicate programs of the federal government, the ones that would reach too few, and so on. A generalized sense of their *criteria* helps the group raise appropriate questions.

The members cut down to about six proposals and consider that all *could* work and *would* stay more or less well within the BOUNDARIES, and that each represents a significantly different method.

STEP IV. SELECTING "BEST" PLAN FOR MANAGING THE PROBLEM

A. Comparing alternatives (on criteria) to select "best" plan

The group members take up their first two plans on the list: Plan A and Plan B. They review the purpose and structure of each carefully: who is to do what? when? where? paid how? with what expectations?

They begin the comparison of plans A and B on the first criterion, UTILITY. What will plan A likely accomplish versus what plan B will likely accomplish? How much of the problem would plan A be likely to encompass in contrast to how much plan B would be likely to cover? In this point-by-point comparison they begin to see that plan A has potentially stronger claims but will reach fewer of the youths than plan B. Thus, their judgment of plan A as superior is tempered by their realization of its narrower scope, and they decide to call plan A superior but only moderately so.

Similarly, they pit plan A against plan B on *feasibility* and, after careful, impartial weighing of the two, they decide that plan B is slightly superior on this criterion.

On *promptness*, they find that plan B could go into effect much more quickly but that its results would be so long in coming that plan A—though needing more time to be started would begin bringing results almost at once—must be considered much superior.

On *congruency with BOUND-ARIES*, they reason about both private and public rights and welfare, and conclude that, whereas both plan A and plan B would safeguard private rights sufficiently well, plan A would be likely to endanger public welfare a little too much but plan B would not. Hence, they decide that plan B is slightly superior here.

Collecting these decisions—plan A moderately superior on *utility* and highly superior on *promptness*; plan B slightly superior on both *feasibility* and *congruency* — they seem to be ready to decide on plan A. Yet they stop to ask themselves which of the four criteria are most important in judging their plan. They reason that perhaps *promptness* may be of special importance in this situation but that all are very significant. Hence they feel assured that plan A is "best" though yielding—but only slightly—to plan B on two of the criteria.

B. Comparing "best" plan with untouched symptoms

But the group members need to make one more check. Returning to the symptoms they listed earlier, they see the items: vandalism, tire slashing, car theft, attacks on the elderly and the alone, shoplifting, assaults in school halls, and the like. They realize that jobs for youth may well turn those who hold the jobs from such acts but that those still not afforded employment will continue these crimes. They ask themselves whether plan A should be tried since it will not truly *manage the problem*, and decide that, even so, some youths may be salvaged, their crimes not committed, and the public safer now and richer (with participating citizens not adult criminals) in the future. Therefore, the group affirms its choice of plan A as the "best" plan.

This has been an abbreviated demonstration of how the Problem Management Sequence could be applied to a real social problem. Planning the installation of the "best" plan, whether by the same group or by some other agency, will again require the use of the Problem Management Sequence.[22] The planners could phrase its new question in the form of: How can we best put plan A into operation?

2.3   **CONCLUSION**

To be effective for group thinking, communication needs to be characterized by *sound* thinking and *systematic* thinking. For sound thinking the group needs reliable information, a group thought-line developed by cooperative idea-production and idea-correction, and appropriate use of levels in resolving differences. At certain points, tests of evidence and reasoning need to be applied in detail; at other points, where understanding and agreement can be more readily reached, the group will need less rigorous use of these tools. As for systematic thinking, the group members need to understand and utilize the series of thought-movements that make up the Problem Management Sequence. They should consistently give attention to describing and analyzing a problem thoroughly before seeking out ways to manage it and choosing the best among the alternatives by careful comparison on standards they have formulated.

If the steps of the PMS are taken carefully and if the group builds with evidence and reasoning (appropriately tested) upon what has gone before, the group should reach a worthy conclusion. It should be emphasized, however, that not all situations will require use of the full series of steps, nor will all situations require use of all the subpoints in the outline. Nevertheless, a clear grasp of the total sequence is an invaluable asset to the group members in knowing what they can or cannot afford to omit. Nor should each aspect be given an equal amount of time on every discussion question; what time is *needed* on each aspect should be spent there, insomuch as is possible. What aspects should be taken up and how much time each should be given should be answered on the basis of the requirements of the specific problem and situation.

Groups truly cannot afford to muddle through on important problems. Effective group process is the product of choices based upon understanding of procedures as well as of the problem itself. The PMS is our recommended, comprehensive procedural guide.

FOOTNOTES — CHAPTER 2

1. Ivan D. Steiner, in *Group Process and Productivity* (New York: Academic Press, 1972), p. 7, uses other terms for this explanation but focuses similarly on the *materials* of thought and the *organization* of thought: "Task demands specify the kinds and amounts

of resources that are *needed*, and the utilization pattern that is required if maximum productivity is to be obtained."

2. Dean C. Barnlund and Franklyn S. Haiman, *The Dynamics of Discussion* (Boston: Houghton Mifflin Company, 1960), pp. 175–177.

3. Jan Tinbergen, *Economic Policy: Principles and Design* (Amsterdam: North Holland Publishing Company, 1956).

4. David Braybrooke and Charles E. Lindblom, *A Strategy of Decision* (New York: The Free Press, 1963).

5. Amitai Etzioni, *The Active Society* (New York: The Free Press, 1968).

6. John Dewey, *How We Think* (Boston: D. C. Heath & Company, 1910), pp. 72–78.

7. An interesting method of locating problems was presented by Lester Bittel in *Management by Exception: Systematizing and Simplifying the Management Job* (New York: McGraw-Hill Book Company, 1964), pp. 5–6, "Comparison of actual performances with expected performance identifies the exception that requires attention. . . . *Decision making* prescribes the action that must be taken in order to (1) bring performance back into control or to (2) adjust expectations to reflect changing conditions or to (3) exploit opportunities." Bittel reports (pp. 10–11) that Bell and Howell, Smith-Corona-Marchant, and St. Regis Paper Company are examples of companies that have used the method with success.

8. Gerald M. Phillips points out in *Communication and the Small Group* (Indianapolis: The Bobbs-Merrill Company, Inc., 1966), p. 83, that decision makers need "observable, manageable causes."

9. Braybrooke and Lindblom, p. 24, point out that in decision making "our difficulties are augmented because policy-making is not simply a pursuit of objectives but is rather an expenditure of some values in order to achieve others." In their introductory chapter, the editors of *Human Judgments and Optimality*, Maynard W. Shelly, II, and Glen L. Bryan, eds. (New York: John Wiley & Sons, Inc., 1964), p. 10, declare that "We need to know what goals we must surrender or modify as a consequence of a decision that permits us to achieve (perhaps) some present goal. . . . If, therefore, we are to preserve our principal values over any period of time, many of our choices must be reasoned choices, and we need a language by which to reason out decisions that will not have unwanted implications."

10. Norman R. F. Maier, *Problem Solving and Creativity in Individuals and Groups* (Belmont, Calif.: Brooks/Cole Publishing Company, 1970), pp. 468–470. This book by Maier is filled with extremely useful insights as is his *Problem-Solving Discussion and Conferences: Leadership Methods and Skills* (New York: McGraw-Hill Book Company, 1963).

11. Alex F. Osborn, *Applied Imagination: Principles and Procedures of Creative Thinking* (New York: Charles Scribner's Sons, 1953), pp. 300–301.

12. Gary A. Davis, *Psychology of Problem Solving* (New York: Basic Books, Inc., 1973), p. 96.

13. Andre L. Delbecq, Andrew H. Van de Ven, and David H. Gustafson, *Group Techniques for Program Planning: A Guide to Nominal Group and Delphi Processes* (Glenview, Ill.: Scott, Foresman and Co., 1965), p. 8.

14. Edward de Bono's interesting and useful methods for generating new ideas and different ways for viewing problems can be found in *New Think* (New York: Basic Books, Inc., 1967) and in *The Mechanism of Mind* (New York: Simon and Schuster, Inc., 1969).

15. William J. J. Gordon's plan, labeled "synectics," is explained and commented upon in Davis, *Psychology of Problem-Solving*, pp. 123–124.

16. James J. Cribbin, professor of Management at St. Johns University, says the "principal characteristics of innovation are a dissatisfaction with the good enough and a focused concern for improvement. It is difficult to create or invent something that is entirely new. It is relatively easy to improve what already exists. Creativity may be more thrilling, but innovation is more realistic in the average firm or department." *Effective Managerial Leadership* (New York: American Management Association, Inc., 1972), p. 239.

17. William J. J. Gordon, "The Operational Mechanisms," in *Synectics: The Development*

of Creative Capacity (New York: Collier Books, 1961), pp. 34–56.

18. Etzioni, *The Active Society*, pp. 286–287.

19. Maier, *Problem Solving and Creativity*, pp. 273–274. Maier points to some research indicating the value of "second" decisions. "Continued searching tends to lead to less obvious discoveries and these are likely to be the more innovative possibilities."

20. Etzioni, *The Active Society*, pp. 282–309, presents his mixed-scanning approach to decision making.

21. The group should, however, take advice from the Preface to *Androcles and the Lion* by George Bernard Shaw, in *Complete Plays with Prefaces* (New York: Dodd, Mead and Co., 1963), V, 421. Shaw wrote "The open mind never acts; when we have done our utmost to arrive at a reasonable conclusion, we still, when we can reason and investigate no more, must close our minds for the moment with a snap, and act dogmatically on our conclusions. The man who waits to make an entirely reasonable will dies intestate."

22. Phillips, *Communication and the Small Group*, p. 89, recommends the use of PERT (Program Evaluation and Review Technique) for groups which must arrange an operations plan. He writes, "A planning group using PERT is able to detect impending bottlenecks, allocate personnel appropriately, estimate reasonable deadlines, determine starting times, and investigate the logic of the program. Complex operations must be handled by a computer; for most groups, however, the arithmetic of PERT is simple enough to be done with paper and pencil."

Etzioni, *The Active Society*, pp. 287–288, lists several considerations for plan implementation in his "mixed-scanning" approach. Information on PERT and Etzioni's suggestions are detailed in Part Three of this book.

CHAPTER 3
THE TEAM WORK

A discussion group assembles for a purpose, and to serve that purpose the members of the group seek to work as a TEAM on their TASK. The university women's crew swings through the Montlake

Cut ahead of their rivals, the coxswain chanting and all the oars dipping and rising in precise unison. The crew members may not be equal in physique or personality and the demands on the person plying each oar in that shell may not be exactly the same, yet oarswomen and coxswain are working together in maintaining the beat.

The changing of a group of people, who are often unacquainted with each other, into an effective TEAM is a drama in itself; nevertheless this transformation needs to be seen as a means-to-an-end, not an end-in-itself. The end toward which the TEAM WORK moves is the effective handling of their common TASK, no matter what that task is.

Does the group, then, take steps to become a TEAM, and only upon becoming a TEAM then turn to its TASK? Or does the group, almost at the very outset, turn to its TASK, and in the process of struggling together toward the handling of that TASK, shape itself up as a TEAM? In an emergency, the case is pretty clear: doubtless the move into the TASK would come almost at once, for every member would yield to the necessity for cooperation at the highest level. But in more relaxed, less urgent situations, more time would probably be spent at the outset in building their relationships as a TEAM. Group members often engage in social talk, passing the before-the-meeting minutes informally and pleasantly, before sitting down at the table to work. And these initial interchanges begin to build the TEAM. How much time the group can afford for these pleasantries will depend upon the group, the leader, their common purpose, and the urgency of the situation.

A group becomes a TEAM—in the sense in which we are using the term—when the members, though remaining separate individuals, together constitute something more, achieving an added identity. The members recognize themselves in combination as something in addition to individuals. Each member of a TEAM feels that he or she POSSESSES something—partnership and belongingness—in the team, and also OWES something—probably both loyalty and effort—to the team. The bond stretches both ways; cohesiveness has developed, the tendency to stick together. But in a TEAM, coordination is also present, the willingness to "work together" toward a common goal. The members of the TEAM understand and accept the personal efforts that team membership demands of them; organized and motivated, they are a TEAM.

3.1   **A SHARED GOAL**

Members of such a TEAM will experience a cohesiveness

that should greatly facilitate their productivity. Although research studies with "laboratory" groups have not shown a strong positive relationship between cohesiveness and productivity, the results of the field studies with "real" groups clearly support this relationship and demonstrate the necessity for TEAM WORK.[1]

Without the pursuit of a common goal, a TEAM does not exist; the added identity does not arise. Each person on the TEAM must not necessarily be doing precisely the same thing; rather, what the person does is his or her contribution toward that goal that all the team members are seeking in common. The team leader and the team members have the same goal though their efforts to achieve it cannot be exactly the same; the efforts of a member with years of experience on similar tasks and the efforts of others with wide theoretical knowledge will not coincide though all share the goal. Indeed, Marvin E. Shaw[2] summarizes results of research studies that demonstrate that individuals in a group contribute differently to the group product, depending upon their unique abilities and capacities, and that groups composed of persons with diverse but relevant abilities perform more effectively than groups composed of members having similar abilities.

It is important that everyone on the TEAM put his or her efforts—whatever they are—on seeking the same goal. If several members are seeking personal goals—a soapbox for their personal gripes or enthusiasms, a possible contract for their company—instead of the declared *group goal*, they likely will not only be unsatisfied themselves but will tend to prevent the group from becoming a TEAM. The importance of a shared goal is revealed in a study of seventy-two decision-making conferences in business and government. The investigators found that when groups had a high proportion of members demonstrating self-oriented needs—dependency, status, dominance, aggression, and catharsis—the members were poorly satisfied with the process as well as with the product of the discussion.[3] Such personal motivations constitute a "hidden agenda" and tend to result in actions that interfere with the group's work on its shared goal.

3.2   **A SHARED PROCEDURE**

Various participants often arrive each with a private view

about how the group should proceed to seek its shared goal. These individual opinions (especially when not brought to the attention of the group) tend to influence the members' contributions and may create conflicts among group members that are hard to explain, yet must be ironed out before the group can act as a TEAM. Suppose that one member is deeply involved in finding out why the breakdown has occurred, whereas another keeps suggesting new pieces of equipment that might get the operation in gear again. They will frustrate each other and everyone in the group by pulling at cross-purposes.

We observed one group in a mid-American city discussing the problem of juvenile crime; the participants could not seem to understand each other and the discussion bogged down. Then they found that some members were asking what causes *in society* were producing the problem and seeking solutions that the community at large could institute, whereas other members were looking for causes *inside the juveniles* and seeking internal solutions, psychological ones. When the procedure was straightened out, each approach was taken up in turn, and the members were able to function together again. Both in the meeting as a whole and at all major points within it, a group needs to share a procedure in order to qualify as a TEAM. A group working in a so-called permissive manner, that is, giving no attention to any step-by-step procedure in its inquiry, would not be considered a TEAM. Maier and Maier's early study contrasting such a procedure-by-steps with an unordered one provides strong evidence for the procedural approach for bringing high-quality solutions.[4] In discussion workshops over the years, the authors have seen groups (without instructions to decide on procedures) start, not by defining the task and goal, and then undertaking to follow an agreed-upon procedure, but by stating solutions and conclusions, then floundering, drifting, and repeating until expiration of the time for discussion leaves them without a decision.

3.3   **TEAM FUNCTIONING**

Effective functioning by the TEAM leader is basically a matter of helping the members focus their efforts fully on the common TASK. This exacting, exhilarating responsibility is given extended treatment in Chapter 4, "Leadership Work."

The present chapter suggests the nature of effective functioning by the team members themselves; it explains in detail three actions to be taken by the members in the team interaction: volunteering, cooperating, and listening.

3.31 Volunteering

Each member must recognize the continuing responsibility to put his or her thoughts before the group without being specifically urged or requested to do so. This does not violate the member's right to remain silent or to choose the time and manner of contribution; yet the member must accept constant responsibility to help provide the material on which the group efforts converge. In a discussion group on the handling of library materials by Bookmobile attendants, one member listened very alertly to all suggestions made but offered none; eventually others began to watch that member a bit furtively as they gave their ideas, and finally the discussion dwindled to an unclear decision and much dissatisfaction. In a group planning the reorganization of a voluntary agency, one member did not contribute verbally at all until the group was well on its way to some preliminary decisions. During this time, however, she had paid close attention to each speaker and had nodded affirmingly at many points. But she had offered nothing of her own. When at last she made a comment, there was a quick focus of attention upon her and members vied eagerly to agree with her point of view. Whether or not her ideas were valuable seemed less important to the group than that she had given something of herself to the common effort. Neither the silent person in the library materials discussion nor the tardy joiner in the reorganization discussion was accepting responsibility for contributing ideas frequently; in neither case did the group become a TEAM and thereby become able to handle ideas dependably.

Members must volunteer when something they know or surmise may help the group effort. Not only the products of their research and preliminary thinking—valuable groundwork, for sure—but also the additional thoughts springing up in their minds from the suggestions of the others in the group should be offered. The garden experiment seen on a vacation trip last year to upstate New York suddenly becomes relevant, and the member brings the gist of the experience to the group's attention. When preparing for the discussion on possible economies in watering home gardens, a member may have not considered important a hunch that spot-watering might be worthwhile, but now, in the earnest, congenial exchange of ideas in the group, mentions the idea and someone else brings in the tremendous success of the Israelis with drip irrigation; the group is off on a new tack. When members are willing to volunteer what may or may not be of use to the group, with the intention of freely offering their knowledge, experience, and clearest thinking to the group, they build together a thought-line that is as rich and reliable as they possibly can. Members should not be hesitant to express their thoughts, provided they are working in tune with the group goal. Catching the attention of the others, who are also engaged in formulating new suggestions, members should begin to put their dawning ideas into words. The group thrives on the enthusiasm of members who speak out: "What about this . . .?" or "How about . . .?" or "Maybe we should take a look at . . .?" or "That makes me wonder about . . ."

Thus, volunteering means a willingness to try an idea out with the group before the member is completely sure of it. Feeling that one must always be *right* in ideas offered to the group, a member will tend to hold back and thus deprive the group of many suggestions, worthy ones as well as useless ones. And sometimes an interpretation, wrong in itself, can give a listener precisely the clue he or she needs to make a remarkable breakthrough for the group in its thought-line. We recall the incident in George Kelly's comedy, *The Show-Off*, in which Joe, the young inventor, is telling his mother how his braggart brother-in-law, Aubrey Piper, had mixed up the story of the "Rust-Preventive Solution." Joe says:

> And it was the way he got it mixed, Mom, that gave me the idea. *He* said,—that it was a combination of chemical elements to be added to the metal in it's *molten state*, instead of applied *externally*, as they had been doin'. And I *landed* on it—the way Howe did when he dreamed of puttin' the eye in the point of the needle instead of the other end. That was exactly what *I'd* been doin'—applying the solution *externally*—in a mixture of paint. But the next day, I tried adding parts of it to the molten state of the metal, and it did the trick. Of course, he didn't know what he was sayin' when he said it—[5]

The member must dare to present his or her thoughts without

having had the opportunity to frame them completely or to test them adequately.[6]

Each member must be alert to notice when something is needed for more effective group functioning—more information, a different line of thought, a deeper probing, a gathering up of what has been said—and then attempt to fill that need. One useful way of categorizing the needs for which members should be constantly on the watch is as follows:

Group TASK Needs	Group MAINTENANCE Needs
Ideas initiated: more needed	Individuals welcomed as members of the group
Ideas probed: a deeper look needed	
Ideas developed: carried farther	Individuals harmonized with each other
Ideas synthesized: pulled together	Individuals oriented to the group[7]
Ideas summarized: items collected	

Other valuable contributions that members can make are asking questions, giving short affirmations (words, nods, smiles, and the like) of belief and approval, offering helpful proposals or interpretations of terms—suggestions that enforce or assist in others' contributions without interrupting their flow. One member says, "Remember that report we had last June?" Several murmur "Yes" or "That's right," and the member continues with a feeling of having touched base with the group; if the responses are vague or negative instead, the member is alerted to the need to provide a quick resume´ or characterization of the report.

These contributions should be inserted into the group thought-line with care, however, for doing *too much* may be as detrimental as doing too little. A harmful result that often comes from a member's overparticipation is the undue amount of influence that he or she gains in the group's work. For example, the classic experiment by Henry Riecken with thirty-two groups demonstrated that the "biggest talker" obtained acceptance for a good solution (supplied to him secretly by the experimenter) over two-thirds of the time, whereas the "small talker" (provided with the same solution) did so less than one-third of the time.[8] A member *can* volunteer too much and fill too many needs.

Also, in volunteering, the member needs to avoid wordiness, the urge to monopolize, and a feeling of defensiveness in contributing ideas; the member needs to avoid thought-stopping clichés such as these:

> Figures don't show anything! You can always lie with statistics!
>
> Well, there are two sides to every question, and one is probably as good as the other.
>
> We just don't have enough information to make a decision here. Who are we to presume to decide such an issue?

At the same time, the member needs to express friendliness toward other participants but without sounding patronizing; often it is the sound of the voice and the look on the face rather than the words that show how genuine a comment is. If someone says, "Joe here has an idea," you cannot judge the attitude without seeing and hearing the speaker. If George pushes his chair away from the table or if Mary consistently avoids the eyes of the leader, each is volunteering a message to the group, one that needs to be noted and handled in line with the group's purpose and the individual member's welfare.

Performing these member functions voluntarily is not a matter of adhering to a checklist of DOs and DON'Ts; it is a matter of judgment. Contributions are helpful *if* they are suited to the immediate situation and overall purpose. While volunteering his or her best efforts, a member must avoid throwing the others in the group off balance by overzealousness. The member who gives too many facts, or asks too many questions, or summarizes too often for the group, or is overly concerned with the swift passing of the time—such a member, no matter the value and appropriateness of his or her contributions, is shortchanging the group by destroying its sense of members working together, of being a TEAM with every member necessary for the good of the whole. Watching the reactions of the others more carefully would probably suggest to a member the need of drawing back a little and letting others take more of the work on their shoulders.

Although the discussion subject should usually receive the member's main attention, something in the immediate situation—a phrase used, a tone of voice, a facial expression, a gesture—may alert the member to a feeling of strain in the group about the situation in general or about his or her participation in particular. For instance, a sense of personal responsibility for the success of the group may cause the member to try too hard and talk too forcefully so that others withdraw more and more into silence. If so, the member should realize that for the group to achieve its goal he or she may need to hold back, at least temporarily. To sum up: each member must volunteer ideas to the group, but must also use good judgment in introducing them so as to avoid dominating and thus disrupting the group effort.

Each member should begin to volunteer early in the session so that the group sees him or her as a fully participating member. If a member waits too long before making any contribution and actually seems uninvolved, others will begin to speak past the nonparticipant. Moment by moment it will become harder for the silent person to break in and be listened to. From the very outset—through brief assists on the ideas of others as well as more sizable attempts of his or her own to carry forward the line of thinking—each member should take a vigorous part by *volunteering*.

This is the TEAM obligation of each member of the discussion group. Then the TEAM is able to function like an effective search party in a heavily wooded area. Each searcher covers a different territory, but a shout from one collects them all at that point where the clue has been discovered, and all—no matter what their previous individual labors have been—start off anew from this discovery. Graham Wallas, in a frequently quoted comparison, declared that "a group of people . . . engaged in dialectic can, like a pack of hounds, follow up the most promising idea which occurs to any one of them."[9]

This TEAM obligation of each member needs to be fulfilled with a lively sense of communication; the member communicates vividly by

| (1) Using transitional phrases | Expresses the relationship his or her idea has to the thought-line that has been already built by the group unless the linkage will be easily clear. Frequently builds phrases around words such as: *result, effect, cause, example, implication, underlying assumption, condition, side effect, exception, application, alternative.* |

(2)	Expressing ideas clearly	Speaks with enough vigor to be heard by all members. *Comes to the point* and uses familiar terms.
(3)	Watching the listeners	Needs to understand whether others are truly understanding the thought being verbalized so any confusion can be quickly cleared up. Needs to be aware of someone else's desire to talk.

Truly, each member needs to volunteer frequently, openly, relevantly, vividly, and as concisely as is appropriate; thus, the member assumes a TEAM-member's obligation to offer ideas for the group's consideration and to do so with the group's goal in mind.

3.32 Cooperating

Each member has a second TEAM obligation: to *cooperate* with all other participants in bringing out the best information anyone has and in thinking dependably upon it. It is easy in groups to feel that responsibility is spread and that someone else will do the information-gathering and processing. But *all* are responsible; it is better that several have an item or idea of importance than that no one have it. A member should not only initiate or volunteer any idea or piece of information that seems useful and relevant but also should contribute where possible in working with the others upon ideas before the group. This means that the member will

restate

clarify

substantiate

extend

request explanation or give it

modify an idea pro or con

accept or reject an idea

synthesize ideas

summarize ideas[10]

Such interaction on ideas will require of each member at least these two important attitudes: OPEN-MINDEDNESS toward ideas and SUPPORTIVENESS toward members.

Open-mindedness. Each member needs a large measure of OPEN-MINDEDNESS toward the ideas of others as well as his or her own. John Dewey, a leading exponent of pragmatism, pointed out that open-mindedness is

> very different from empty-mindedness. While it is hospitality to new themes, facts, ideas, questions, it is not this kind of hospitality that would be indicated by hanging out a sign: "Come right in; there is nobody at home." It includes an active desire to listen to more sides than one; to give heed to facts from whatever source they come; to give full attention to alternative possibilities; to recognize the possibility of error even in the beliefs that are dearest to us.[11]

Open-mindedness means the "active desire" to give any idea fair consideration, to understand it fully and examine it without bias. It means willingness to grapple with a new idea and to cooperate in finding as nearly as possible where the truth really lies. The difficulties in accepting a new viewpoint are explained by Walter Bagehot, a prominent political writer of nineteenth-century England:

> One of the greatest pains to human nature is the pain of a new idea: it is . . . so 'upsetting'; it makes you think that after all your favorite notions may be wrong, your firmest beliefs ill-founded; it is certain that till now there was no place allotted in your mind to the new and startling inhabitant, and now that it has conquered an entrance you do not at once see with which of them it can be reconciled, and with which it is at essential unity.[12]

Sometimes, however, a member gives careful consideration only to ideas with immediate appeal and fails to pursue vigorously ideas that do not at once stir imagination and interest. For instance, in a discussion on improving the rehabilitation of prisoners, he or she may fail to give fair consideration to a proposal for changing the parole system. This neglect may arise from a lack of interest in a measure that comes so late in the process of rehabilitation, or the member may believe that public apathy would ruin the plan's chances of success, or may simply fear "letting prisoners out too soon." In such cases the member lacks an "active desire" to consider a rather unpalatable suggestion, one not sufficiently developed, seemingly hard to handle, or somewhat disturbing. Or the member may neglect the parole suggestion because it was contributed by someone who has been reticent in volunteering ideas or who has phrased a suggestion poorly. By overlooking the idea because of its lack of immediate appeal or its contributor's lack of influence, the member has failed in open-mindedness. *Open-mindedness means fairness of consideration, not hasty, uncritical rejection.*

Nor, on the other hand, should the member accept too quickly a new, unexamined idea. The novelty of the idea may be attractive or there may be a need to make quick progress in the group or the member may merely desire to be considered a cooperative member—but these are not good reasons for accepting an idea without considering it. Nor should the fact that the idea has been proposed by the most affable person in the group be a good reason for the uncritical acceptance of the idea. It is easier to agree with statements made by persons we find interesting and likable than to see the merit of ideas suggested by persons who are less pleasing to us; yielding to such impulses, however, is a denial of open-mindedness.

Nor is the fact that the idea has been vigorously championed by the most articulate or the most experienced member a good reason for its acceptance. In fact, the possession of a great sweep of experience or the holding of some high position in the world's affairs or of some distinguished title may create a status for that individual in the group that could harm the group's cooperation.

An example of the harmful effects of status difference arose in a gathering of young widows to plan the organization of a local unit of Parents Without Partners. Their chairwoman introduced all those present and then emphasized how fortunate they were to have as one of their number a woman who had been instrumental in establishing a phenomenally successful group in an Eastern seaboard city and would be of invaluable help to this group. The others seemed to feel stifled by the generous introduction given to the person with such outstanding achievement. Furthermore, this woman seemed to feel invited to guide the group's thinking at every point. A wiser introduction by the chairwoman would not have silenced the others and would have tended to protect the newcomer from falling into this unfortunate posture.

Whether status is dangerous in a particular situation seems to depend largely on how the person with the high status handles group relationships. Some years ago a captain in the Navy, two lieutenant commanders, a lieutenant, and an ensign were called to Washington, D.C., to meet as a committee on a vital military matter. Walking down the corridor to the conference room, the captain led the way. At the rear of the little procession, the lieutenant leaned back to say—half under his breath—to the ensign, "They won't get a word out of me!" But the captain, as he reached the door of the meeting room, took off his hat and tucked it under his arm. Turning to the others, he said genially, "Off with the rank. Come on, men, we have a job to do." Even the ensign talked in that committee.

Whoever accepts an idea without careful consideration—for whatever reason—has failed in open-mindedness. *Open-mindedness means fairness of consideration, not hasty, uncritical adoption.*

Being open-minded not only requires of a group member fair consideration for the ideas of others, it also asks objectivity about one's own ideas, admitting to self and others that one may be wrong. Benjamin Franklin's plea for the adoption of the Constitution revealed his willingness to doubt his own beliefs:

> I have experienced many instances of being obliged by better information or fuller consideration, to change opinions even on important subjects, which I once thought right, but found to be otherwise. It is therefore that the older I grow, the more apt I am to doubt my own judgment, and to pay more respect to the judgment of others. . . .[13]

And the renowned Judge Learned Hand said that "the spirit of liberty is the spirit which is not too sure that it is right."[14] One who is fiercely committed to one's own ideas cannot truly have an attitude of open-mindedness toward the ideas of others. If conclusions on a matter are presented as if they were final, then their modification or rejection is likely to be viewed as a personal attack requiring self-defense; defensive response denies the very essence of the discussion process, that of cooperative idea building. This lack of objectivity and open-mindedness can destroy the team nature of the group effort.

Instead of militantly defending his or her own idea, the member would accomplish more by explaining it further so that the other members can examine it fairly. He or she should join with the others in seeking out whatever weaknesses it may have and suggesting appropriate changes. In fact, although perhaps unable to spot weaknesses in his or her own idea,[15] the person is particularly well suited to help in its modification and should not deprive the group of assistance through over-sensitivity, misconstruction of others' motives, or petulance. The member's attitude toward ideas should surely be one of true open-mindedness, a demonstration of a genuine desire to search for truth and an ability to respect it wherever it arises in the interaction of the group. Researchers have found that those discussions in which the members lost themselves in the work of the group to such an extent that they later found it hard to remember *who* had said *what* were highly satisfying to the participants. And our own experiences bear out these findings. Actually, the group member should conduct himself or herself in the spirit recommended by Montaigne in his *Essays*, Book III, Chapter VIII:

> When a man differs from me, he raises my attention, not my anger; I advance toward my opponent and profit from his instruction. The cause of truth ought to be the common cause of both of us.

Having presented an idea, the truly open-minded member views modification of that idea as a valid part of the group's progress toward its goal and, as a fully cooperating member, he or she gives all assistance possible.

An honest skepticism toward personal infallibility, however, should not impel a member to abandon an idea quickly at the first sign of criticism. The member should not withdraw with an abrupt loss of confidence in the idea or with a feeling of being rebuffed by the group, nor should the member seek to get out of the spotlight of group attention as quickly as possible. If the ideas are the result of careful research and thinking, they have some value that deserves the consideration of the group. The member should resist any tendency to abandon his or her ideas too quickly: perhaps the group needs further explanation or needs to focus on the ideas longer to perceive their actual worth. Thus, a member ought neither be overly defensive of ideas nor abandon them too quickly; staying between these extremes is one of the most important aspects of open-mindedness.

Open-mindedness must not be seen as a passive willingness *to let things change*; it is rather an "active desire" to see things improve under the cooperative action of the group. Such co-operation will involve enough use of diversity to make maximum use of resources but enough dependable agreement to resolve issues and move on. Though holding in mind the less-than-hoped-for experience with magnet schools in a much smaller neighboring city, the planners can agree to match their plan to the situation in their city as they have discovered it. Such cooperation will mean that all needed roles in the group are taken, by one member at one point and by another at the next. No member will be responding excessively to a "hidden agenda," that is, out of personal loyalty to an external group or doctrine that thwarts his or her honest cooperation with the group on its purpose and may actually cause friction and lack of harmony in its functioning.

Such cooperation will mean that the norms that have developed in the group are widely honored by the members and are stretched only when such stretching serves the group purpose; for example, all the group members will listen gratefully and often to the most experienced member in a time of emergency or will defer their primary task momentarily in calmer times to rebuild the self-image of a shaken member. Such cooperation means that one member's work substitutes for another's; each uses the advance made by the other. In a world hunger study group, one member points out the development of protein-calorie malnutrition in babies as a consequence of the shift from breast to bottle; another inserts the qualification "by mothers in low-income groups" and the first nods and moves on to mention the accompanying reduced immunity to disease. It does not matter who voiced the thought; that it was built into the group thought-line is the point. Such cooperation is TEAM work.

Supportiveness. No matter how open-minded the attitude of the members is toward ideas, the group can be severely handicapped in its cooperative interaction if the members do not maintain mutually *supportive* attitudes. Supportive attitudes that enable others to do their best work on the TEAM include *acceptance* and *expectation*.

An accepting attitude by one member toward another means a welcoming of the other into full-fledged partnership in the work of the group. Acceptance of the person does NOT mean uncritically accepting his or her ideas—these must be judged on their own merits. It means, rather, demonstrating good will toward the individual, inviting him or her to participate in an atmosphere of general and generous receptiveness. Not only friendly words but warmth of facial expression and of voice will tend to make the person feel that contributions are truly wanted. Furthermore, such a welcoming attitude suggests the recipient's worth in this group while appreciating loyalties that may be felt to other groups and other causes.

This extension of sincere friendliness by words and manner must not be transitory. Unless an accepting attitude is regularly shown, it will be seen as a reward for a particular behavior or opinion, and those who value the supportive relationship most highly will be likely to alter their contributions to bring this fostering touch back again. The consequent distortion of the thought-line is obvious. Acceptance is not an attitude to be turned on and off; it should be steady and dependable; otherwise it may produce as many problems as it seeks to solve.

And this accepting attitude must be shown toward *all* members impartially, insomuch as this is possible. Unless an overall atmosphere of common trustfulness and supportiveness prevails, the group is not truly a TEAM. If the acceptance is extended to certain members only, their participation and influence in the group may eventually come to dominate the discussion and shut the others out. Likewise, if acceptance is shown to all in the group but one, such pointed exclusion is likely to stop his or her contributions or to arouse overt belligerence. Obviously, limitations of acceptance—through favoritism or thoughtless neglect—inhibit the effectiveness of the whole group; acceptance must be impartially extended to all members.

The second component of an effective attitude toward other TEAM members is that of *expectation*. In speaking and listening, a member needs to show that he or she expects the others' efforts to be wholehearted and their motivations sincere, and regards them as responsible members of a cooperating team. Extending confidence to all implies that, despite differing status among members in the group, and despite differing degrees of experience with the matter at hand, the member regards *all* other members as valuable partners in the group's work and solicits and appreciates the efforts of all.

The effect of an attitude of *expecting the best* becomes clear when contrasted with an attitude of *expecting the worst*. We have all seen members with negative attitudes reacting with barely suppressed groans to some talkative, overly forceful, or somewhat contentious individual. But we can notice how much more effective is the attitude of the member who sincerely values all contributions and solicits the group's attention to them. By acknowledging the potential worth of all ideas, such a member supports and encourages the participation of all other group members, thus building and sustaining the TEAM.

A member reveals beliefs and attitudes about the group and the task by *words* used in phrasing contributions to the group thought-line and by *appearance* and *manner* while making them. Actually, he or she can encourage group cooperation in many ways:

(1) By saying, WE, OUR, and US

Others are included as partners with an opening such as this: "Our idea that . . ." or "Do you suppose that we should . . ."; these first-person terms must be a natural outgrowth of true feeling about the group or they will be considered insincere and be resented.

(2) By phrasing ideas tentatively, often as questions

The member reaches forward with a thought but asks all the others to reach ahead, too, and then to test the thinking. He or she does not say, "My own opinion is that we should . . ." but rather, "One way we might consider is. . . ."

(3) By avoiding belligerent phrases and manner

Saying "Correct me if I'm wrong" almost dares others to find error. Saying crisply "I disagree with you!" indicates a fixed position already taken and readiness to challenge all opposition. Saying "You didn't understand my point!" misplaces the responsibility for clarification, arouses group tension, and denies cooperation.

(4) By expressing friendliness

Words of honest appreciation of others' efforts and feelings, sensibly introduced, are helpful to cooperation; but overuse or

superficial use destroys cooperation. Supportive eye contact, the understanding or
appreciative smile, the cooperative tone of voice, posture of
body—these manifestations encourage group cooperation.

3.33 Listening

Listening is an extremely important component of TEAM
WORK, not only because it plays a part in the *volunteering*
and *cooperating* components but because its power is often
not well understood. Fortunately, the average listener can hear
and comprehend many more words per minute than a speaker
can say—four or five times as many. The effective listener
needs this time advantage to absorb and scrutinize the ideas
offered; but even with these extra moments it is sometimes
hard for the listener to keep up, for he or she is also reacting
to cues from the speaker's words, voice, and manner and to
the nonverbal cues of the other listeners as well.

Good listening is hard to do. Sometimes a speaker's words
or thoughts arouse strong personal emotions that keep the
listener from really attending to the meaning intended; sometimes new ideas are piled on too rapidly by various members
before the listener has moved on from an earlier idea. Sometimes the listener needs to have a point clarified but cannot—or
does not—break in to ask; sometimes the speaker's voice or
manner contradicts the words used and confuses the listener.
But the members need to learn how to handle distractions and
conflicting information. If they do not succeed in listening
effectively to the thought and feeling expressed, the listening
members tend as a result to bring up ideas that have been
already suggested, ask for clarification of points already explained, or lose track of the development of thought entirely.
And they may also miss important signs of attitudes arising in
the group, attitudes that may seriously endanger the cooperative interaction on their TASK.

Hence, each member must spur himself or herself on to
grasp ideas quickly, and to be willing, when necessary, to stop
the flow of the speaker's ideas and request an explanation. For
example, a member may ask, "Did I get this straight? Are you

saying that . . .?" And the member as listener must exert self-discipline enough to resist pleasurable tangents, to conquer the temptation to be reminded of that favorite story. The listener needs to interpret voice and gesture as sensitively and objectively as possible, and to listen responsibly because the listener's inner thought-line and the group-developed thought-line need to correspond as closely as possible. Only then do the members of the group have a chance to utilize fully each other's potential as a TEAM member.

The members' responsibilities include *listening to understand, listening to evaluate, and listening to provide support for the speaker.*

Listening to Understand. Each member must understand the speaker's remarks reasonably well before attempting to criticize or evaluate them and be willing to hear the speaker out but ask for clarification if the meaning is unclear.[16] While absorbing the speaker's words, the listener needs to be vividly alert to the speaker's meaning, measuring the facts and opinions given against his or her own, and singling out any discrepancies. This kind of mental sorting and rearranging keeps the listener's personal thought-line consistent with that developed by the whole group and also suggests points to raise, questions to ask, and information and insights to add.

Listening to Evaluate. Only when the speaker's meaning truly emerges should the listener evaluate with any great confidence. Even then the listener should hold back from any firm acceptance of the judgment that is beginning to form in his or her mind until he or she is reasonably sure of what is really being said. To evaluate effectively, the listener must observe the rules of good reasoning: distinguish carefully between facts and inferences, apply the tests of logic to the speaker's reasoning, and hold the judgment being formed as tentative.

Listening to Provide Support for the Speaker. A listener has a certain amount of responsibility to help a speaker express his or her ideas clearly; the cues that the listener provides should increase the speaker's power to get his or her ideas understood and should give encouragement toward the best possible contribution. To provide such support for the speaker, the listener needs to fulfill such obligations as the following:

> (1) Give attention willingly and consistently. A speaker who does not have to strive for the listeners' attention will have more mental energy to devote to the development

of the idea itself. And the speaker is further encouraged if, when distractions in the group occur, the listeners resist being drawn away from what is being said.

(2) Be easy to talk to. The listener should show—by facial expression, turn of head, set of shoulders, and the like—a sincere attempt to understand what the speaker means, and a willingness to allow the speaker freedom of expression.

(3) Avoid responses that are distracting to the speaker. If the speaker sees deadpan faces, giving no reaction at all, or observes responses disturbing to thought or self-confidence, the speaker will be handicapped in presenting ideas well. The following table of adverse and facilitating responses may serve to indicate the crucial importance of listening responses in TEAM effectiveness.

No group can be an effective TEAM if members are contributing only when they are talking. As listeners, they not only upgrade or downgrade the work of the one who is speaking at

ADVERSE FACTORS

1. Absence of any observable response

   In this case the speaker is deprived of the feedback needed to monitor his or her own contribution: Have I been clear? Am I believed? Am I invited to continue?

2. Presence of nonfacilitating responses

   a. *Competitive responses*
   The listener may draw attention away from the speaker and the speaker's ideas by some unexpected action; the listener may talk to a companion on seemingly unrelated matters, or may point out something in the room in an attention-getting fashion. Such actions may seriously affect the attention of the speaker and weaken the presentation.

   b. *Threatening responses*
   The listener may divert the speaker's attention, damage self-confidence, or arouse anger by a thunder-cloud face, a clenched fist, or low mutterings.

   c. *Ego-maintaining responses*
   The listener may be so eager to maintain harmony with the speaker that an exaggerated show of approval and agreement calls attention to itself and away from the group thought-line.

   d. *Anticipatory responses*
   The listener may nod vigorously and frequently as though beating the speaker to the point being made and may show readiness to interrupt, not for the purpose of assisting but to take over the conversation.

FACILITATING FACTORS

The speaker is provided with feedback that demonstrates fair play and dedication to the group purpose. Such responses take at least three forms.

a. *Meaning-oriented responses*

The listener shows that he or she is putting all resources of intellect and experience at the service of the speaker. Whether these responses are of understanding, questioning, agreeing, or differing in information or interpretation, they are cooperative attempts to aid in the TEAM effort. Facial expression and posture reveal a sincere desire to interact fully with what the words, voice, and manner of the speaker are communicating.

b. *Initiative-yielding responses*

By appearance and manner, the listener shows an intention to give the speaker a full chance to express a view and to understand what the speaker really means. Others may follow this example.

c. *Distraction-resisting responses*

The listener keeps eye-contact with the speaker and shows continued interest in the ideas being presented despite unexpected noises or movements in the room or outside. This is a pointed "I'm interested in what you are saying" demonstration by the listener.[17]

the moment but are preparing themselves well or poorly for the verbal contributions that they make—or should make—the next moment.

3.4   RISKS IN TEAM WORK

Working on an effective TEAM is, by its very nature, a source of pleasure and satisfaction to the participants. Sometimes, however, this sense of accomplishment and feeling of strong satisfaction may build, when poorly handled, into a sense of euphoria that is dangerous. This heady feeling may have very harmful results in the group interaction, such as (1) resisting contrary facts, (2) suppressing differing opinions, (3) making riskier decisions, and (4) stereotyping group roles. Group members, knowing these tendencies, can take steps to prevent or counter them.

3.41   Resisting Contrary Facts

As persons talk with others of like mind only and become

isolated from differing views, they become firmer in their own resolve, and they tend to value their cohesiveness highly. Irving Janis in his book on the faulty use of group methods entitled *Victims of GROUPTHINK* illustrated his thesis by telling of fiascoes in governmental decision-making groups. He pointed out that in-group pressures can lead to a "deterioration of mental efficiency, reality testing, and moral judgment,"[18] He explained further that individuals emerge who act as self-appointed "mindguards." They see themselves as protecting the group from outside information that might suggest contrary positions and thus weaken the group agreement: such individuals may censor or distort incoming information in order to protect the group's cohesiveness. The maintenance of the TEAM has become more important than the TEAM goal itself.

How can a TEAM protect itself against these dangers arising partly from its very successes? The team needs to learn to monitor itself and to take rigorous steps against any tendency to see its chosen position as having *no faults at all*. Outside experts can be called in to set forth differing views with vigor and depth. And within the group, any member can call attention to the group's need to remain open to opposing ideas until the very last moment; such insistence may succeed in getting the potential "mindguards" to win their standing in the group by revealing instead of concealing important facts known to them alone.

Another way to get a reanalysis of the favored solution (and thus break the illusion of having found the *right* solution, one that must not be challenged by new facts) has been suggested by Norman R. F. Maier, as discussed on page 41. He recommends that, after choosing a first solution, the group move to form a second decision, and he notes that in his experience this second solution can often be better than the first. Maier explains the value of the second solution as follows:

> The procedure of requiring groups to find a second solution caused them to return to the problem where they may have found the remaining obvious alternative unattractive. This required them to do one of three things: (1) modify their previous solution, (2) improve the undesirable alternative, or (3) innovate in some other way. The assignment of obtaining a second solution, therefore, tends to initiate activity in the area of *developing* alternatives rather than *choosing* between obvious alternatives.[19]

Janis agrees with the idea of seeking a second solution:

> After reaching a preliminary consensus about what seems to be the best policy alternative, the policy-making group should hold a "second chance" meeting at which every member is expected to express as vividly as he can all his residual doubts and to rethink the entire issue before making a definitive choice.[20]

There is no doubt that the TEAM must find ways to destroy any reason that members might have for holding back any contrary facts.

3.42 Suppressing Differing Opinions

Janis also suggests that just as group cohesiveness may cause participants to feel that they are entirely correct and really invulnerable, so it also may cause the group to apply pressure on individual members to conform to group norms and not deviate greatly from them. Members will tend to engage in self-censorship; they will hold back on their commitment until they see the direction in which the group is moving and will then declare for that direction without mentioning their earlier views lest they disturb the group movement and lose status as a full partner. As individuals engage in self-censoring and all speak the same piece, they can easily be misled into believing that there are no deviating opinions; if none is heard, then none exists.

What can save the TEAM that values its cohesiveness from these capitulations to conformity? Two procedural steps can offer help: (1) getting the problem carefully described before turning to solutions and (2) developing strong alternatives and keeping them alive long enough.

The tendency to begin suggesting solutions as soon as a problem is announced is strong in all of us. But this tendency must be carefully resisted. Members who present their favorite solutions at the very outset tend to remain so attached to them that they find it hard to look at other proposals fairly. Also, if the group begins to consider solutions before clarifying the situation that the solutions are supposed to remedy, they are depriving themselves of the only means by which they can decide among those proposals. A group must be problem-minded before it is solution-minded.

The group must also be strongly committed to the *value* of

looking at other sides than the one most familiar or most favored. Maier described a human tendency when he pointed out that "after a suggested solution has achieved enough valence, then resistance to it disappears and then the group seeks further justification for that solution, and search for other alternatives is inhibited."[21] The necessity of finally making a choice (or two choices) should not begin to close doors against other possibilities too soon and likely will not do so if the group has made creative production of alternatives a norm. If group members are not acting sufficiently well as critical evaluators of their own thinking, they may ask one or more members to act as "devil's advocates." Janis warns that such a procedure must be a "genuine effort," not just a token bow in the direction of thorough consideration of all possibilities. He says that

> The most effective performers in the role are likely to be those who can be truly devilish by raising new issues in a conventional way, low-key style, asking questions such as, "Haven't we perhaps overlooked . . .?" "Shouldn't we give some thought to . . .?"[22]

This recommendation of giving sustained attention to alternatives does not deny that there is a point at which the group makes its choice and moves forward.

But these specific recommendations will really be unnecessary if the members of the group make appropriate and full-fledged use of the Problem Management Sequence. Careful attention to the first two steps—describing and analyzing the problem—will keep the group problem-minded for a profitable time. And thorough, tough-minded but imaginative work on the third and fourth steps—proposing alternative solutions and selecting the "best"—will cast all members as critical evaluators. Differing opinions will not be suppressed, but invited and valued.

3.43   Making Riskier Decisions

Another tendency of groups is to arrive at riskier decisions than the members of the group would if they were working as individuals. A number of related studies of this phenomenon provides valuable insight into how it works in groups.[23] For example, one study concerns the question of whether an electrical engineer should accept a job with a newly founded company offering a larger salary and the possibility of becoming a shareowner, or remain with a larger company now paying him a modest salary that will probably not be increased much. Estimates from discussions on several such cases suggest that groups will generally accept riskier decisions than will the group members when responding as individuals. This finding tends to counter the common view of groups as great levelers, who usually choose a middle-of-the-road course. Several reasons can be suggested for the tendency of groups to choose riskier solutions:

(1) That risking is a value in our society and we are stimulated to it in the presence of others

(2) That persons willing to take risks will be more persuasive in group interaction

(3) That spreading responsibility among all members of the group encourages the let-George-do-it tendency so that rarely does a member call a halt to the escalation, half realizing, perhaps, that resentment would follow such action.

Whatever the reason in a particular case, group members are well advised to be aware of the group tendency to a riskier decision and to be willing to give special attention to its claims and its hazards.

3.44   Stereotyping Group Roles

When TEAM members have developed a cohesiveness of some strength through their interaction, they tend to feel a compulsion to turn to the same person to play the same roles repeatedly. They wish to continue their successes. For example, if one person gets the reputation of being the person with the information, or the person who will know what procedure ought next to be followed, or the one who can always synthesize well what has been said, no other person gets a chance to perform these functions. On many occasions others could probably do these tasks equally well, or better; furthermore, the variety of functions would liberate the group from the crushing pattern into which it has fallen. Courageous members should buck the hurtful group norm that has developed; encouraged by the perceptive leader, others should begin to move in to play these roles and to approve each other in these efforts. Unless the stereotyping tendency can be offset, the group will be robbed of the fullest use of its potential.

3.5   **CONCLUSION**

If a group of people have a SHARED GOAL and a SHARED PROCEDURE, they have the potential for working as a TEAM. Only when the members function as a TEAM, however, by appropriate volunteering, cooperating, and listening, will they have the potential of being a highly effective TEAM. And, if they are to become effective as a TEAM, the members must be aware of, and take steps to prevent or counteract, certain risks that can result from effective TEAM WORK.

FOOTNOTES – CHAPTER 3

1. Marvin E. Shaw, *Group Dynamics: The Psychology of Small Group Behavior*, 2d ed. (New York: McGraw-Hill Book Company, 1976), p. 234.

2. Shaw, *Group Dynamics*, pp. 233–235.

3. N. T. Fouriezos, M. L. Hutt, and H. Guetzkow, "Measurement of Self-oriented Needs in Discussion Groups," *Journal of Abnormal and Social Psychology*, 45 (1950): 682–690.

4. Norman R. F. Maier and Richard A. Maier, "An Experimental Test of the Effects of 'developmental' vs. 'free' discussions on the Quality of Group Decisions," *Journal of Applied Psychology*, 41 (1957): 320–323.

5. George Kelly, *The Show Off: A Transcript of Life* (Boston: Little, Brown, and Co., 1924), pp. 117–118.

6. Ernest Dichter, noted for over thirty years in motivational research, explained: "Creativity can be engendered and developed if we train ourselves not to be afraid of our own thoughts. Utter honesty and understanding of one's real motivations as far as this is possible are requirements for such an achievement. The desire to be always right often leads to an overcautious selection of the great variety of ideas floating around in one's mind. By this premature selection process we often lose some of our most valuable ideas. To associate freely, therefore, and permit almost all your thoughts to come out into the open either for yourself or in discussion is one of the prime prerequisites for the development of creativity."—*The Strategy of Desire* (Garden City, N.Y.: Doubleday & Co., 1960), p. 74.

7. It is the philosophy of this book that members should think of themselves as *filling group needs* rather than merely *playing roles*; filling needs suggests adjustment to situation, whereas playing roles describes the action without reference to the situation in which that action is taken. A list of roles that members tend to play was developed by Kenneth Benne and Paul Sheats and is frequently quoted in discussions of group process:

GROUP TASK ROLES:

Initiator-contributor	Information seeker	Opinion seeker
Information giver	Elaborator	Coordinator
Orienter	Evaluator-critic	Energizer
Procedural technician	Recorder	

GROUP BUILDING AND MAINTENANCE ROLES:

Encourager	Harmonizer	Compromiser
Gatekeeper-expediter	Group observer-	
Follower	commentator	

"INDIVIDUAL" ROLES:

Aggressor	Blocker	Recognition-seeker
Self-confessor	Playboy	Dominator
Help-seeker	Special interest	
	pleader	

—"Functional Roles of Group Members," *Journal of Social Issues*, **4** (1948): 41–49.

8. Henry Riecken, "The Effect of Talkativeness on Ability to Influence Group Solutions to Problems," *Sociometry*, **21** (1958): 309–321.

9. Graham Wallas, *The Great Society* (New York: Macmillan Publishing Co., 1914), p. 246.

10. These categories are presented in the article entitled "Categories for Analysis of Idea Development in Discussion Groups," by Laura Crowell and Thomas M. Scheidel in *The Journal of Social Psychology*, **54** (June 1961): 155–168.

11. John Dewey, *How We Think*, 2d ed. (New York: D. C. Heath & Co., 1933), p. 30.

12. Walter Bagehot, *The Works of Walter Bagehot*, Forest Morgan, ed. (Hartford, Conn.: The Travelers Insurance Co., 1891), Vol. IV, *Physics and Politics*, Chapter V, "The Age of Discussion," pp. 547–548.

13. *The Records of the Federal Convention of 1787*, Max Farrand, ed. (New Haven: Yale University Press, 1937), rev. ed., Vol. II, pp. 641–643.

14. Quoted in *The New York Times*, April 11, 1959, p. 12.

15. In an early and highly significant study on this point, Marjorie Shaw conducted a study of groups and individuals who were to meet a task in which each separate step had to be correctly taken before the right answer was obtained; she found that other members were three times as likely to detect errors in a mistaken idea as the person who had originally contributed the idea. See "A Comparison of Individuals and Small Groups in the Rational Solution of Complex Problems," *American Journal of Psychology*, **44** (July 1932): 491–504.

16. The contribution to the study of listening made by Carl R. Rogers and F. J. Roethlisberger in the early 1950s has not lost its point. Rogers suggested that the tendency to evaluate before understanding is the primary barrier to communication, especially where emotions are strongly involved, and has explained:

    > Real communication occurs, and this evaluation tendency is avoided, when we listen with understanding. What does this mean? It means to see the expressed idea and attitude from the other person's point of view, to sense how it feels to him, to achieve his frame of reference in regard to the thing he is talking about.

    —"Barriers and Gateways to Communication," *Harvard Business Review*, **30** (July-August, 1952): 19.
    And Roethlisberger, considering communication in the industrial context, urged the same view: "The biggest block to personal communication is a man's inability to listen intelligently, understandingly, and skillfully to another person."—*Ibid.*, p. 24.

17. Quoted and paraphrased from S. Frank Miyamoto, Laura Crowell, and Allan Katcher, "Communicant Behavior in Small Discussion Groups," *The Journal of Communication*, 7 (Winter 1957): 151–160.

18. Irving L. Janis, *Victims of GROUPTHINK* (Boston: Houghton Mifflin Co., 1972), p. 9.

19. Norman R. F. Maier, *Problem-Solving Discussions and Conferences: Leadership Methods and Skills* (New York: McGraw-Hill Book Company, 1963), p. 120.

20. Janis, *Victims of GROUPTHINK*, p. 218.

21. Norman R. F. Maier, *Problem Solving and Creativity in Individuals and Groups* (Belmont, Calif.: Brooks/Cole Publishing Co., 1970), p. 250.

22. Janis, *Victims of GROUPTHINK*, p. 215.

23. Nathan Kogan and Michael Wallach, "Risk Taking As a Function of the Situation, the Person, and the Group," in *New Directions in Psychology* Vol. III, G. Mandler, ed. (New York: Holt, Rinehart, and Winston, 1967), pp. 111–278.

CHAPTER 4
LEADERSHIP WORK

If a discussion group TEAM is to handle its TASK effectively, one additional factor must be present—LEADERSHIP. The essential functions of leadership are to assist in developing a group into a team, and to focus the efforts of that team upon its task. Ralph Stogdill, professor of Management Science and Psychology at Ohio State University, suggested that "Leadership implies activity, movement, getting work done. The leader is a person who occupies a position of responsibility in coordinating the activities of the members of the group in their task of attaining a common goal."[1]

A chairman of the board, a sales manager, a college dean, and an army general are all examples of leaders that come readily to mind. Each of these persons, by virtue of the position held, has a job of leadership to do and will do it more or less well. In other situations, persons may be elected or appointed to serve for more temporary periods as leaders of community, social, and church organizations. A person chairing the school board, a League of Women Voters discussion leader, and a chairman of the local Rotary Club, are examples of persons serving for a time as group leaders who may be called upon periodically to fulfill the functions of developing a team and helping it focus on a task. These leaders would also have a job of team leadership to do and would so it more or less well.

In most task groups, such as those mentioned, one person would serve as leader, either ex officio or by election or by some other means of appointment. This does not mean, of course, that they are the only persons who can provide leadership. Although not every comment in a group meeting can be considered an act of leadership, there are many contributions made by members that lead to significant insights, turns of thought, new lines of inquiry, and useful summaries and syntheses—acts that fill important group requirements exactly when they are most needed. Such contributions clearly are acts of leadership, which can be made by any group member at any time. One member, alert to the momentary needs of the group, may emerge to a leadership role to fill that need, and then move back again to the fully engaging membership role.

A single leader, however, will usually offer most of the necessary acts of leadership during a group meeting. If, in fact, some member other than the designated leader persistently performs such leadership acts, a harmful, competitive situation may develop. Even worse, the group can also lose the specialized functions of one participant who could better fill a valuable group member role. The values of maintaining stable and consistent good leadership are supported by the research synthesis of Professor Stogdill:

> When successful and unsuccessful leaders change places, formerly ineffective groups tend to gain in performance and morale under successful leaders, while formerly effective groups tend to decline in performance and morale under unsuccessful leaders.
> Groups that change leaders frequently or experience high rates of personnel turnover tend to suffer a reduction in productivity.[2]

Norman Maier, who is experienced in management training programs in eight countries outside our own, distinguishes the functions of a discussion group leader from those of the other members:

> A leader is needed who plays a role quite different from that of the members. His role is analogous to that of the nerve ring in the starfish which permits the rays to execute a unified response. If the leader can contribute the integrative requirement, group problem solving may emerge as a unique type of group function.[3]

Group leadership is a specialized function; it is a motivating and cementing function that is essential for group success.

Some researchers have suggested that there are dual leaders in many groups: an instrumental or task leader and an expressive or social-emotional leader. For example, in some early studies with Harvard undergraduates working together in discussion groups, Robert F. Bales[4] found differences in the persons rated high on "giving ideas and guidance" and persons rated high as "best liked." Some have interpreted these findings as indicating a need for these two types of leaders—task and social-emotional—in each group. Amitai Etzioni,[5] an eminent theorist in societal and political processes, has suggested that homeroom teachers should play the expressive (social-emotional) role, whereas classroom teachers play the instrumental (task) role. He further argues that a shop foreman would have a difficult time playing the task and social-emotional roles at the same time. But in the case of the teachers, one role is played in one setting and the second role is played in another setting; the roles are sequential rather than simultaneous. And a shop foreman is not quite the same as a discussion group leader. The foreman is a director who knows best what the goal is and how to get there. This is known apart from the work group and before it ever assembles. There is little relation between a foreman and our conception of a group leader who assists group members in moving toward *their* answer to *their* problem.

The task leader who cannot also play a social-emotional role to some degree cannot be a very effective leader of any sort. In a more recent description, Bales asserts that a good leader must have some ability to play both roles:

> The acknowledged leader of the group, if there is one, is likely to be found somewhere on the work-acceptant end of this dimension. Usually he is also somewhat on the dominant side, and somewhat on the positive side in his behavior. A task leader who is simply dominant and work-acceptant with no positive component in his behavior, is likely to encounter trouble. He is likely to be identified sooner or later as an authoritarian autocrat, and to suffer a revolt in which he is provoked into negative and dominating behavior.

The successful and acknowledged task leader is usually positive in his behavior rather than negative, and so is able to inspire enough liking and admiration to keep the coalition around him strong. He needs also to be work-acceptant in a task-oriented group, but should not be too impatiently so.[6]

It is undoubtedly difficult to manage both task and social-emotional roles extremely well. Nevertheless, this double requirement is one of the most appropriate challenges for a leader, who must learn to respond in both roles simultaneously but with one role then the other predominating as the situation in the group changes. Actually, the leader cannot help the group work on its TASK without the very ideas expressed, words used, tone of voice, and whole visible manner having some effect on the social-emotional climate of the group. Nor can the leader turn from the task for a moment, intending to build more cohesiveness in the group without that act having some effect upon the way the members see the handling of the task. These roles—task and social-emotional—are not mutually exclusive; whatever the leader does at any particular time has both a task and a social-emotional significance.

What further complicates the situation is that all the members will not read the leader's acts the same way: a deft and accurate summary of the causal factors that the group has developed will seem appropriate and helpful to most of the members (largely a task response by the leader, with an accompanying good feeling), but coercive and arbitrary to the member whose idea has been bypassed without—to his or her way of thinking—enough consideration (largely a social-emotional response tied to a task matter).

Thus the leader must emphasize the role that is thought to be more important at the time but must realize that (1) how the secondary role is played is also important, and (2) what is actually done and which role is emphasized will not be interpreted in the same way by all members of the group.

Some persons have suggested that leaders should be chosen to fit a certain job, or the job selected to fit the leader. But most situations do not offer a wide selection of ready jobs and ready leaders at the right level awaiting an easy matching. Nor do most discussions make the same demands of the leader at every point. We have greater confidence in the idea of leadership as being located primarily in one person who unites the TASK and TEAM roles in the proportion to fit the immediate circumstance, shifting those proportions when the situation within the meeting changes. Filling the functions as TASK focuser and TEAM developer, the leader sees neither the achievement of the group nor the human relations in the group as his or her full job. Rather the leader seeks to be sensitive to, and able to provide, whatever emphasis is needed at the moment to promote cohesive and effective group effort.

Professor Stogdill, who has experienced both the academic and business worlds, seems to support this view that most real situations require leaders with both task and team abilities:

> A business executive once told the author, "You psychologists keep telling me that I have to choose between a soft headed or a hard headed form of leadership. It seems to me that there is a golden mean somewhere between these two extremes, and I prefer it." It may well be that the businessman had better intuitive insight into the nature of leadership than the researchers. Certainly, the thinking of behavioral scientists on the subject has been characterized by dichotomized and bipolar conceptualizations of the problem. These seem totally inadequate to account for the complexity of leader behavior.[7]

And James J. Cribbin, in his *Effective Managerial Leadership*, points out strongly:

> The executive must appreciate the fact that his personality and his psychological history predispose him to engage in certain types of activities—maintenance, mediative, pro-active, or what have you—and make it difficult for him to carry out others. Hence, he must discipline himself to do what must be done rather than take easy refuge in what comes naturally or what he prefers to do.[8]

4.1   REALITIES THE LEADER MUST FACE

Anyone undertaking to lead a discussion group must understand at least four basic realities of that task:

4.11 That a Leader Must EARN the Role

One may be given a task with a group or may stand automatically in the position of headship in a group, but these factors do not actually make that person the leader; the leader relationship with the group must be won, and, to a certain extent, must be won again each time the group meets.

Being seen in the role of group leader means that the person's competence, purposefulness, fairness, and trustworthiness are recognized by the members and, as a consequence, they will let him or her act as their focuser. They see this LEADER as being competent and purposeful with respect to their task, and fair and trustworthy in his or her relationships with them.[9] The would-be leader must build these group opinions in order to become the true, accepted, and valued LEADER. Speaking from a business framework, Cribbin has put the matter clearly: "He must simply accept the fact that his *legal* right to manage others does not qualify him to lead them. He must earn a psychological and sociological right to do so. Influence is merited and gained, not coerced and demanded."[10]

Often a brief "honeymoon" period occurs at the outset of the meeting, a preliminary time when the members give the aspiring leader the benefit of the doubt, noting successes with approval and overlooking fumbles or mistakes. Such a period tends to ease the task of EARNING the leadership role. The earlier that genuine workmanlike relationships are established, however, the better it is for the group.

And if a person comes to be the leader of an already established group, an additional aspect has to be watched: too sudden changes in procedure or relationships would seem to be characterizing the group's earlier operations as weak or wrongheaded. Actually, the new leader's actions should be seen as "merely an extension of the organization's usual way of doing things."[11] Nevertheless, the new leader's true strength and purposefulness must not be lost upon the group even during these early, transitional minutes.

Whatever the specific situation, the matter of EARNING the role of leader is a delicate, important first step.

4.12   That the Leader Must Reconcile the Group Goal and Individual Member Goals

Certain members sometimes feel that full and open participation in the work of the group is likely to be harmful to their own interests; they fear that the decision of the group will cut down their own individual opportunities, or their enjoyments, profits, or the like. An ambitious commercial fisherman, for example, might well feel wary of the recommendations likely to come from an ecology-minded group of which he is an active member. The leader must find ways to widen the fisherman's feelings of responsibility and, at the same time, keep the environmentalists aware of the many types of rights involved in the problem.

Writing on "Political Justice," Alan Gewirth, professor of Philosophy at the University of Chicago, pointed out that one of the functions of a "just" government is that of enabling the "intermeshing of individual interests and contributions to society which makes compatible with one another private and common goods. When properly developed it includes governmental concern for moral, intellectual, and even aesthetic common goods."[12] That is, the act that serves the individual must at the same time serve society; and, conversely, the act that serves society must at the same time serve the individual.

The pioneering anthropologist Ruth Benedict studied many island cultures and was puzzled by one particular phenomenon: whereas on some islands the people were happy and prosperous, on other islands, under similar conditions of climate and vegetation, the people were poor and warlike. She came finally to the view that a nonaggressive society was distinguished from a warlike one primarily by virtue of having a social order in which "the individual by the same act and at the same time serves his own advantage and that of the group."[13]

Similarly, at the level of the discussion group, the leader must—to the extent that it is possible—create and maintain the conditions under which all of the members can feel that their personal interests will not be seriously endangered if they work openly and fully toward the purpose of the group.

4.13   That Each Task of Leadership Is Different

No leader can succeed by using the same style of leadership with all groups. Of course, he or she cannot stop being the same person, but must be that person responding to a particular situation. The demands upon leadership are not the same from group to group, nor in the same group on a different problem or even at different points in the same meeting.

When a group of Seattle citizens met for the first time to begin a lengthy study of ways of checking pollution in Lake Washington, the leader faced a far different situation from that which he faced with the same group members six months later when their efforts were beginning to pay off and they felt like a triumphant team. That "team" still needed a leader to focus their efforts, but the needs were much different. Suppose that this same community leader was also chairing a lay group in his church, a group requested by the senior pastor to articulate the wishes of the congregation on the musical program for the coming year. The group has been appointed to include persons widely different in age, interests, and degree of involvement in the church life; the group meets but once; the leader knows most of the members but not all; they have never worked together before; the group is to make no real decision but only to organize and report the ideas voiced in the meeting. The problem of the leader here is clearly different in many ways from that in the community group at any point in its working life; in both situations the leader must analyze the potentialities and wishes of the group in terms of the task before the members and mobilize the abilities and motivations of them together as well as possible. At times, for example, he or she must be quick and decisive; at others, deliberate and open. The leader must realize that each task of leadership is different, that one leadership style is not appropriate for use everywhere and at every time.

4.14   **That Even Good Leadership Cannot Make Every Group Successful**

The quality of leadership is not, of course, the only influential factor in a group's achievement: conditions both outside and within the group itself may make any high degree of success virtually impossible. If, for instance, members come to a community group meeting pleading the needs of their particular neighborhoods, each may resist favorable consideration of other neighborhood situations as potentially endangering financial aid for his or her own area. Or, and let us give a more specific instance, if Smith has seen Collins pull shabby deals in city politics and now encounters him in a discussion group, Smith may not be able to discount his feelings enough to think openly with the group on any subject at all. Or perhaps several people in a group may have no respect for the discussion process itself and consider decision making by individuals infinitely superior to the—as they see it—"watering-down" process of a discussion group.

Faced with any such disturbing conditions in the group but feeling strongly that the group purpose is legitimate, the leader must assess the situation fairly and recognize those areas in which progress *can* be made. At times the seemingly unmanageable conditions only await a leader who is patient, sensible, purposeful, and resilient; though unable to bring the group onward to high success, he or she will have brought off the situation as well as was possible.

What, then, are the components of discussion leadership, this indispensable group function, as performed by a single leader?

4.2 BASIC COMPONENTS OF GROUP LEADERSHIP

The leader's work in a discussion group consists of interlocking parts: *inner work* and *outer work*. The leader observes and analyzes silently the ongoing work of the group on its task and the interaction by which the members do the work. These inner assessments, which are constantly altered by new observations, are the basis for the leader's overt actions—what is said and what is done; from the *inner work* springs the *outer work*.[14] Neither *inner* work nor *outer* work is easy. Theodore M. Mills suggests that in the leader's *knowing* dilemma he cannot be "omniscient," so he must be "humble"; in his *doing* dilemma, he cannot be "omnipotent," so he must be "imaginative."[15]

We cannot, however, think of *inner* and *outer* work as being done in turn, first one then the other; both are done *all the time* the group meeting lasts. Every member also proceeds by means of *inner* and *outer* work, but the group responsibilities of members are somewhat different from those of the leader. It is the leader's handling of *inner* and *outer* work that is of concern here.

4.21 The INNER WORK

Although no amount of preparation before the group meeting can take the place of vigorous, on-the-spot INNER WORK throughout the session, it is nevertheless true that appropriate preparation can increase the likelihood that the INNER WORK can be effectively done.

The leader's inner work takes the rational thinking form: observation, analysis, choice of action-to-be-taken. But in group interaction the leader never has a chance to focus completely and only on observation of *one* matter, analyze it, and then select an action-to-be-taken about it. Instead, the leader is, at one and the same moment, busy at the observation stage on several matters, at the analysis stage on others, and the choice-making stage on still others. But let us examine these stages separately.

Observation. Once the discussion begins, the group members react to their purpose and interact with each other and with the leader. Alert to verbal and nonverbal cues that reveal the members' attitudes, the leader notes incidents that reveal the special feelings of the members involved. And throughout the discussion the leader carefully observes the condition of the group's work on its task.

Norman R. F. Maier, out of years of interest and experience here and abroad with leadership of discussions and conferences, states forthrightly: "The first step in conducting a discussion is to determine the state of mind of the conferees."[16] The leader observes how the members feel in general about the group purpose and topic, and about their own participation: do they assume responsibility or leave it to the leader? Are they ready to work? The leader notes their relationship with each other, especially with those whose status is different from the others, observes their degree of acquaintance and liking, their willingness to develop a working relationship with each other, and their attitudes toward him or her as leader, and toward themselves as a team. The leader notes carefully how they feel about differences in viewpoint, in depth of experience, and in ways of saying things. And, as host to the group members,[17] the leader notes whether they are comfortable, whether the lighting and air are sufficient, whether all can see the charts displayed, and, especially, whether they can see *each other*. These indications—and many more—the leader notes for what they have to tell of the general attitudes of the group members.

But the leader will also be alert to the "quiet ones" who tend to be "left behind" in adult groups;[18] he or she will be alert to catch incidents and postures that reveal specific feelings of individual members. Is someone feeling squelched or bypassed by the group? Is someone reacting so negatively that a chain reaction is likely to begin? What about that "guarded expression of resentment"[19] that Maier emphasizes? Has someone heard a favored idea or person stigmatized and is rising to a heated defense? What about that sudden move to formality in addressing another member, the "Mr. Austin" instead of the previously used "Bob"? Or in the opposite direction, from "Dr. Smith" to "Well, Jack, you know how it is!" What about that repeatedly expressed concern that time is running out? Whether members' feelings are evidenced through their movement and posture or their words or the inflection and timing of what is said, or perhaps the drumming of fingers or shifting of chairs, the leader has information to process by INNER WORK in order to handle the OUTER WORK effectively.

But the leader will notice not only attitudes of the members but also indications of how the work of the group on its task is going. The leader will indicate whether the group is proceeding without enough dependable information, or whether it is mired down in a fruitless line of thought. The leader hears and remembers the potentially valuable idea that is being lost through having appeared too early in the group's thought-line, and notes a suggestion that is being rejected without consideration because of the stigmatizing term thrown at it; the jibe of "panacea!" or "pie in the sky!" has downed many a useful idea. The leader's attention is caught by actual agreement existing but not yet realized by the members, and by voiced agreement that is based upon a misunderstanding of others' meaning. If the solutions suggested are weaker than they need be or fewer than appropriate, the leader is aware of the group's inadequate coverage. He or she is watchful of the group's rate of progress, alert both to a tired or discouraged slowness, and to a precipitate, headlong dash that does not allow sufficient clarification and development of ideas by the group. Responsible for the TEAM's attention to its TASK, the leader is alert to all manner of verbal and nonverbal cues.

Analysis. Alertness is only the beginning. The process of analysis is a continuing activity: what has produced these emotions, these cues that deserve attention? Are their causes group-relevant so that the leader (and the group) could remove or alter them, or are the causes unrelated to the group or its topic so that the leader and members have no power over them and must work around them as constraints? This analysis is not only ongoing but open to change.[20] A new bit of evidence may change the leader's interpretation: what had seemed a member's dominating behavior is now seen as springing from an unusual store of information rather than from a wish for power in the group.[21] The leader's analysis must be quick and as perceptive as goodwill and some knowledge of human motivation can make them, but constantly updated as new observations are made.

Choice of Action-To-Be-Taken. But this openness to change in interpretation must not make the leader slow or indecisive in choosing the OUTER WORK to undertake. Quickly surveying the options—of words, turns of thought, inquiries or examples, movements of eyes, head or hands, a bit of humor or a coffee break—the leader selects the best item of OUTER WORK that can be mustered at the instant and performed with appropriate attitudes and integrity.[22]

And even as the leader makes the chosen remedial move, the INNER WORK continues: how is this chosen action succeeding? how can I modify what I am now doing so that it will result in the best TASK WORK and the best TEAM WORK by us all, yet without serious damage to any member's self-image and future cooperation?

4.22 The OUTER WORK

Out of this INNER WORK the leader will act; even the timing of the selected action is a judgment made on the basis of this inner scanning and analysis. The leader institutes or initiates a remedy through ideas and attitudes manifested by language, voice, and body. For example, the selection of words in summaries, in forward-inviting questions, and in any leadership actions is significant; the sound of the leader's voice reveals response to the situation; posture and movements in listening and talking are also *acts* by which the focusing task is done. Spontaneous in words by necessity, close physically to the group, the leader has little chance of masking his or her true feelings—full sincerity is essential.[23]

All the leader's attempts to focus the group on its purpose with greatest effect and to bring remedial action when necessary are forms of this OUTER WORK. The leader cannot retreat from choice. To do nothing at a given moment when action is necessary is itself a choice. On the other hand, too precipitate or too delayed action are both poor choices, no matter how well the action itself would otherwise fit the needs or use the opportunities arising in the group. Some of these choices will be intuitive instead of reasoned ones. But it is clear that the effectiveness of leadership acts will depend upon the quality of the INNER WORK and upon the timing and manner of execution as well as the quality of actions in the OUTER WORK. These resulting *acts* will take two forms: keeping the members TASK-oriented, and keeping the members TEAM-oriented.

TASK-orientation. A group's thought-line is constructed by the addition of many diverse elements whose meaning and importance may be differently evaluated by the various members of the group. The members' individual efforts must be coordinated and that is largely the task of the leader. Stogdill summarizes research showing the value of structure and task coordination and suggests that "The hypothesis that job structuring reduces follower satisfaction and group performance is contradicted by research findings. Group members exhibit a desire for structure that lets them know what they are expected to do."[24] The necessary structuring and coordinating work of the leader consists primarily of two simultaneous and highly related functions: managing the thought-line and building the thought-line. In the *management* function the task is to serve as overseer and administrator, but in the *building* function the leader will be working with the stones and mortar, albeit with a somewhat closer grip on the blueprints than the other group members have.

1. *Managing the thought-line.* The leader's work here has several subfunctions, such as

> *Locating*—Where are we now?
>
> *Summarizing*—What have we accomplished?
>
> *Opening*—What shall we do next?
>
> *Tracking*—How can we all get back on the same line?
>
> *Pacing*—How can we spend our time where we need it most?

The leader uses each of these subfunctions to establish or regain a desired state of affairs and sets in motion appropriate procedures for accomplishing the needed changes.

Locating

> *What the group may need*:
>> Clear understanding of what the line of thinking is at the moment, its *present status*; where we are.
>
> *What the leader can do*:
>> Leader can say something like, "Are we saying, then, that ..."
>>
>> If in doubt, the leader may say openly to the group, "Let's see, what are we saying?"

Summarizing

> *What the group may need*:
>> Clear understanding of the salient points that have been established so group members can move forward efficiently and will feel motivated to do so.[25]
>>
>> Summaries are needed at many points within the discussion—at junctures, or at any point where grip on the

forward movement seems to be slipping away from the members, or when some disagreement arises as to what has been agreed upon.

What the leader can do:

Welcome effective summaries volunteered by members.

Phrase own summaries as questions to involve members and bring correction of any errors; for example: "We said, didn't we, that . . .?" or "Our proposal has three parts—do I have them the way we want them?—one was. . . ."

Summarize, where possible, in group-developed terms, that is, using group "handles" that provide quick, easy recall plus a feeling of group cohesiveness. Use effective language other group members have used (without attaching individual names).

Opening

What the group may need:

Smooth transition into a new aspect of the subject.

Movement into a relevant *next* inquiry.

Clear relationship of *next* inquiry to preceding work so that members will have a sense of *linking* and are more likely to be motivated in understanding the new aspect.[26]

What the leader can do:

Follow whatever summarization is needed with a suggestion—usually an invitation in question form—that the group move into a specific next portion of the topic, as "Can we move now to . . .?"

Move (like an effective chairman in a parliamentary body) *promptly* from summary statement to this subsequent invitation in order to keep group momentum and interest; for example, with *no delay* after the summary, "Perhaps we are now ready to suggest causes of the problem as we have described it; what might we say is one of the causes operating here?"

Tracking

What the group may need:

Though sidetracking occurs frequently in discussions (sometimes with benefit to the group),[27] an effective return to the main line must be made.

A useful idea, arising before its proper time in the group deliberations, must be brought back for consideration at the appropriate point.

What the leader can do:

Without rebuke or undue emphasis, help the group return from a tangent to the main thought-line: "I wonder whether we're getting off the track a little here? We were trying to. . . ."

Avoid too abrupt a return, especially when the chief tangent-goer is a new person, or someone shy or with a low self-image. Sometimes the leader allows the group to remain a few minutes on a tangent, even taking part in the excursion, in order to meet other group needs.

Clarify the point in the group inquiry to which it is appropriate to return.

Defer the too-early idea and bring it back at an appropriate time. The leader who defers a point should jot it down so that it is not forgotten.

Pacing

What the group may need:

To move at a pace appropriate to the complexity of the issue, seeking to save time on quickly understood parts in order to spend it on baffling ones.

To avoid hasty movement that bypasses relevant issues and treats others scantily, or that leaves many members without sufficient understanding.

What the leader can do:

Set an example by the pace of his or her own contributions, thus tending either to speed up or to slow down the overall movement of the group.

Synthesize a slow movement of thought and invite the group on to a more important aspect.

Break into a runaway interchange with a quick "Just a minute! I wonder whether we're not moving a little too fast here. Could we take a closer look at this one idea about . . . before we move on?"

Demonstrate by the alertness of his or her own contributions that ideas can *catch fire* from one another.

---

2. *Building the thought-line.* In the crucial matter of the actual ideas developed in the thought-line, the leader plays a very important role. While stating the problem at the outset and while working with the group during the discussion, the leader needs to hold back carefully personal contributions and favored solutions where they might stifle the group's freedom of thought. Yet the leader must contribute to the drawing out and molding of the group's ideas. This is a highly creative form

of activity, one that demands great energy and astute reasoning skills. The leader's work in building the thought-line has several subfunctions:

Spinning—gathering and using ideas

Shaping—attending to quality and scope of the ideas

Testing—working for dependable idea-development

Completing—fulfilling the task

As with the other TASK-orientation function (managing the thought-line), the leader uses these subfunctions to fill group needs.

Spinning

What the group may need:

To share more information, experience, hunches, inferences, questionings, and the like.

At some points to develop "handles" (words or phrases as useful labels) for their developing thoughts to capture what they mean.

To be more investigative, creative, and open.

To use whatever technical methods will assist them in their thinking.

What the leader can do:

Show quick interest in ideas offered by members, especially by attention and facial response.

Use group-developed "handles" but avoid letting one be assigned too early;[28] at times the leader needs to use a more fully descriptive set of terms such as "specially equipped schools for pupils' interests and needs" instead of echoing a member's phrase that is perhaps less familiar to some others, "magnet schools."

Be prompt with appropriate questions (usually *to the group*, as "Shall we . . .?" instead of *to individuals*) to serve many purposes, such as for clarity, idea-development, exemplification, and focusing.[29] Effective leadership also uses the question to upgrade a contribution, that is, to lead the speaker to more originality and greater sweep of thought; for example, "Oh, that's a new angle! Could you carry that forward a little?"

Have charts, maps, computer printouts, and experts present in person, when useful to the group.

Hold a view voiced by a minority before the group long enough that any value it has can be utilized,[30] for example, "Let's give this suggestion a real look. . . ."

Shaping

What the group may need:

To work with its materials, discovering areas too thinly analyzed and remedying the oversight.

To cut its list of alternatives to a manageable size and then move into rigorous comparison.

To strip off again the clutter of less essential aspects and get to the heart of the matter.

To upgrade its alternatives—if proposed solutions are not promising enough—by wider search and by creative development.

What the leader can do:

Avoid taking over the shaping process from the members too much; for instance, the leader must not give the impression that he or she is *much ahead* of the others in thinking on the matter.[31]

Introduce principles of screening to reduce an overlong list.[32]

Initiate inquiries that the group needs to make and does not make at its own instigation; for example, "Could we hazard some guesses as to the long-range results of such a move?"

Set up the conditions in the group that allow and stimulate creative thinking by the members.

Testing

What the group may need:

To accept responsibility for having enough facts readily available for consideration and for seeing that these facts are accurate and relevant.

To iron out differing interpretations and lines of thought-development, weighing them against experience, recommendations of experts, and good sense.

To understand what they are doing so that misinterpretations of their common work do not handicap development at the time or produce confusion later.

What the leader can do:

Initiate application of appropriate tests by raising questions and by recommending tests of evidence when necessary.

Use visual means (chart board, overhead projector, and the like) to get difficult sets of data or relationships before the group.

Assist in working out differences of interpretation, helping the group to move to chief points of difference,

and keeping the thought separated from the member
who brings it out and focused on the idea itself.
Thoughts should not be labeled as "Mary's suggestion"
or "Bill's plan."

Remain alert to indications that ideas are not being
similarly understood in the group, and raise questions
on what the *group understanding* actually is: "Do we
mean by this. . .?"

Completing

What the group may need:

To handle all necessary aspects of its task more appropriately, fulfilling each (where sequence is involved)
sufficiently to serve as the springboard for the subsequent one.

To complete its task within the time available or allotted.

What the leader can do:

Bring to the group's attention any segments of the ideas
(or of the task as a whole) that the group is bypassing;[33]
it is best to do so in question form so as to allow the
members to be in on the procedural decisions.

Watch the overall expenditure of time with great care,
asking himself or herself at all points whether the group
is spending its energies on what is most important, that
is, whether the apportioning of time matches the
importance of the topics.

Assist the group to pace individual contributions appropriately and to move from one aspect to another of its
work effectively by the pacing of comments, and by
the manner shown in listening and responding.

TEAM-orientation. Since the purpose of any group meeting
is to work together on a common task, it is extremely important
that the members become a TEAM in action and in feeling.
Only then can their combined efforts be superior to the work
of individuals acting alone.[34] The leader must serve an enabling
function in building this TEAM-orientation, helping the members achieve *full* participation, *voluntary* participation, and
cooperative participation.

Enabling Full Participation

What the group may need:

To have ALL members giving their best, not holding back
what might be of help in the group effort.

To have members freely offering to the group their information, experiences, intuitions, fantasies, worries, and humor.

What the leader can do:

Build a group climate in which such participation is genuinely expected, a strong group morale.[35]

Demonstrate integrity[36] and competence, setting a standard for the members.

Provide easy openings for contributions by questions to the group, a tentative approach, and by an "asking face."

Encourage the members' desires to know the ideas of the others, realizing and prizing differences.[37]

Emphasize the fluid nature of the thought-line developed so far, holding it open to members' thoughts: "Is this what we've been saying then . . .?"

Listen supportively to the person who has a different view,[38] letting all members know that all sides of an issue are considered relevant.

Give members continuing assurance that their presence and efforts are valued; help them release feeling in harmless channels; help them retreat from an overstated position without losing self-esteem.[39]

Slow up a thought-line that is being moved to certainty too quickly: "Let's hold up our decision for just a minute here; have we thought about . . .?"

Enabling Voluntary Participation

What the group may need:

To speak up (not waiting to be called on, nor asking permission to speak by signaling the leader), threading their contributions into the group thought-line.

To speak up to meet a need or to take the opportunity to contribute to the group purpose.

To make known personal ideas and feelings, expressing self in line with the goals of the group.

What the leader can do:

Enable each member to give openly to the common task and to feel a valued part of the process; leader looks evocatively at each and shows a continuing interest in the person as a team member.

Value the insight and effort of each, not yielding a greater measure of interest to someone who has spoken often or well, or who holds or represents authority, or over-doing a response to a quiet person who finally speaks up.

Avoid labeling a thought by the contributor's name; speak

of it rather as "our idea that . . ." and thus a legitimate part of the *group* thought-line.

Echo the key words tentatively of a member's contribution that is incomplete or lacking in forcefulness in language, voice, or manner, thus holding it before the group the necessary moment longer.

Move into a series of negative statements (made by members) that are beginning to produce a spiral of negativity; pose a question *to the group* to steady the group and keep the way open for other sides or other aspects.

Speak up quickly if a "communication squeeze" has developed, with a few members talking only to each other, thus offering the chance to help build the thought-line to others who have been squeezed out; for example, "Can we hold up just a minute? I was wondering whether there were some other ideas that might need to be brought in here?"

Take pains to share affirmation around the group, showing clearly that any idea is to be considered by all. The leader needs to counter any tendency of quieter members to talk only to the leader, to status members, or to more talkative members.[40]

Make widespread volunteering possible *early* in the meeting lest the difficulty of volunteering increase too much to be overcome.[41]

Foster an atmosphere in which *working for the group* and *being true to one's own ideas* are possible at the same time.[42]

Note any silence (no one volunteering) that becomes destructive of group relationships or wasteful of too much time, but avoid calling on someone or proceeding to give answers to the group; rather, begin to collect the thought-line orally and to talk forward a bit in a tentative way with good spirit, watching the members for growing responsiveness and pausing expectantly to let someone continue the thought-line forward without a break.[43]

Expect and encourage volunteered contributions from members in order to keep from dominating the work too much.[44]

Enabling Cooperative Participation

What the group may need:

To add to the group-developed thought-line, catching up the line with no break and then letting others catch up and carry on with their contributions.

To thread in, at times, helpful words or explanations within others' comments.

To have all members listening to the same speaker at the same time; side conversations are seldom useful or appropriate.

To have each member make a continuing, strong effort to understand the true intent of the persons speaking, granting them their own way of phrasing ideas.

To express differences of fact or opinion by showing first how far the thought-line (as developed by the group) seems correct, then raising a question about the aspect that the speaker sees differently; that is, make it a natural thing to affirm as far as possible, then differ (with a question) where necessary.

To listen supportively to whatever person (member or leader) is speaking, giving that person full attention and respect.

To avoid falling into conflict when members see an issue differently; rather to put the issue out in the middle of the table and treat it as fairly as they can from each of the opposed viewpoints in order to work out the difference fruitfully.

What the leader can do:

Show interest in the responses of all members, whether or not they are taking part in the current exchange; always widen the circle of active response; each person's contribution is shown to be wanted.[45]

Find ways to articulate the goal often, realizing that a clear goal-centeredness invites the group to work at its most effective organization, that is, where what is said by one is thereafter the property of all as if each had made the statement; thus, the leader makes a practice of saying "we" and "our" in referring to task, accomplishment, difficulty, and the like.[46]

Recognize the common enterprise on a common task: "Our view so far, then, is. . . ."

Rephrase a disparaging remark of a member to take out the sting, especially if the sting is directed to another member.[47]

Move an issue away from competing members or factions by stating it clearly, then inviting any and all comments on one side and then any and all on the other side, allowing no rebuttal meanwhile.[48]

Demonstrate from the outset of the discussion *good*

listening, eliciting similar attention to the speaker from others.[49]

Avoid giving special treatment to anyone, that is, exceptional praise, a show of familiarity, or the like.

Stimulate all to enjoy their sense of group achievement and pleasant interaction through the leader's own honest enjoyment and appropriate interjected remarks.

4.3   **CONCLUSION**

The leader of a discussion group plays the major part in focusing the TEAM on its TASK. He or she welcomes leadership acts by members, unless the member, by doing these acts too frequently, destroys the cooperative effort of the group by challenging the leader's focusing role too much.

Certain realities of group functioning are: (1) that a leader must *earn* the role; (2) that the leader must reconcile the group goal and individual member goals; (3) that each task of leadership is different; and (4) that even good leadership cannot make every group successful.

The leader performs his or her function in INNER WORK (observing, analyzing, choosing the action-to-be-taken) and OUTER WORK on both the TASK level (managing the thought-line) and the TEAM level (enabling full, voluntary, and cooperative participation). Suggestions are made as to what the leader's observation and analysis might reveal at a particular point in the work of the group, and as to what some of the possibilities are among which the choices of action-to-be-taken can be made. Leadership is always a creation of and for a particular group with a particular purpose at a particular time in its interaction.

FOOTNOTES – CHAPTER 4

1. Ralph M. Stogdill, *Handbook of Leadership: A Survey of Theory and Research* (New York: The Free Press, 1947), p. 63.

2. Stogdill, *Handbook of Leadership*, p. 176.

3. Norman R. F. Maier, *Problem Solving and Creativity in Individuals and Groups* (Belmont, Calif.: Brooks/Cole Publishing Co., 1970), p. 441.

4. Robert F. Bales and P. E. Slater, "Role Differentiation in Small Decision-Making Groups," in *Family, Socialization, and Interaction Process*, T. Parsons and R. F. Bales, eds. (New York: Free Press, 1955), Chapter V.

5. Amitai Etzioni, "Dual Leadership in Complex Organizations," *American Sociological Review*, **30** (1965): 688–698.

6. Robert F. Bales, "Communication in Small Groups," in *Communication, Language, and Meaning*, George A. Miller, ed. (New York: Basic Books, Inc., 1973), pp. 214–216.

7. Stogdill, *Handbook of Leadership*, pp. 405–406.

8. James J. Cribbin, *Effective Managerial Leadership* (New York: American Management Association, Inc., 1972), p. 47.

9. E. P. Hollander has described the two dimensions involved in building status in a group framework as "the behavior of the object person in accordance with interpersonal expectancies, and his contribution to group goals." In *Leaders, Groups, and Influence* (New York: Oxford University Press, 1964), p. 157.

10. Cribbin, *Effective Managerial Leadership*, p. 20.

11. Humphry Osmond, *Understanding Understanding* (New York: Harper & Row, Publishers, Inc., 1974), p. 201. Dr. Osmond is a renowned British physician and researcher in psychological medicine. Not only does he hold that such a new leader should convey the idea of changes as extensions but that he should do so whether the organization is healthy or is failing.

12. Alan Gewirth, "Political Justice," in *Social Justice*, Richard B. Brandt, ed. (Englewood Cliffs, N.J.: Prentice-Hall, Inc., 1962), p. 168.

13. "Synergy: Some Notes of Ruth Benedict," selected by Abraham H. Maslow and John J. Honigmann, *American Anthropologist*, **72** (April 1970): 325.

14. Fred Massarik and Irving R. Wechsler declare that "As an executive faces the myriad decisions he needs to make, it becomes quite clear that he must master two tasks; he must learn to see accurately the human, as well as the inanimate, factors of the total scene; and he must acquire skills of action, which, while based upon accurate perception, tap wellsprings of behavior that ultimately lead to the successful attainment of personal and organizational goals."—"Empathy Revisited: The Process of Understanding People," in *Organizational Psychology: A Book of Readings*, 2d ed. David A. Kolb, Irwin M. Rubin, James M. McIntyre, eds. (Englewood Cliffs, N.J.: Prentice-Hall, Inc., 1974), p. 224.

15. Theodore M. Mills, *The Sociology of Small Groups* (Englewood Cliffs, N.J.: Prentice-Hall, Inc., 1967), pp. 96–98.

16. Norman R. F. Maier, *Problem-Solving Discussions and Conferences: Leadership Methods and Skills* (New York: McGraw-Hill Book Company, 1963), p. 99.

17. Erving Goffman describes a "chief surgeon" as "host as well as director of his operating team." *Encounters: Two Studies in the Sociology of Interaction* (Indianapolis: The Bobbs-Merrill Co., Inc., 1961), pp. 127–128.

18. Sidney J. Parnes reports from one of his groups the interesting insight of one of the discussants that "in the first grade you don't have to teach children the principles of brainstorming. They do it immediately. One thing really woke me up when I did this with a first-grade group. There were five kids, and three of them were very fluent. They could just rattle off ideas for improving a product. There were two very quiet students: one of these would express a new idea, and the three fluent ones would take off on it. Then suddenly one of the quiet ones would come up with a very different idea, which would set the fluent ones off again. These two quiet ones would just change ideas at right angles. I think what happens in adult groups is that the quiet ones are left behind that way—in other words they keep quiet because they are afraid they'll be laughed at, but quiet kids don't do that. They keep speaking up and sending the group down new avenues."—"Research on Developing Creative Behavior" in *Widening Horizons in Creativity*, Calvin W. Taylor, ed. (New York: John Wiley & Sons, Inc., 1964), p. 168.

19. Maier, *Problem-Solving Discussions and Conferences*, p. 109.

20. The leader needs "elasticity" of mind. Charles de Gaulle wrote of Napoleon: "The story of Napoleon's campaigns is rich in examples of the passionate energy with which he sought to master all the circumstances and conditions of his many battles, and, more especially, of the efforts he made to keep accurately informed about the enemy, and, finally, of the elasticity of his conclusions which he reached and adapted to each situation as it arose." *The Edge of the Sword* (New York: Criterion Books, 1960), p. 89.

21. James J. Cribbin, widely known management consultant, author, and lecturer, describes the leader's need to analyze the probable nature of observed behaviors with the question: "What separates the truly innovative man from the mere pretender?" From the chapter "The Manager-Leader: Catalyst for Change," in *Effective Managerial Leadership* (New York: American Management Association, Inc., 1972), p. 243.

    R. B. Cattell warns that "exuberance . . . should *not* be confused with creativity." Quoted in a chapter entitled "Predictors of Creativity Performance" by Calvin W. Taylor and John Holland in *Creativity: Progress and Potential*, Calvin W. Taylor, ed. (New York: McGraw-Hill Book Company, 1964), p. 28.

22. Since the remedial action of the leader is in the nature of a "control," the suggestions of Kenneth E. Boulding (professor of Economics at the University of Michigan) on control systems seem interesting. He says that "the ability to control anything depends on two factors: the magnitude of the thing to be controlled and the skill and appropriateness of the instruments of control." (p. 324.) And he points out further that "the two greatest problems of control systems are first, signal detection, that is, how do we know when something needs to be done, and second, implementation, or how do we know what to do." (p. 326.) In his view "false alarms" are probably better than "failed alarms." (p. 237.) *Conflict and Defense: A General Theory* (New York: Harper & Row, Publishers, Inc., 1962).

23. Georg Simmel, an eminent German philosopher and early sociologist (1858–1918), who saw life as externally manifested in sociology and the arts, wrote as follows: "By the glance which reveals the other, one discloses himself. By the same act in which the observer seeks to know the observed, he surrenders himself to be understood by the observer. The eye cannot take unless at the same time it gives. . . . What occurs in this direct glance represents the most perfect reciprocity in the entire field of human relationships."–"Sociology of the Senses: Visual Interaction" in *Introduction to the Science of Sociology*, R. E. Park and E. W. Burgess, eds. (Chicago: University of Chicago Press, 1921), p. 358.

24. Stogdill, *Handbook of Leadership*, p. 415.

25. Melvin Sorcher and Herbert H. Meyer, psychologists with the Behavioral Research Service of the General Electric Co., have pointed out the motivational value of articulating subgoals so that members can measure their accomplishment and feel a sense of completion.–"Motivating Factory Employees" in *Human Relations and Organizational Behavior: Readings and Comments*, 3d ed., Keith Davis and William G. Scott, eds. (New York: McGraw-Hill Book Company, 1969), p. 47.

26. Walter M. Lifton has emphasized the importance of the leader's "linking function." *Groups: Facilitating Individual Growth and Societal Change* (New York: John Wiley & Sons, Inc., 1972), p. 166.

27. A tangent may reveal an aspect of the context of the group's topic that might not otherwise come to their attention. Furthermore, the tangent may alert the leader to the tangent-goers' attitudes and give him or her help in the INNER WORK.

28. Mary Henle, in talking about a person working inwardly on his or her own ideas, has made an explanation that is clearly parallel to comments made in the group setting: "Welcoming a new idea is, of course, much more than not forgetting it. It involves first of all formulating it. Words are brought forth to cloak the idea, one and another is tried on for fit. Here it is important to avoid giving the newcomer a premature clarity which may distort or even destroy it."–"The Birth and Death of Ideas," in *Contemporary Approaches to Creative Thinking*, Howard E. Gruber, Glenn Terrell, and Michael Wertheimer, eds. (New York: Prentice-Hall, Inc., 1962), p. 42.

29. In his *Effective Managerial Leadership* (New York: American Management Association, Inc., 1972), pp. 174–177, James J. Cribbin gave twenty types of questions for the leader (with examples), but concluded: "The variety of questions that the manager-leader has in his armory is not of primary importance. The essential thing is that he master the art of asking the right question of the right person at the right time and in the right way. His real purpose is not merely to secure the desired information but additionally to help others learn and to build a more cooperative relationship with them."

30. Norman R. F. Maier and A. R. Solem in an important early study found that more valuable results were reached in groups with leaders who stimulated consideration of

divergent views than in those without such stimulation.—"The Contribution of a Discussion Leader to the Quality of Group Thinking: The Effective Use of Minority Opinions," *Human Relations*, 5 (August 1952): 277–288.

31. Leslie E. This, in *The Leader Looks at the Art of Listening* (Washington, D.C.: Leadership Resources, Inc. 1972), p. 7, declared: "Try not to understand things too soon; do not permit yourself to get too far ahead of the speaker."

32. Norman R. F. Maier recommends screening solutions suggested for consideration on the basis of two negative and two positive principles. He explains:

> The two negative principles that screen out solutions may be stated as follows: (1) solutions transferred from other problems should be rejected: (2) solutions supported by facts or by interpretations of facts that are challenged by other members of a group should be rejected.
> The two positive principles that select solutions for consideration may be stated as follows: (1) solutions founded upon any of the unchallenged facts or unchallenged interpretations of facts (taken from the problem situation) should be selected for consideration and evaluation; (2) when exceptions to a trend in results can be satisfactorily explained, solutions based upon the trend should be selected for further consideration.

Problem-Solving Discussions and Conferences (New York: McGraw-Hill Book Company, 1963), pp. 237–238.

33. William C. Schutz characterizes the group leader as the "completer" and declares that "the prime requisites for a leader are: (1) to know what functions a group needs; (2) to have the sensitivity and flexibility to sense what functions the group is not fulfilling; (3) to have the ability to get the things needed by his group accomplished; and (4) to have the willingness to do what is necessary to satisfy these needs, even though it may be personally displeasing."—"The Leader as Completer," in *Small Group Communication: A Reader*, 2d ed., Robert S. Cathcart and Larry A. Samovar, eds. (Dubuque, Iowa: William C. Brown, Co., 1970), p. 395.

34. Peter Drucker in *The Practice of Management* (New York: Harper & Row, Publishers, Inc., 1954), p. 341, says that "The manager has the task of creating a true whole that is larger than the sum of its parts, a productive unity that turns out more than the sum of the resources put into it."

35. The vital importance of morale-building acts by the leader is expressed in relation to the work of a *new* leader but is certainly true of any leader: "If there is one skill without which a new leader's failure is assured, it is the capacity to assess, raise, rebuild, and foster morale. As Napoleon said, morale is to the physical as ten is to one." Humphry Osmond, *Understanding Understanding* (New York: Harper & Row, Publishers, Inc., 1974), p. 198.

36. "But when all is said and done, developing men still requires a basic quality in the manager which cannot be created by supplying skills or by emphasizing the importance of the task. It requires integrity of character." Drucker, *The Practice of Management*, p. 348.

37. Ralph Waldo Emerson told of the elderly Quaker who said, "It is the not-me in thee which makes thee valuable to me."

38. "The principal lesson of the Bay of Pigs, it seems to us, is that a President must always seek out and weigh carefully the advice of 'no men' who are not swept along by the popular passions of fashionable viewpoints of the day," Editorial, *The Seattle Times*, April 16, 1971.

39. Thomas C. Schelling, Harvard Professor of Economics, declared: "If one can demonstrate to an opponent that the latter is not committed, or that he has miscalculated his commitment, one may in fact undo or revise the opponent's commitment." *The Strategy of Conflict* (Cambridge, Mass.: Harvard University Press, 1960), p. 34.

40. Robert F. Bales found in his research studies on the dominance hierarchy that "the lower person addresses a little more, generally, to the higher person than the higher person addresses to him."—"Communication in Small Groups," in *Communication, Language, and Meaning: Psychological Perspectives*, George A. Miller, ed. (New York: Basic Books, Inc., 1973), p. 212.

41. The response that a group makes to the long-delayed contribution of a quiet member may be unjustified: either too accepting because the group has at last gotten him or

her to talk, or too rejecting because his or her nonconformity (lack of involvement) had started too early and persisted too long. E. P. Hollander in *Leaders, Groups, and Influence* (New York: Oxford University Press, 1964), Preface, p. x, said that "early nonconformity . . . diminished considerably the ability to influence the group to accept what were in fact good solutions."

42. James J. Cribbin, *Effective Managerial Leadership*, p. 242, stated: "More imaginative ideas have been done in by the negative attitudes of authorities than by lack of evidence." He pointed out further (p. 243) that "openness, flexibility, and sensitivity [are] essential to innovation."

43. "It appears that if silences become too long, interpersonal relationships are strained, uncertain, and perhaps threatened or beyond repair." Thomas J. Bruneau, "Communicative Silences: Forms and Functions," *The Journal of Communication*, **23** (March 1973): 29.

44. James J. Cribbin, *Effective Managerial Leadership*, p. 238, said: "It is always wise and often necessary for the manager to have other people serve as his corrective mirror lest he become the victim of his own views, preferences, and aversions."

45. Gordon L. Lippitt and Edith Whitfield explain the relationship between a member's identity and his or her cooperative action in *The Leader Looks at Group Effectiveness* (Washington, D. C.: Leadership Resources, Inc., 1961), p. 5: "Perhaps the most effective cohesiveness is that which enables members to work together in an *inter-dependent* way, where each member feels free to invest himself and to make his contribution toward the work of the group, while retaining his individuality."

    The members need to feel themselves "enlarged" in the cooperative undertaking. John Dewey, in his essay, "Democracy and Education," says: "To be a recipient of a communication is to have an enlarged . . . experience. One shares in what another has thought and felt, and in so far, meagerly or amply, has his own attitude modified. Nor is the one who communicates left unaffected . . . Except in dealing with commonplaces and catch phrases, one has to assimilate, imaginatively, something of another's experience in order to tell him intelligently of one's own experience. All communication is like art."

46. Ernst Cassirer, German theorist on scientific knowledge, wrote: "The thought of one partner is kindled by that of another. And by virtue of this interaction each constructs for himself a 'shared' world of meaning within the medium of language." Ernst Cassirer, *The Logic of Humanities*, Clarence Smith Howe, trans. (New Haven: Yale University Press, 1961), p. 113.

47. Norman Maier suggests: "If the situation can be blamed for an outbreak, if the foreman restates an attack so as to remove the sting, or if he protects the person who might otherwise go to his own defense, disagreement may be prevented from disrupting constructive problem solving." *Problem Solving Discussions and Conferences*, p. 128.

48. Irving J. Lee has explained how to move a group effectively into agreement in his article entitled "Procedure for 'Coercing Agreement' " in *Harvard Business Review*, **32** (January–February 1954): 39–45.

    Rensis Likert says that ". . . the stimulation of diversity yields new insights and fosters creativity." *New Patterns of Management* (New York: McGraw-Hill Inc., 1961), p. 25. And again (p. 132): ". . . groups can contribute significantly to creativity by providing the stimulation of diverse points of view within a supportive atmosphere which encourages each individual member to pursue new and unorthodox concepts."

49. W.J.J. Gordon, in his "Operational Approach to Creativity" in *Harvard Business Review*, **34** (November–December 1956): 41–51, explains that the riskiness of the speculative approach demands an atmosphere free of criticism; discipline is necessary to get group members to defer solutions.

    Mary P. Follett, in her pioneering work, *Creative Experience* (New York: Longmans, Green & Co., 1924), p. 174, declared: "Our 'opponents' are our co-creators, for they have something to give which we have not. The basis of all cooperative activity is integrated diversity."

    La Rochefoucauld (1665) wrote: "The reason why so few people are agreeable in conversation is that each is thinking more about what he intends to say than about what others are saying, and we never listen when we are eager to speak."

PART TWO

The Chronology

CHAPTER 5
PREPARATION FOR THE MEETING

5.41   On the TASK WORK

5.42   On the TEAM WORK

5.5   Conclusion

We have all seen things like the following happen:

1.   A person was asked to chair an open but small meeting set to begin at 1 P.M. A small room with a table and ten chairs was reserved. Fifteen people had arrived by 12:55 and a *last-moment search for another room was started*. One person was left behind to bring any late arrivers to the new room; those who went on ahead "stalled for time" until all were finally assembled. A half hour was wasted, and, worse, the momentum of the meeting was lost. The group had also been inadvertently divided into subgroups—those who were early and those who came later. The effect was much the same as if one or two persons had missed the previous meeting and must be filled in on what they missed while the others in the group wait.

2.   A short course on group decision making was being presented. A carefully prepared and edited tape recording was made at 3.75 ips to illustrate a number of important concepts, and the opening session of the workshop was planned around the use of that tape recording. When the time of the meeting came, it was found that the only available tape recorder would play only 7.5 ips tapes. *That meeting had to be restructured on the spot without the use of the recording.* The question arises: How much more valuable could that session and the ones that followed have been had the proper tape recorder been on hand at the initial meeting?

3.   A group began a working session on prison reforms that were needed in the state. As the discussion began it became apparent that *no one present had the necessary specific information* about the state's *current reform efforts* to permit the group to proceed. Without knowing the *status quo* they were hard pressed to be specific about what the exact nature of the problem was or what would constitute new approaches to remedy it.

4.   A ten-member group met periodically to discuss current best-sellers. The task objective was to explore some of the major ideas in the work and to draw out implications and possible applications in their own lives. As one meeting got underway,

the leader for the evening discovered that *only three persons* had read the book. Among those who had not read it were two persons on whom the leader had especially counted to provide spark and some novel ideas for the session.

In these situations—and dozens of others in which arrangements, equipment, information, preparation, and the like are inadequate— groups cannot do their best nor can they feel satisfied about what they have done. Although failure is possible for any group at any time, the more about an upcoming meeting that can be anticipated, thought through, and planned for, the more likely it is that the meeting can be productive and worthwhile. Such preparation done or instigated by the leader or other planners prior to the meeting in- volves a number of matters, such as preliminary decisions on the discussion question, the meeting time and place, and the group size and composition. Preparation for the meeting should also include notification and involvement of the members and specific arrange- ments for the carrying-on of the meeting. Even though the situation may require that persons other than the leader handle some of these matters, one important aspect must be handled by the leader alone: personal preparation for the leadership job.

5.1   PRELIMINARY DECISIONS

What is the group to talk *about*? Should it be some *topic* of interest or concern? But if the members are to talk *about* a topic, that is precisely what they will do, go round and round ABOUT the topic without getting anywhere. The planning must result in a *wording of the question* that will enable the members to get under way together. Such phrasing would point right to the matter they are to discuss and do so unambiguously and concisely.

Points to the Matter. Suppose a citizen group intends to talk about reducing juvenile crime. But juvenile crime *where*: in their own city? in their state? in the nation as a whole? These qualifying words would lead to quite different discussions. The differences in the problem, in the resources available for rem- edying it, and the solutions that would be appropriate are very great. To the extent possible, the more that the scope of a problem can be narrowed, the more limited and specific will be the resulting group discussion. But, in every case, the planners must decide what is their charge and mission, and must phrase the discussion question at the appropriate level; they must indicate clearly what question they want the group to answer.

Suppose the question posed were: What are the causes of juvenile crime in Seattle? That phrasing asks only for a listing, a bill of particulars, not for a solution to the problem. If a solution is desired, the question should *not* ask just for a listing. Of course, if this discussion desires only a determination of the causal factors (and that could be a worthy question), the phrasing suggested would be appropriate.

Or suppose that the question were phrased as: Should juvenile offenders in Washington State be required to receive psychiatric counseling? That is a straightforward question, and it can be answered with a simple Yes or No. But such phrasing is not appropriate for problem-solving discussion groups. It does not ask the group to compare psychiatric counseling with any alternative methods before deciding, and it focuses attention at the end of the decision-making process without adequate thought on the earlier stages. Furthermore, such phrasing tends to lock the members into their preconceived opinions of whether the answer should be Yes or No, and tends to make them try to persuade each other rather than cooperate in building a group answer. This type of phrasing should be avoided for a discussion group.

The statement of the question should point directly at what the group is to discuss. If finding a solution to recommend or act upon is what is intended, then something along the lines of: How can we best reduce the incidence of juvenile crime in Seattle (or Washington State, or the USA)? is appropriate. If the group is talking about one part of a problem (without choosing or building a solution), then: How bad is juvenile crime in Seattle? or What are the causes of juvenile crime in Washington State?, or What is being done today to reduce the incidence of juvenile crime in American cities?, or How successful has the Los Angeles plan of reducing juvenile crime been? are suitable questions. Not only must the phrasing be appropriate to the thought process necessary to achieve the group purpose but it must also delimit the scope of the problem to be discussed so that the group does not attempt an impossible job. Appropriate settlement of these matters is of extreme importance in preparing for a successful meeting.

Does So Unambiguously and Concisely. Definitions of key terms in the question will be needed in the discussion, and the leader should bring alternative definitions to the meeting for initial consideration and group agreement. In the juvenile crime question, for example, who is a "juvenile?" Does this mean youth from birth on or from, say, eight years old? And an upper limit must also be set. The term used in the question need not itself necessarily spell out these limits, but it should *be definable*. The leader is responsible for giving these matters of definition some early and careful thought, and for suggesting some possible definitions for the group's thought in the event that adequate definitions not be contributed by members. All this for the word *juvenile*. Next could come the word *crime*.

Nor must the statement of the question be long and involved; it must catch up the point intended not only with definable terms but without clutter. Unnecessary words must be omitted so that the important words stand clear. The statement should not be "How can the caring citizens of King County see that their children have better educational opportunities?" but perhaps, "How can educational opportunities for children in King County be improved?" Here the three parts stand out: What? (educational opportunities) For whom? (children in King County) The goal? (improvement). This question asks for ways, several ways perhaps, but does not ask the group to decide among the ways. Were a choice desired, the question could read: "How can educational opportunities . . . best be improved?" and the group would then choose among the alternatives or build a composite solution.

5.12   The Meeting Time and Place

When and where the group will meet are also important questions for the leader (or other planners) to decide.

When. How soon? How long? How often? These questions and others need thoughtful handling. Sometimes group meetings, especially in business, government, education, and church settings, are scheduled at stated intervals, with the hour and duration of the meetings being known to all members. In such cases flexibility lies more in tailoring questions to fit these expected meeting times than in time changes. A university departmental staff would not expect to settle the matter of all graduate requirements for the master's degree in one ninety-minute meeting, but perhaps one or two aspects of these requirements could be handled.

On the other hand, making arrangements for a newly constituted group involves a number of important issues.

1. *Single or series*? Shall the new group meet once or hold a series of meetings? Often, of course, only one meeting is intended: an interested group of citizens can meet to ask themselves: What is the best way to get more Precinct 32 voters to the polls in November? But either the question or the group purpose may indicate the need for a series of meetings. The question of how to handle the present sharp increase in shoplifting goes too deeply into the social structure of our day to be handled in a single meeting, and a topic such as developing a better community spirit in the neighborhood would surely demand a series of meetings.

   If the meetings are to be arranged in a series, how far apart should the meetings be scheduled? In our experience intervals between meetings of more than one week require too much repetition and rebuilding of previous meetings at the outset of all later meetings. A concentrated series of meetings, such as every morning for a week or a workshop weekend at a conference site, sometimes achieves much more work and strengthens the impact. But if the meetings are to be held on consecutive weeks, the series should last no longer than six or eight weeks. Although governmental bodies meet over lengthy periods and study groups sometimes maintain long-term interest by taking a new topic (book, noted person, historical period, scientific achievement) for each meeting, less cohesive and dedicated groups should hold to something like eight weeks as the upper limit; if the members then wished to go on, they could decide to take on a new series.

2. *Next week or next quarter*? Despite the dictum "Strike while the iron is hot" (which is, of course, not a bad practice), the group may need *lead time* for preparing or shifting schedules. For example, if a floor manager in a department store sees a problem developing, the staff may be summoned to meet right after lunch; on the other hand, if these employees are to consider better use of existing facilities in displaying merchandise, they may need time to visit other stores or to consult trade maga-

zines. The leader as planner will base the choice of time for the meeting primarily upon the urgency of the problem but should also consider the time needed for appropriate preparation.

3. *Time of day*? Situations vary so much from one another that only a vague outline for making choices can be suggested. What will disrupt the members' schedules the least, avoid meal preparation times, or steer clear of regularly scheduled office-conference hours? On the other hand, what will utilize energies the best? Certainly not scheduling a meeting for the sleepiest time of the day, or when fatigue has set in, or at that precious morning hour when the demands of the day need to be noted and scheduled. Getting the most effective hour for the meeting is worth every effort it takes.

4. *How long*? Should the meeting last one hour, two hours, or longer? A subtle adjustment is needed here between what must be accomplished and what the capacities (mental, emotional, and physical) of the members are for sticking to the task.

The leader (or other planners) will be asking questions such as the following:

> Will the members be stimulated by the question at the outset, or will their enthusiasm and motivation have to be built?
> Will much information need to be presented (by members or the leader) before the thought-line can even begin to take shape, or will the facts need only be *called to mind*?
> Are the members accustomed to working through a problem rather than jumping too quickly into solutions?
> Do the members take pains to look at alternatives before making up their minds on *one*?
> How TASK-ready are the members likely to be?
> Have the members ever worked together before and effectively?
> Or are they strangers or perhaps know each other by name only, and so will need more time to become TEAM-ready?

These matters all relate to the gearing up of the group at the outset of the meeting.

There is also the factor of slowing down (within the session or as time is drawing to a close), of letting up on effort out of fatigue, diminution of interest in the topic, frustration over slow progress, or returning concern, even anxiety, about external matters.

These expenditures of the group's time must be foreseen

as much as possible and allowed for in deciding how long the meeting must last for the group to accomplish the task.

Another matter for decision is whether there should be *rest breaks* during the meeting time. If so, at what point in the deliberations? How long? Should coffee be provided? The leader should probably consider a break desirable if the group thought-line would not unravel too much in the recess, and if the members can and will go at the task afterward with renewed vigor and without too much loss of time and team feeling. If a break is planned, should the time be announced at the outset (that is, will the anticipation of the break do more good than harm in the group work)? or should the time be left open so that the leader can sense the moment in the discussion when the break will do the most good and the least harm? The minutes to be spent in the break must be counted in when planning the overall length of the session.

With the task necessities in one hand, as it were, and the human limitations in the other, the leader as planner weighs the situation as well as possible, decides, and makes the necessary preparation. A "wrong" decision here—to have or not to have a break, to have it at a particular time or of a particular length—may be realized and changed in the meeting. If it is carried out when the realities of the meeting itself have shown it to be unwise, the break may cause serious harm to the group achievement.

Where. Where shall the meeting be held? There is considerable evidence that people work better when they are in pleasant surroundings. A quiet room of ample size but not so large as to dwarf the group at its work, with good lighting, comfortable seating, fresh air, and appropriate temperature are all factors to which the leader should attend in doing the planning. Less than excellent accommodations cannot defeat a good group, but they can seriously damage the work of a weaker one and can subtly drain the energies and less subtly try the patience of any group. All of us know how soft, cushiony chairs and a country club atmosphere tend to undermine the work aspect of a meeting.

In business the place of meeting often brings in a prestige factor; the member who travels the least distance to attend the meeting or who is able to show the sumptuousness of his offices when he hosts the meeting may be given the edge in the discussion. The leader must make arrangements that will tend to keep the entire group in the best condition to do its work well; if one building and room would favor certain members and make others an out-group, a neutral setting must be found. Groups will often enjoy the generosity of a member who is able to offer them splendid accommodations, but such enjoyment must not be allowed to harm the work the members do together.

Another important factor to be considered is the table arrangements (whether a single table or several smaller ones) that would best allow the members to do their work.

The single table should be of a size and shape that will let all participants see and hear each other easily. An oval-shaped table is *excellent* and a rectangular one is only adequate. A round table sounds superior but, except with relatively small tables and small groups, it has one serious disadvantage: if the group is much larger than five, the sight-lines across the necessarily larger round table are too long to give the feeling of close cooperation that is essential for good team functioning. If several tables are used for a single group, the tables should be arranged so that all participants (as with the single table) can see and hear each other easily. Placing these tables to approximate an oval and seating participants only along the outside edges often achieves this purpose.

Some have suggested that having no table at all brings the members into a more friendly relationship; we hold that a task group usually needs a table to emphasize the members' concerted attack upon that task and to provide a working space for their materials. Only when the primary task of a group is to *build group relationships* might it be better not to use tables, for without a table each member could have a *full* view of all the others.

5.13   The Size and Composition of the Group

How well the factors of size and composition are handled will have a great deal to do with how well the group can function. Sometimes there is no chance to seek an optimum number of members or the most advantageous composition of the group. For example, a person who wants to gain the cooperation of his or her staff must have the whole staff present (or their representatives), whether they make up a group of five or fifteen people. And a precinct committee set up to evaluate the procedures that were used in the primary election campaign just completed will be as small or as large as the number of workers dictates. Nevertheless, when flexibility is possible, the optimum size and composition of a group should be approximated.

Size. What is the optimum size for a discussion group? What number of participants will best implement the discussion process? The nature of the group's TASK will make a difference. If the group is to *make a decision*, it must have a chance to tap the information and thinking powers of every person in the group in order to make the soundest judgment possible. On the other hand, if the purpose of the group is to study a question for individual enlightenment rather than group decision or action, there is less necessity that everyone assist so fully in producing the group thought-line. Despite the fact that an individual's development will no doubt be greater if he or she frequently enters the group interaction, yet the individual's inner and silent investment must not be completely discounted. The enlightenment group can thus have more members than the decision-making group.

What are the disadvantages of having a decision-making group that is too large or too small? The leader as planner must realize that in too large a group (1) the opportunities for each member to speak up will be fewer; the more aggressive members will speak up and tend to speak more while the quieter ones speak less or not at all; (2) splinter groups are likely to arise; and (3) consensus is extremely hard to achieve. If the group is too small (1) there is likely to be too narrow a view of the problem; (2) the members are likely to feel pressed into speaking when they don't really wish to speak at the time; (3) everyone is too visible so that what is said is too easily and closely connected to the speaker; and (4) the group often cannot afford a focusing agent because with so few members the leader must play a member role.

If a group seeking only enlightenment on a problem is too large, its value is reduced, probably for all present, but the damage is not as great as it would be in a decision-making group. If the enlightenment group is too small, the contagious enthusiasm that makes such a group come alive overworks the few members; they have no rest from participation. Also such a group is too much at the mercy of chance; there may be no one present (other than the leader) with enough spark or information or vision to carry the ball. To have the leader provide most of the energy in an enlightenment discussion is like saying: "You've *got* to have a good time!"

If the leader is arranging a decision-making group, it is best to have *five* to *seven* members, counting himself or herself as one. Several researchers, having found that members are generally less well satisfied in groups that are larger or smaller than five, have reasoned that *five* may be the optimum number. From his classic experiments at Harvard University, Robert F. Bales[1] considers *five* the optimum number and *more than seven* too many for his task groups. Bales further points out:

> There seems to be a crucial point at seven. Below seven, for the most part, each person in the group says at least something to each other person. In groups over seven the low participators tend to stop talking to each other and center their communications on the few top men. The tendencies toward centralization of communication seem to increase rather powerfully as size increases.[2]

Research studies have indicated that a group of *four* tends to set two pairs of people against each other, and that a group of *three* tends to make one member a "slider" who sides now with one and then with the other of the group members, each of whom tries to win his or her approval rather than trying to solve the problem together. Arranging a group of *five* avoids both of these invitations to alignment and contention; five is probably the smallest number in which the psychological forces tend to foster cooperation instead of setting the stage for contention.

Our experience underscores the effectiveness of having seven members in a decision-making group and brings us to prefer it to the even-numbered six-member group or the often too small five-member group. Generally speaking, a decision-making group should be large enough to bring in a sufficient variety of ideas and lines of thinking, and small enough to function efficiently on its task.

How much larger can a group meeting for individual enlightenment be? Since it is not necessary that everyone speak or that the group move to a reliable consensus on its topic, the planner of such a session could well extend the cutoff point beyond seven, perhaps even to as many as fifteen or twenty members.

Composition. As explained previously, some groups are made up of persons whose positions on a staff or as representatives of other groups give them automatic membership in the group, which is then as predetermined in composition as it is in size.

Where choice is possible, the leader as planner needs to do what can be done to put together a group with a high chance of handling the task successfully. The planner seeks to put together a group whose members together possess all the information necessary to the performance of their task, plus the ability to interpret and use it. Furthermore, the planner seeks to keep knowledge and ability distributed generally through the group, realizing that where great differences raise prestige barriers, communication and cooperation are likely to suffer. In considering the actual membership of the group, the leader tries to think of persons who will view the process as the cooperative framing of an understanding or an answer and will be willing to put their differing abilities and knowledge to imaginative use.

The leader knows the necessity of building in diversity (of information, thinking patterns, attitudes) so that the many-sided consideration of problems, which is the essence of discussion, may occur. If there is no way of knowing the members directly, the leader can yet reach for valuable differences by selecting persons whose occupation, activities, age, and sex suggest possible variations in viewpoint and information. The leader realizes, for example, that a particular physician and a particular librarian may be more similar in beliefs and information on this special subject than that same physician and another physician, or that the young management consultant may actually be more conservative than the older one. But the attempt to develop diversity is made.

When the leader knows to some extent the people from whom the group is being chosen, it is possible to build in diversity with a surer touch. A minister of a large city church desired input on his preaching from the members of his congregation in a discussion setting. He invited three couples:

1. One young: husband in banking, wife a new mother.
2. Another in early middle years: husband a high school science teacher, wife a speech therapist and singer in a church choir.

3. An older couple with family grown: husband in investment banking, wife with the telephone company.

He also invited five single people:

1. A young woman graduate student.
2. A rising, young, male lawyer.
3. A middle-aged widow who had gone back to a job in
   working with medical records.
4. A mechanical arts and recreation instructor in an experimental high school.
5. A retired woman professor.

The minister knew that these people differed in experience,
training, and interests and he realized that a group needs
sidesteppers (members who can turn the group to an entirely
different tack) as well as *fluent-developers* (members who are
quick to add details, make adjustments, give ideas shape), to
use the terms suggested by Parnes.[3] The minister knew that the
group needed reality-testers as well as vision-builders, boundary-
testers as well as mainstreamers. Looking ahead, the leader
asked himself: what about *social skills*? in what interactional
ability must we have someone especially strong? Doubtless
he decided upon having at least one very articulate person, the
kind who catches up the entire group by the way he or she
grasps and phrases ideas, and is ready and willing to speak up.
Doubtless he also wanted to have someone who was a morale-
builder, a person with that special warmth, that open goodwill
that binds a group together. Not that the minister, the leader,
could not provide these assets for the group but he realized
that someone *in the group* needs to be doing these things too
so that the members will be certain to see them as member
functions also. By giving this attention to diversity, the leader
has attempted to build in those conditions that characterize
creativity—*flexibility*, *fluency*, *originality*, and *elaboration*—as
well as the socialization skills of organization and cooperation.[4]

The leader seeks for the group people who are already interested in the subject or who are capable of becoming interested. It may be less obvious that the leader watches the matter
of interpersonal relationships; that is, where the choice is
between two persons with the positive characteristics mentioned the leader avoids certain disruptive types: the dogmatic
and the counterformer. No group works as well when it in-

cludes a person who is overpositive and opinionated, who considers that he or she comes to give advice rather than to cooperate with equals. Nor does a group work well when it has a member who is against everything, who sees the negative aspect unrelentingly.[5] Nevertheless, if such a dogmatic or counterforming person is truly outstanding in a desired positive trait, the leader may choose the person anyway, counting on a generally strong group and an alert leader to provide a buffer against this person.

The leader should not think that people whom he or she has seen work in a fair-minded and purposeful way in one setting will necessarily act similarly in a different group or toward a different purpose, despite their potential for doing so. Nevertheless, upon that potential for mutual trust and cooperation, the leader rests the group's chances.

5.2   NOTIFICATION OF THE MEMBERS

Word of the meeting must reach the prospective members early enough to allow them to adjust their schedules and make the necessary preparation. If someone cannot come, the leader may want to substitute someone else who can bring information, experience, and clear thinking to the meeting in his or her stead. Furthermore, if a member has a completely different approach to the subject or access to extremely unusual and important information, he or she can then make these known to the leader *before* the meeting rather than dropping this information like bombshells during the meeting. For example, if this member wanted to talk about the United Nations' role in the milk-for-babies-in-the-Third-World problem rather than the multinational corporations' role, this suggestion could be made when it could be considered fairly rather than at a time when the suggestion would throw the group off course, catch the leader relatively unprepared, and make the leader seem to be a dictator. On the other hand, if the member had unusually good material to offer, it is possible to let the leader know at a time when the leader could work it more effectively into the agenda. Of course, members will, throughout any discussion, bring up material unknown to others; this is one of the obvious great sources of group effectiveness. But the ideas referred to here are large in scope and shattering in their significance; the leader needs to be alerted to them, if possible, during the time of preparation. The leader is fortunate if the notification of the meeting to the members will alert the member to his or her own gold mine of information and induce the member to tell the leader of it before the meeting.

Some situations do not require a written notification of a meeting, such as when the group has met before, or when telephone or direct contact has set time and topic well enough, or when the work will go forward upon present information. Many situations, however, call for written notification to achieve such purposes as these:

1. Clarify time and place of meeting.
2. Announce formal statement of question.
3. Declare the format of the meeting.

Where the format of the meeting will differ from the usual round-table discussion, the members should be notified as to what to expect. For example, if the leader thinks it desirable to give extended opening remarks—perhaps bringing the group up to date on the local situation or presenting data that is not available to the members—before opening the question for discussion, this planned use of the first fifteen or twenty minutes by the leader should be made known to the members in the notification. Or, if the leader is arranging to bring one or more experts to the meeting to give an explanation or background information for the use of the group, the name and qualifications of the experts should be included in the notification.

Where desirable, the notification may serve the following additional purposes:

1. Identify the members of the group.
2. Include materials on the topic.
3. List useful sources on the topic.
4. Set up the agenda for the meeting.

5.21   Identification

Showing the caliber and diversity of the participants by giving the names and qualifications of the participants in the notification may heighten the potential value of the meeting in the eyes of the members. Such information on past accomplishments is certainly unnecessary where the members know each other professionally, as in 1958 when six eminent scientists met at the University of Colorado to talk about creative thinking: Jerome Bruner of Harvard, Richard Crutchfield of the University of California, Mary Henle of the New School for Social Research, Robert B. MacLeod of Cornell, David C. McClelland of Harvard, and Herbert Simon of the Carnegie Institute of Technology. Obviously, the notification to these thinkers whose careers were well known to each other would not list their respective publications and honors. But if, when Jerome Bruner was on a lecture tour and a number of men and women from a half dozen disciplines—from architecture to astronomy—were gathered to enjoy discussion with this team-oriented thinker, the notification should surely carry the names, interests, and accomplishments of the group members. In many situations, however, it would be neither necessary nor possible to list the participants in the notification.

5.22 Materials

When an information base for the discussion is essential, the leader should consider assembling well-presented materials to inform and stimulate the members. Materials that give a one-sided view should be avoided, and clearly written articles or easily understood charts or graphs that fulfill all the tests of reliable information and sources should be chosen. Nor should too much material be sent, surely not more than could or would be read by most members. When information on the discussion topic is included, the notification must reach the participants early enough so that it can be used; getting excellent reading materials too late is highly frustrating. Even if the members do not—for lack of time or of initial interest—go into the materials very thoroughly, yet this care to provide a start to their thinking will show the importance of the meeting; it invites involvement. But the tone of the notification should not imply that the materials provided form the complete basis for the discussion; members should feel encouraged to go beyond these pieces of information rather than be discouraged from doing so. A list of additional sources will help to suggest further study.

5.23 List of Sources

Suggestions of books and articles on the subject are often

helpful in enriching the background of the members and in raising issues for their consideration. Usually no more than a half dozen sources should be noted, and probably the most valuable one or two sources should be pointed out. The leader should also limit the list to books and magazines that are likely to be available in local libraries and bookstores. A brief annotation on each item would help the member to choose with more assurance among these suggestions.

5.24 Agenda for the Meeting

A brief list of subtopics—often in question form—will be helpful to apprise the members of the lines of thinking the discussion will probably take. If a citizens' group were to discuss the question: What is the best way to handle the infant milk crisis in Third World countries? in a series of six meetings, the notification might indicate the topic for each meeting:

Meeting	Date	Topic
1	Oct. 4	How serious is the shift from breast to bottle feeding?
2	Oct. 11	What has caused the shift to bottle feeding?
3	Oct. 18	How useful is regulation of advertisement and distribution of commercial infant milk as a way?
4	Oct. 25	How useful is education of health professionals and mothers as a way?
5	Nov. 1	How useful is self-determination and self-reliance as a way?
6	Nov. 2	What part can we as American citizens play?

Or if the group wanted to talk only about the part being played in the shift by the advertising of the multinational corporations as a single-meeting topic, the notification might include such subtopics as these:

Question: How are multinational corporations expanding their Baby milk markets in Third World countries?

Subtopics: 1. Advertising to the public.

    2. Advertising to health professionals.
    3. Advertising through health professionals.
    4. Advertising by health professionals.
    5. Advertising to shopkeepers.

Whether the leader was preparing the notification for the series or for the single meeting, it would be helpful to add a brief list of easily obtainable sources. And the leader may also want to consult the *Cornell International Nutrition Monograph Series*, especially No. 2 (1975) "The Promotion of Bottle Feeding by Multinational Corporations: How Advertising and the Health Professions Have Contributed" by Ted Greiner, and No. 4 (1977) "Regulation and Education: Strategies for Solving the Bottle Feeding Problem" also by Ted Greiner. Knowing that local libraries or bookstores would probably not have these monographs, the leader could reproduce several items to be included with the notification to the members.

If the question has been talked about superficially in the media and the leader needs to invite the members to begin thinking about the question at a deeper level, or if the question is especially emotional or controversial, the leader should consider spelling out some of the subtopics when announcing the agenda.

5.3   SPECIFIC ARRANGEMENTS FOR THE MEETING

The leader (or the other planners) can do a great deal more to set the stage for a successful meeting than merely arranging for an appropriate time and place and sending out the notification. The leader can think through carefully whether having information available would help, what pieces of equipment might be useful, and whether experts on the subject might be needed and, if so, who they might be.

5.31 Information

Grade school teachers meeting to plan better bus-boarding procedures should need no specific preparation for the meeting; their past experience will provide the information that is most needed. In other groups, members will have done some preliminary reading and thinking on the question before the meeting. Even so, the leader needs to consider what graphs, maps, sets of figures, and summaries of reports should be made available to help the group in its deliberations. The materials put before the members must not be so detailed or complex as to be baffling and time consuming. So the leader seeks out the relevant portions and finds a way to present them quickly—as photocopies, flip charts, overhead projections, slides, or movie strips—to all members of the group. At times the leader would want a photocopied graph, drawing, or set of data for each individual in the group to look at separately. At other times the leader might plan to hand out only one copy for every two members so that members will cooperate in looking at the materials even as (or perhaps before) they cooperate in talking together.

5.32   Equipment

Whether the piece of equipment is a chalkboard, a tape recorder, a projector, or a film—the equipment must be in position, tested, and adequate to the use to be made of it by the time the group assembles. Hence, the leader (or other planners) must have arranged for its use, its placement in the room, and its testing. Although a telephone call to the custodians at the meeting place on the meeting day will give the leader some assurance of the equipment's presence and usability, it is also important for the leader to arrive early enough to be sure that the equipment is there and ready to use.

5.33   Experts

If the understanding of the group is likely to be enhanced by having one or more resource persons present at the time of the meeting, the leader needs to choose persons not only with the experience and information that will be helpful but the resource persons must understand that they are *providing grounds* for the group's thinking rather than *substituting* their own for it. Whether such an expert would remain throughout the discussion after giving an initial presentation of information would depend upon the expert's schedule and upon the likelihood of his or her being needed for additional facts at later points in the group's thinking.

The leader must think of the possible impact of the expert upon the self-confidence of the members. The leader's introduction of the expert and attitude as leader toward the expert would be large factors in the expert's usefulness to the group. If it seems, however, that the presence of an expert would make the members reluctant to offer their ideas, the leader might consider putting before them material prepared by the expert rather than having the expert actually come to the meeting.

5.4   THE LEADER'S PERSONAL PREPARATION

We are *not* thinking here of the leader's reading of a shelf book on theories of leadership, although many of us do so (with profit) from time to time. We are concerned in this desk book with specific preparations made by the leader for this job as he or she sees it. Such preparations would relate both to work on the TASK and work with the TEAM.

5.41 On the TASK Work

At two earlier points in this chapter we have mentioned aspects of this preparation: the leader notifies the members of the meeting, often including information or lists of sources and often subquestions that are likely to come up, and the leader arranges to have specific materials in front of the members at the time of the meeting. Of course, the leader is preparing himself or herself as well as the members in readying these materials.

In addition to materials that the leader thinks would be helpful for the members to read before the meeting or to see while they discuss, the leader needs to possess appropriate knowledge for every important turn of thought the group will likely take during the discussion—information on the symptoms, the present programs being used, the plans that have failed and the ones that have succeeded, and the dangers inherent in doing anything at all. Such information is needed for two reasons:

To cover any gaps that may occur in the members' knowledge.

To alert the leader to any pieces of information that are questionable as to their accuracy, recency, typicality, or scope.

Suppose that a citizens' group, busy in its discussion of the activities of multinational corporations in developing countries, worries over the content of breast milk in areas where the protein factor in the daily diet is low, and thinks that the surge to bottle feeding is probably a good thing for that reason. If this were the group consensus, wrong though it is, it will be built into the thought-line unless the leader knows and can offer to the group the information that the protein factor of the mother's diet has little effect upon the content of her breast milk. It is true that the milk she produces is less in quantity but the protein, lactose, and fat components are hardly changed at all.[6] Thus, the leader's information would have filled a gap in the group's knowledge and have enabled them to correct their thought-line.

Or suppose that the group undertaking the series of meetings on the *infant milk crisis* were talking about the possibilities of regulation of advertising by the multinational companies, and a member points out that some of these companies have seemed to develop a conscience, that Abbott and Bristol Myers, for example, have worked out codes of ethics that would stop mass media advertising in Third World countries. If the leader knows that this report is correct *so far as it goes* but that the codes do nothing to stop the use of milk nurses and the distribution of free samples,[7] the leader can point out the false implication that the group might reach.

How to present these corrective items so that the leader's contributions will not submerge the work of the group is another matter that the leader must handle within the meeting itself.

When preparing notes for his or her own use during the discussion, the leader moves from the general structure suggested in the phrasing of the question. If a short listing were being sent out in the notification, the leader would amplify that set of subquestions or subtopics in order to have a basis for deeper questioning and a reservoir of relevant information. The leader should consider:

1. Are all four steps of the Problem Management Sequence involved in handling the discussion question? Or is only some portion necessary?
2. How deeply into the subpoints under the steps should the listing go? For the material sent with the notification? For the leader's own preparation?

There are many times when the full PMS will not be possible, and there are times when not all four major steps are necessary. The PMS may not be possible because the time may be too short, or because the participants simply are not able to meet the demands. The PMS may not be necessary because the question being discussed involves only a portion of the full sequence.

Nevertheless, the leader who really grasps the pull and haul of the Sequence, who knows how ideas fit together, and who sees how the subordinated parts provide depth and breadth in the inquiry, will be prepared to know

1. *How to manage group time*: that is, which inquiries can be omitted or treated lightly, if necessary, and when enough work has been done on a particular aspect.

2. *How to ask questions* that advance the thought-line dependably: that is, ones that link what has been done with what must yet be done, ones that recommend themselves to the members by their very reasonableness.

3. *How to detect tangents*: that is, to distinguish unfruitful movements of thought from fruitful ones.

4. *How to keep the group steady on its course*: that is, how the little relates to the large and how to use the built-in safeguards to shallow or narrow thinking.

Thus, the leader's personal notes need to follow the PMS structure carefully in order to provide steady footing in the busy, sometimes highly confusing interaction that takes place in the group.

5.42 On the TEAM Work

The leader in the premeeting planning needs to think out how well acquainted the members of the group will be. Will they need to be introduced? What are the pertinent factors about their experience and interests? Might it be better in this situation to get right to the TASK (after names are exchanged) and let acquaintance and trust grow in the course of their work together? How much warming up will it take for this particular combination of individuals to work well together, that is, what is their degree of TEAM-readiness? If some preliminary warming up seems to be needed, what small inquiry—responded to by each at random or around the table—would open up the group to each other and give a few moments of pleasant interaction? Some groups try questions such as:

1. Where were you when . . . (you heard the news of Kennedy's assassination; or the earthquake that struck two years ago?)

2. What is your first memory of . . . (Thanksgiving? winning a prize?)

Many of the decisions the leader makes in other parts of the preparation will provide groundwork for the development of the TEAM. Out of his long experience in industrial management, James J. Cribbin says:

> Historically, there has been far too much talk about dealing with individuals, but relatively little stress has been given to the importance of team building. One can manage people so that the work progresses in a coordinated way, as, for example, in a concentration camp. It is a far cry from this to managing them so that they are stimulated to cooperate willingly with each other, to offer mutual help spontaneously when needed, and to have pride in their workforce—to think of themselves as damned good.[8]

For what problems of TEAM building, then, can the leader make preparation? Probably no reports of research studies are needed to make the point that he or she must--during the meeting—find ways to fulfill as well as possible the *social needs* of the members: for attention and approval; to belong and feel welcomed; to contribute and be heard. What the leader does need is to stir up in himself or herself (if the feeling is not present already), a sense of the worth of each individual who will be attending the meeting—both basic worth as a human being and potential for contribution on the question at hand. If the leader knows the members personally, the setbacks or handicaps they have faced as well as the contributions they have made can be brought to mind. If the leader doesn't know the members, imagination can suggest how various people might feel about the subject for the discussion and about coming to a meeting to talk about it in a group.

On the other hand, the leader needs to heighten in himself or herself a sense of the importance of the problem itself and a sense of the opportunity the leader and the group will have in going at the problem together.

But if the leader knows the group or particular individuals

who will be members of the group, he or she realizes that certain individuals tend to create problems by their aggressiveness, their antipathy to certain others, their closed-mindedness, and their impatience, and knows also the likely effect of such behaviors upon the group in their TASK and their TEAM work. The leader thinks ahead of ways the situation can be structured to prevent or minimize this harm to the group.

We are told that Aneurin Bevin when he was prime minister of Great Britain used to arrive early to decide where his cabinet ministers should sit at the table; he was attending to inter-relationships that might work for good or ill at the cabinet meeting. Thus, for example, the leader can sometimes plan seating arrangements that will not place likely opponents directly across from each other at the table.

The leader must plan to set the stage in his or her opening remarks for full and creative interaction among the members. The overall purpose in these initial comments is to enable the group to work effectively on its job and to *stimulate* it to do so. While serving this composite purpose, the leader can work generally to alleviate undue tensions, open minds toward new ideas, and make cooperation the expected and desired relationship. But, if the leader knows or surmises that there will be status problems in the group or self-serving behaviors by certain members, attempts can be made to forestall the difficulties:

status problem	*preventive steps*
dominance by the status person, or his or her mere presence	plan to speak in "we" terms, including all equally by voice and manner
withdrawal or competitive responses of others	plan to tell a relevant incident that shows the common lot of humanity
	plan to give an example of the innate intelligence of untutored men and women (without pointing the moral)
	think out a means of address for all members alike, with no deference for status person but no impertinence either (neither address the mayor as

individual prominence problems

recognition-seeking by members (one or more) idea-possessiveness of members

Mayor nor call him Wes too familiarly)

plan to tell incident from history or literature where involvement in a great cause meant freely accepted anonymity for the individual

seek out examples to give in which significant improvement came through modifications made by others

explain the steps taken by the Board of Consultants in preparation for formation of the U.N. Atomic Energy Commission to handle idea-possessiveness[9]

And certainly the leader can include appeals to the interests and values that the "problem person" is thought to hold without directing them pointedly to this person. Probably the leader should prepare more approaches than can possibly be needed, allowing the opportunity to choose and shape materials and manner to meet the situation as it develops in the group. The leader prepares to help the group become and remain an effective TEAM.

5.5

CONCLUSION

When the leader (or someone else) plans the meeting, certain important preliminary decisions must be made: stating the discussion question, setting the meeting time and place, and planning the size and composition of the group. The leader notifies the participants appropriately and makes specific arrangements for the meeting as to information, equipment, and resource persons. And the leader undertakes the personal preparation that will ready him or her for a crucial role in the TASK work and the TEAM work of the group.

FOOTNOTES — CHAPTER 5

1. Robert F. Bales, "In Conference," *Harvard Business Review*, 32 (March-April 1954): 48.
2. Bales, "In Conference," p. 48.
3. Sidney J. Parnes, "Research in Developing Creative Behavior" in *Widening Horizons in Creativity*, Kelvin W. Taylor, ed. (New York: John Wiley & Sons, Inc., 1964), p. 168.
4. E. Paul Torrance concerns himself with these factors in his extensive studies on creativity. See "Creativity Research in Education: Still Alive," in *Perspectives in Creativity*, Irving A. Taylor and J. W. Getzel, eds. (Chicago: Aldine Publishing Company, 1975), p. 291.
5. For the "counterformer," see R. S. Crutchfield, in *Contemporary Approaches to Creative Thinking*, Howard E. Gruber, Glenn Terrell, Michael Wertheimer, eds. (New York: Prentice-Hall, Inc., 1962), pp. 126, 137–139.
6. Henri L. Vis, Michael Bossuyt, Philippe Hennart, and Michel Carael, "The Health of Mother and Child in Rural Central Africa," *Family Planning*, 6 (1975): 437–441.
7. Ted Greiner, *Regulation and Education: Strategies for Solving the Bottle Feeding Problem* (Ithaca, N.Y.: Cornell University, 1977), p. 25.
8. James J. Cribbin, *Effective Managerial Leadership*, p. 107.
9. Norman Cousins and Thomas K. Finletter, "A Beginning for Sanity," *The Saturday Review of Literature*, 29 (June 15, 1946): 9.

    Our first joint decision, then, was to liberate all our discussions from idea-possessiveness. No point would be argued down; we agreed that we would attack the problem inductively, working from the ground up, assembling all facts pertinent to the problem as a basis for conclusions, implied or implicit. We agreed that all questions coming up were to be considered as being brought up by the group as a whole rather than by any single member. If a member had an objection to any one point, it was regarded as something that troubled the group as a whole....

CHAPTER **6**
THE FIRST FEW MINUTES

6.1 Before the Call-to-Purpose

    6.11 Initial Impressions upon Members

    6.12 Initial INNER and OUTER Work of the Leader

6.2 The Leader's Call-to-Purpose

6.3 The Leader's Opening Remarks

    6.31 Sufficiently Informative

    6.32 Climate Setting

    6.33 Stimulating

    6.34 Inviting

6.4 The Leader's Handling of the Early Interchanges

    6.41 First Test-Point: Immediately After the Leader's Invitation to Begin

    6.42 Second Test-Point: Immediately after the First Member Contribution

    6.43 Third Test-Point: Making the First Synthesis

    6.44 Fourth Test-Point: Handling the First Member Challenge

6.5   Moving Out of the First Few Minutes

6.6   Conclusion

What happens during the first few minutes of a group discussion will definitely do much to establish the pacing and practices the group will follow throughout the rest of the meeting.[1] All participants, and especially the leader, must be alert and careful during these significant initial moments (whether three or thirty minutes) between the time when the group members begin to arrive for the meeting and the moment when they have actually begun to work and could be said to be thinking together. *What happens* during this period, and *how it is interpreted* by each group member will be important; Plato says in *The Republic* that "The beginning is the most important part of the work." The leader must make good use of this period in order to build a productive, satisfying TASK/TEAM relationship.

The initial period makes special demands on the art of leadership. Most often these minutes are an unstructured, easygoing, informal, and less work-oriented time. As such, it is easy to allow matters to drift and take their own course. But norms, relationships, and patterns of behavior are already beginning to emerge and they may well need direction and guidance. Cliques may be forming that will be more difficult to break up at a later point; for example, all Boeing engineers who have worked in the Wichita plant understand certain problems the same way. Some members may be adopting roles that could become fixed; after one engineer pointed out the flaws in the first plan mentioned, he might be expected (by himself and others) to take the lead in pointing out the defects in the plans that are considered subsequently. Other members may start to become isolates even at this early stage when it would be relatively easy to draw them into the group; it would not have taken much to hold back the fluent-developers long enough to draw in someone who had tried three times without success to add a thought, and others would then have been more likely to look to him or her more frequently for comments. Even though these moments constitute a very short portion of the total group time, they are too important to be permitted to drift by. Remedial actions not taken now may be virtually impossible later.

Perhaps more than at any other time in group work the leader must here take an appropriate stance somewhere between (1) stepping aside and letting matters take their own course and (2) playing a dominant role and imposing an authoritarian and rigid control. Achieving that proper balance is the true art of leadership.[2] As has been stated, effective leaders are rarely at one extreme or the other, but rather seek an appropriate point between the two (and a changing point at that) throughout the group process, according to the needs of the moment. In these first few minutes the leader is establishing some measure of credibility and rapport with the other participants, and, in this activity, the demands for maintaining an appropriate positioning are paramount.

Then too, there are certain *irreversibles* in group process that the leader must consider at this point. The procedures of an effective working group can often move from greater leader control over procedures to lesser control, from more rigid rules for participants to more flexible ones, from more leader-centeredness to more member-centeredness; but it seems rarely possible, and then very difficult, to move in the opposite direction. Many teachers have struggled without success to gain control over a classroom process in which they had forfeited control during the initial stage. We are not, of course, talking about extremes. Within that middle ground (where most groups operate) the frequent trend is from greater to less leader control. The initial control by the leader helps to set the patterns and procedures and, if well done, will establish an atmosphere in which overt control is less needed. An able leader can adapt to this lessened need. It is not that guidance and control are given up by the leader, but rather that initial interactions have set the pattern, and thus control from the leader becomes less needed by the group members. These patterns must be established early, that is, started in the first few minutes of the discussion.

6.1   BEFORE THE CALL-TO-PURPOSE

The dynamics of the meeting actually begin before the meeting as such starts at all. The very gathering of the group at the place announced, the random greetings and conversations, and the finding of seats all begin to set the stage for the meeting.

6.11 Initial Impressions Upon Members

Each member learns a great deal upon entering the room and looking about. A first glance will reveal table, chairs, special equipment, and general decor—a setting that will suggest to the member something of the nature of procedures he or she may anticipate. The member will note the groupings and activity of other persons who are already in the room, including the person who will be leading the group meeting; these observations will indicate something of the relationships to be expected. From the tone of the conversations about the room the member can sense even more fully the atmosphere in which the discussion will start. Observations and inferences about the *procedures*, *relationships*, and *atmosphere* influence each member as the group is called to its purpose.

The situation is complicated by the fact that every member has had different previous group experiences and may have different expectations of this particular meeting. So these initial impressions differ from member to member, each observing and interpreting them in the light of his or her own expectations of

> *group discussion*, ranging from
> > an experience in creative interaction
> > to
> > an exercise in futility and frustration
>
> *leaders*, ranging from

democratic	fair	effective
to	to	to
dominating	partisan	incompetent

> *himself or herself as participant*, ranging from

informed	effective	appreciated
to	to	to
uninformed	ineffective	bypassed

Certain of these expectations will in the members' eyes be proved right or wrong by what occurs in these first few minutes. The leader will note the members' expectations as well as possible, using what is seen and sensed to guide his or her actions and attitudes during these first important minutes.

6.12 Initial INNER and OUTER Work of the Leader

No matter how insightful and thorough the leader's preparations are prior to the actual assembling of the group, much of that work had to be done more or less in the dark. No amount of information on the achievement and reputation of the various members can really prepare the leader for these people as actual team members. But now—as one member and another and then still others enter the meeting room, make themselves known (or do not), and take places in the group—the leader can begin to get specific information to fill out and correct his or her premeeting assessments.

And even as the leader is inferring the members' degree of task-readiness and team-readiness, the members are making certain preliminary judgments as to the leader's style and competence, judgments based on the leader's entrance, greetings, voice, gestures, and movements. One who saw Lyndon Johnson when he was a senator come to the Senate floor before the members were called to order and drop down on a desktop to talk face-to-face with a shorter colleague would form a distinct impression of Johnson's leadership style.

One of the leader's most difficult tasks in the first few minutes is to translate *INNER work* quickly into *OUTER work*. At the same time as these swiftly decided-upon behaviors are being put into effect, it is necessary for the leader to continue (and even heighten) the INNER work. The leader must gather feedback information as to how the initial efforts are being received and responded to, and then further shape the guidance in task and team work in the light of that information. These readings of others must be essentially correct and the leader's behavior exhibited for others to read must be appropriate and genuine. Writing about how a manager and staff see one another, James J. Cribbin emphasized how crucial it is that each see the other accurately.[3]

If an isolate is observed, for example, during the period of mixing and milling, the leader must consider whether to do anything about it, and if so, what and how. And if anything is to be done, it must be done immediately or the moment will be lost. Perhaps the leader will strike up a conversation with that member or introduce the member to others in the room. Or the leader may decide to do nothing at the moment, knowing that such special action might make the member feel even more separate and inadequate.

These observations provide the leader with a basis for two important preliminary assessments of the group members:

1. TASK-readiness: How ready are they? Have some brought resource material? Do they seem to have a genuine interest and purpose?

2. TEAM-readiness: How effectively are the members relating to each other? To the leader? Are they forming up as one team or as subgroups?

Having made these tentative judgments (to be updated throughout the discussion) and having by voice, manner, and movement established himself or herself as the person performing the specialized role of leader, the leader can turn to the call-to-purpose, the opening remarks, and the handling of the early interchanges.

6.2   **THE LEADER'S CALL-TO-PURPOSE**

The leader may have talked easily and casually before this point to several persons nearby in the room, moving from circle to circle with introductions and light talk, but the break from casual chatting to the calling together of the members as a *discussion group with a purpose* needs to be clear-cut and recognized by all for the summons that it is. Avoiding the formal "call to order" used in parliamentary bodies, the leader calls the group to work with that degree of formality appropriate to the specific situation, shading all the way from "Members of the Planning Committee" to "Well, let's get at it."

Sometimes the appropriate moment for the call-to-purpose is hard to determine. The time *announced* is, of course, the *natural* and *desired* moment. To begin promptly is to allow full time for the group's work, to underscore the purposefulness of the group, and to establish an expectation of promptness throughout. But short delays occasioned by situations or events beyond the leader's control—a tardy delivery of essential equipment, a last member's imminent arrival, and the like—must be taken in stride. It is unsettling for members to see the leader become rattled by minor disturbances at this early point in the meeting.

In making the call-to-purpose the leader will do well to see that some fitting, noticeable physical change accompanies the words such as taking a seat, turning from the display board directly to the group, or breaking off conversation with members and moving to the table. The leader's words and manner should reveal purposefulness and an expectation that all participants will recognize as a signal that the meeting is about to begin.

6.3 **THE LEADER'S OPENING REMARKS**

What should the leader say, then, in the first few minutes? What form should the leader's OUTER WORK take? To build the necessary TEAM/TASK relationship the leader needs to make *opening remarks* that are (1) sufficiently informative; (2) climate setting; (3) stimulating; and (4) inviting. INNER WORK will not only help in the decision as to *which* of these four qualities needs the most emphasis in this particular situation but *how* each of the four can be best achieved in this situation. Achieving one of these qualities may contribute to the achievement of the others.

6.31 **Sufficiently Informative**

The members pick up certain clues about how the meeting is likely to go from the room arrangements, the casual remarks they have exchanged as they assemble, and the attitudes of the leader. Also they probably know from their notification what the topic is to be and perhaps even what the plan of approach is apt to be. But these impressions and pieces of information are separate and individual; the leader needs to give the members a common focus in these opening moments, and can probably do this best by following the call-to-purpose with a direct statement of that purpose.

Members must know what their task *is*: Are they to examine a plan submitted to them? Are they to analyze a problem and recommend two or three options for handling it? To whom or to what body are they to report? Are they to recommend only, or to make a firm decision themselves? Are they to carry out the decision they make? Will they meet several times or is the entire matter to be settled in this one meeting? How long will the group meet at this time and just what is the specific objective for the meeting? How may all this fit into a larger goal? The members need to know the scope and nature of their task at the very outset. The explanation ought, however, to be relatively brief so that it does not hold back other matters too long, and it should be given in a manner that recognizes the members as partners in the effort.

The leader needs to be sure that all members are acquainted; not all introductions may have been made in the social moments before the call-to-purpose. It behooves the leader to provide facts that will inform all very briefly of the knowledge and experience that each member brings to the meeting without either (1) establishing a hierarchy of worth within the group by emphasizing some over others, or (2) characterizing a person's area of competence so pointedly that that person expects to act as the expert within that area and feels hesitant to speak in other areas. To have the chairman of last year's highly successful fund drive present as a member and to retell the story of the success in detail is to handicap that ex-chairman and everyone else at the meeting. The leader should be working here to establish the group as a team.

Handling information is one of the group's major difficulties; as for the leader, attention to this matter must begin in the opening remarks. The members, through their own experience or study, will have come to the meeting with varying amounts and kinds of information. Throughout the discussion it is to be hoped that members working together can supply much of what the group needs at key points in its inquiry, with the leader drawing out or adding spontaneously what the group lacks. But the information with which the group starts in these first minutes is especially important; the members and leader need to give their attention simultaneously to a particular array of facts. Hence, the leader may hand out copies of prepared material or project a slide, and then direct the attention of all members at the same time to the same materials.

When the leader thinks it necessary to make a presentation of information in the opening minutes, care must be taken to avoid such tendencies as these:

1. To go on too long, thus focusing the attention on the leader for too long a time.
2. To overwhelm the members with more information than they can process within the group interaction.
3. To present the material in a way that seems biased, giving the impression that the leader has a predetermined solution.
4. To make the leader seem to be the expert on substantive matters in the discussion.
5. To present the information in a dull or unorganized fashion.

6. To present aspects of the information that will be needed in later parts of the discussion rather than at the opening.

The leader needs to let the members assist in processing the information presented, thus demonstrating the cooperative nature of the group task.

Usually the members must be informed of the agenda items that will be followed in the meeting or meetings. What lines of consideration will the group task require? The necessary steps can be suggested to the group, and some useful format (perhaps an appropriate portion of the Problem Management Sequence) can be presented. Suggestions made spontaneously by the members can be incorporated if useful, and the whole can be cast into a logical form and agreed upon so that the discussion can begin with common understanding and agreement.

The leader's INNER WORK will be the guide in deciding what attention must be given to introducing the members, explaining the task, presenting basic information, and suggesting the lines of thought-development for this particular situation.

6.32 Climate Setting

Not only what the leader says but *how* he or she says it in those early minutes are extremely important factors in developing an effective group attitude *toward the task* and *toward the idea of working on it together*.

Central in the establishment of this group attitude is the leader's own attitude. In presenting preliminary information to the members, the leader needs to show that he or she is

1. Fair-minded

> The leader shows that his or her mind is not already made up about the problem. Members must feel that the leader is not trying to get their acquiescence but looks forward to their working out the decision together.

2. Desirous of members' participation

> The leader shows confidence that members can and will achieve their goal together, and offers all members freedom to suggest ideas without danger of ridicule or out-of-hand rejection.

3. Willing to lead

> The leader shows acceptance of the special-
> ized role of LEADER. Without overconfi-
> dence the leader will refrain in these first
> few minutes from mentioning any personal
> weaknesses he or she has in leadership
> because the group has not yet developed
> enough cooperative strength and mutual
> confidence to escape feeling threatened by
> such an admission.[4]

If the leader thus lets the members know before they enter the
interchange that their discussion will be guided with friendliness, firmness, and fairness, the chances of starting the discussion
at a relatively high level of cooperation are greatly increased.

In a study based on observations of small-group discussions
in various contexts, Jack R. Gibb[5] distinguished between communication behaviors that are typical of *supportive* climates
and of *defensive* climates in group interaction. Gibb's classification system contrasts six pairs of behaviors, as follows:

Supportive		*Defensive*
Description	versus	Evaluation
Problem orientation	versus	Control
Spontaneity	versus	Strategy
Empathy	versus	Neutrality
Equality	versus	Superiority
Provisionalism	versus	Certainty

Gibb suggests that as comments made in a discussion tend to
be closer to the terms of the left column than to the terms of
the right column, they will be helpful in creating a more
supportive group climate.

Strong, confident members and reticent, inexperienced
members alike should respond better in a vigorous but supportive climate. As the leader performs the fourfold role of the
opening remarks he or she watches to see how the climate is
developing and modifies his or her subsequent efforts, if necessary, to draw all the members into a mutually reinforcing,
cooperative, and purposeful team.

6.33 Stimulating

The members need to *feel* the challenge that is inherent in their task; it is the leader's job to introduce their projected task with such clarity and vividness that its challenge and motivation catches them all. How can this be done? To begin with, the leader's own enthusiasm is likely to be contagious unless

1. That enthusiasm does not seem genuine or —
2. That enthusiasm is too strong too soon and denies the members an opportunity to *build up* interest and concern on their part.

The leader can provide time and opportunity for this buildup by presenting some striking, concrete, and feeling-charged idea or incident, one that is likely to engage the group's interest and imagination.

The leader of a study group on human rights might open with these facts from *Time* (August 16, 1976), p.31, by saying *Time* magazine reports that

> It is one of the grim truths of the second half of the twentieth century that rarely before in history has torture been in such widespread use. Amnesty International, the widely respected human rights organization headquartered in London, estimates that in the last decade torture has been officially practiced in sixty countries; last year alone there were more than forty violating states. From Chile, Brazil, Argentina, Uruguay and Paraguay to Guinea, Uganda, Spain, Iran and the Soviet Union, torture has become a common instrument of state policy practiced against almost anyone [that] ruling cliques see as a threat to their power.

Or the chairman of a school board might awaken the members to a cooperative attack upon their problem by quoting Adlai Stevenson: "The World is too dangerous for anything but the truth and too small for anything but brotherhood." Or a community group studying the needs of the mentally ill may be alerted by the leader's explanation that the mentally ill people in the United States constitute a larger group than those who suffer from cancer and tuberculosis combined. Thus:

presenting
 A piece of unusual information, or
 A quotation from a well-known
  authority on the subject, or
 A vivid comparison,
  etc.,
   that is
    appropriate to the group,
     the task, and the leader;

> suitable in length;
> vivid in the way it is told
>
> *provides*
>
>> good grounding for their movement
>> into the task together.

The effect of appropriately chosen specific materials can be contrasted with a generalized appeal. Suppose that the study group leader had said, "We should all feel concerned with the use of torture as a government policy; we tend to feel that it could not occur in our century but it does, and we must be concerned about it." Suppose that the school board chairman had opened with this brief statement: "We have a problem to solve and we need to cooperate on it." Suppose that the community group leader had opened with a remark that "Mental illness is an important problem in our country, one we can't afford to bypass." In each case, the general statement tells the group members that the problem before them is important, but it does nothing to help them *feel* its importance. This statement does not bring one of man's basic needs compellingly before them. The torture reports shock us with the violation of physiological and safety needs, those most basic needs as Maslow[6] has told us. Stevenson's words challenge us on safety and also on belongingness and love needs, and the figures on the number of the mentally ill also touch our belongingness and love needs. We respond with feeling and perhaps begin to wish to get at the problem. This stirring up of motivation is certainly one of the leader's major tasks in the opening remarks.

As the leader seeks to kindle the members' enthusiasm, he or she must be careful not to talk too long. Instead, alert to the members' aroused willingness and wish to take hold, the leader should quickly provide them with an appropriate question and invite them to begin.

6.34 Inviting

The leader should address an *invitation-to-begin* to all members of the group by asking an appropriate question to start upon. By glancing around at each person, even the ones sitting closest, the leader subtly affirms the responsibility of each member to offer whatever he or she can to the group. This glance is not inquisitorial but genuinely confident of the members' cooperativeness and abilities. If, on the other hand, the leader singles out an individual to make the first contribution, rather than letting anyone who wishes begin the discussion, serious harm can be done to the selected individual and to the whole process of voluntary interaction that should be established. Consider the difficulties created by the leader whose *invitation-to-begin* is directed to an individual:

> *Leader*:   Yes, this problem is right on our doorstep; we can't evade it, so let's talk about it. Joe, you had a lot to do with the cleaning up of the streets after SEA-FAIR this year. What do you think the heart of the problem is?

It is pretty clear to all the others on this clean-up-the-streets committee that Joe is considered as having good information PLUS unusual ability to draw inferences from it. Or the *invitation-to-begin* might have gone like this:

> *Leader*:   Yes, this problem is right on our doorstep; we can't evade it, so let's talk about it. Mary, I know that your City Beautification Action Group has done a lot of research on this problem. Why don't you share some of your findings with us so that we can start off with facts as they really are?

Here Mary is given *carte blanche* to set the group straight now and at any point during the discussion. In both these unfortunate examples, the leader harms the individual singled out; he or she may feel embarrassed or elated by the request and find it hard to move thereafter to a fully cooperative role.

It is important that the expectation be created that all members will volunteer their contributions and that these remarks will be considered valuable for the group to hear. A member should not raise a hand to gain the floor, but should accept the responsibility of threading his or her contribution into the group thought-line.

The opening remarks must not be drawn to a close *abruptly*; rather, the leader lets the members know by words and manner that he or she is finishing and will be turning to them with an invitation for someone else to speak, an invitation such as, "What indication do we have that this problem really exists?"

6.4   **THE LEADER'S HANDLING OF THE EARLY INTERCHANGES**

Nothing the leader has done so far reveals so much to the

members as the responses that the leader now makes to their first contributions. At certain key points in these first few minutes, the group functioning is sure to be tested severely, and the leader must meet these tests as well as possible. Building the expectations that the members will hold of the leader throughout the discussion, the leader can never win so much or lose so much for the successful functioning of the group as at four risky points in the first few minutes: (1) immediately after the invitation to the members to begin; (2) immediately after the first member contribution in the discussion; (3) when making the first synthesis of group thought; and (4) when responding to the first direct challenge to his or her leadership.

6.41 First Test-Point: Immediately After the Leader's Invitation to Begin

If one member begins without hesitation to contribute, and if others yield their attention to the speaker and then respond, this test has been passed successfully. This is likely to be the case if the leader has made useful and stimulating opening remarks, watching the group to see when several seem ready to respond, concluding with a question that is easy to understand and interesting to respond to, and then looking about confidently for someone to begin.

But if a pause occurs, and extends until it becomes uncomfortable and a waste of time and a denial of the desired vigorous interchange, the leader may have failed to be clear and interesting, or may have made a variety of other mistakes, such as these:

made too impressive an opening so that any spontaneous remarks will suffer in comparison;

did not make contact with the listeners while giving the OPENING REMARKS and they don't feel involved;

asked a question-of-invitation they did not expect so they are caught off base when offered the chance to respond;

made their TASK seem too large to be tackled, or their area of decision-making too small to be worth the effort; or

seemed to have figured out the answer already and is merely asking them to make their way to a foregone conclusion.

How can the leader get the interchange started? Not by

answering the question himself or herself. Showing dismay or uttering a rebuke would only deepen the problem. When INNER WORK suggests that the group can afford to wait no longer and that the leader *must* act, it is possible for the leader to try talking with undiminished interest of the area of the problem out of which the "opening question" had been formulated, and watch again for someone's readiness to respond. But if no one yet volunteers, the leader could suggest the need for hearing some brief personal experiences and look expectantly from one to another, then sweep up the gist of the ideas presented and ask a question that would carry forward some thought in these ideas to which the group had seemed to respond. The leader consistently resists calling on some particular person to begin and makes the invitation to all members both clear and personal by glance and inquiring look.

6.42   Second Test-Point: Immediately After the First Member Contribution

The first contribution by a member will be either a comment or a question. If it is a comment, the test for the leader is to *avoid being the one to respond to the comment*. If it is a *procedural question*, the test for the leader is to *reply in an effective way*, that is, in a way that will give the group members confidence in their ability to handle the task and in the leadership being offered them. If it is a *substantive question*, the leader needs to look about the group, letting someone else begin the reply.

Not Responding to the First Comment. It is hard for the leader not to respond! He or she has been speaking animatedly during the opening remarks, and has gained some momentum. Eager to keep a lively pace going, the leader tends to speak again with some half-realized notion of keeping the ball rolling and showing approval for the member's participation.

But the leader *must* resist this tendency to reply, and the tendency may be especially strong for the reason that this first comment is often made straight to the leader. He or she must realize that to reply will focus all the attention again on the leader and may seem to establish a pattern in which the discussion is carried on between the various members, as individuals, and the leader. The pattern may become: member A speaks— leader speaks—member B speaks—leader speaks—member A speaks—leader speaks. It becomes more difficult thereafter to get the members to talk with each other (as well as with the leader), and the wide interchange necessary for good group discussion and thinking together will not occur.

So the leader remains silent and looks invitingly around the group, holding the opportunity open for some member to speak voluntarily and to carry the thought forward. And the leader must keep from prompting the interchange with the empty question: "What does someone else think of that?" This question is more than merely *empty*, it is decidedly *harmful*:

1. It keeps the *leader* clearly in charge, directing the flow.
2. It takes away the member's precious right to volunteer; whoever responds is answering, not offering of his or her own accord.
3. It seems to invite difference or opposition to the position taken by the member, thus tying that member securely to that position.

Replying Effectively to a Question on Procedure. Questions to the leader at this point may be one of at least three kinds: (1) simple request for clarification of a procedure, (2) insistence on justification of the procedure suggested, or (3) suggestion of a drastic change of the announced procedure. In general, the group will tend to gain a sense of confidence in a leader who appears unthreatened, able to share the limelight, and appreciative of others' interpretations. But these three types of questions will need different approaches by the leader.

1. A simple request for clarification of procedure could well be handled by the leader as a logical part of the OPENING REMARKS, a helpful prompting, as it were, to make the procedure more easily understood. Not interpreting the question as an attack on his or her intelligence, efficiency, or status, the leader can reply in stride.

2. An insistence on justification of the procedure suggested by the leader should be treated as the members' right to know not only *what* procedure has been chosen but *why* the particular choice was made. The leader should undertake to explain briefly and without defensiveness. If, however, this first contributor refuses to be satisfied with a reasonable response, the leader must move more strongly. Although there is a need to

avoid crushing the point (and the contributor) peremptorily or harshly, the leader must at this point be forceful enough to return the group without undue delay to an appropriate opening aspect of the problem and to invite all to begin at that point. A combination of firmness and fairness is needed here.

3. A suggestion of a drastic change of procedure calls for rapid and perceptive INNER WORK on the part of the leader. As to the TASK, there is quick thought of how much preparation of information, resource people, and the like would be demanded by the newly suggested approach, preparation that has not, of course, been included in the preparation so far. There is, also, a quick review of the reasons for the chosen procedure. As to the TEAM, the leader considers how important it is in the building of the TEAM that all suggestions be fairly handled, and analyzes as well as possible whether the questioner is sincere (even if perhaps shortsighted) in the suggestion or intentionally disruptive with little concern for delaying or subverting the work of the group or undermining the leader's authority.

The leader's OUTER WORK will reflect both of these considerations. The leader will probably explain the choice briefly and undefensively, a move that may well satisfy an *honest* inquiry but will likely only entice a disruptive member into more vehement inquiries. Some persons want to march to a different drummer. Suggest a trip to the mountains and they want to go to the sea; suggest surfing and they ask for backpacking. They argue that a different approach would be better. And, in some cases, the other approach *is as good as* the one initiated by the leader. But the leader has a considerable investment—gathering materials, organizing information, interviewing resource persons—in the approach being pursued. If the suggested different approach is significantly better, that is one thing, and the leader in many cases may wish to discard the previous choice and move in the better way. But if, as is often the case, the suggestion is merely a perverse fancy, then it can be harmful to the group progress. The leader's reasonable response will help the other members to recognize the challenge for what it is and the leader would be likely to have their backing (or, at least, their understanding) as he or she resists these disruptive efforts and moves past them back to the work of the group. At any rate, such a situation is a true test of the art of leadership.

6.43   Third Test-Point: Making the First Synthesis

When the comments made by the members on their first topic have gone far enough that the members are moving without realizing the fact into another topic, or are simply in need of drawing together what has been said so that they will not be repeating or becoming confused, the leader needs to make a synthesis. By alert INNER WORK the leader will know *when* this point arrives and *what* the upshot of the group's thought so far really is. No doubt the leader will have given the members little assists—nods of support, terms caught from a speaker and fed back into the interchange, full attention to each speaker, and the like—before this time so as to have been an *active* though largely *silent* member of the group. Now, however, the group needs the focusing action of the leader in a synthesis that they will all recognize as accurate. To check the true development of ideas and in order that the members will recognize the TEAM nature of their thought-line building, the leader should phrase the synthesis tentatively, posing it questioningly to the group for its quick appraisal. For example, the leader may ask, "Well, where are we now? We seem to be saying that . . ." or "Is it our position that . . .?" This statement is *not* a review of each turn, twist, and modification of the idea, but the idea in its evolved form. It is not a listing; it is a synthesis, a true composition of the relevant elements.

The leader needs to be accurate on both judgments, the *when* and the *what* of the synthesis. To pull things together too soon will seem to be guiding the thought-line too closely, perhaps seeming to be unwilling to let the group take enough initiative. If, on the other hand, the leader waits too long, making a useful and accurate synthesis of all the diverse materials that have been considered may be actually impossible. If, in making the synthesis, the leader adds to the idea in stating it (thus changing the idea from what the members had developed), the members may be disturbed or come to look to the leader for that shaping-up service, and thus never take their full responsibility or give their full value. And if the leader fails to catch the idea at its fullest development in the synthesis, and the members have to speak up to change the formulation to make it appropriate, the members will tend to lose confidence in their leadership.

6.44   Fourth Test-Point: Handling the First Member Challenge

When some member brings a *direct challenge* to the leader in these first few minutes, an important and difficult test-point occurs. If the member raises strong objection to the leader's remarks or to the procedures, he or she is challenging the leader. If the member makes a bid to take over the leadership, he or she is challenging the leader. At this stage of the meeting the members are only *learning what to expect* of their leader; therefore, how this type of challenge is handled is crucial in the overall success of the group meeting.

With INNER WORK the leader tries to ascertain the member's motivation in making the challenge as well as the other members' reactions to this act of challenge. Whether the act is judged to be self-serving and hostile behavior or merely as a strongly stated but honest concern, the first OUTER WORK may well be to treat the member's act as consistent with group purposes and thus helpful. Without reacting defensively to the challenge, the leader takes as much of the shock out of the situation as possible by attempting to integrate any relevant elements of the member's idea into the flow of the group thought-line. This action will permit the group to move along without a great loss of time, without upsetting the group more than the challenge has already done, and without losing the momentum of thought-development any more than can be helped.

If the challenge is not absorbed by this action, that is, if the challenger persists in making a charge, then the leader must take stronger measures. As agent of the group the leader must be firm to uphold its purposes even while remaining sensitive to the feelings of all members of the team. The leader must not take the challenge personally and thereby lose his or her usefulness to the group. And the leader would hope not to let the challenging member in these first few minutes be typed as a disruptive antagonist and thus be incapacitated from contributing usefully in the group work thereafter. It is hoped that sufficient time will have passed before such a challenge comes (if it does come) so that the members react as a team and swing behind the leader in a reasonable handling of this issue, and will do so without ostracizing the challenger for the outbreak.

These tests of leadership emphasize the fact that leadership is not so much a position to be held as a job to be done.

6.5   MOVING OUT OF THE FIRST FEW MINUTES

For the leader these first few minutes are surely a period requiring special alertness and careful action. For the members these minutes are also a time of testing: testing how their efforts are received, what freedom in speculation and procedures they have, and how safe it is to reveal their thoughts and feelings.

When the members begin to forego their strong personal concerns over these matters and to lend themselves cooperatively to sincere work on the problem, the leader can sense that the first few minutes have passed and that the members have moved on into the discussion proper. Actually, it is not so necessary that the members themselves be aware of this transition. The leader, seeing that the group has passed through the first few minutes, is ready now to address the full measure of INNER and OUTER work to the ongoing duties of leadership throughout the meeting.

6.6   CONCLUSION

The impressions that the members receive even before the meeting starts are important and lasting. The leader makes tentative judgments of the situation and strives to establish himself or herself appropriately in the role of leader. Having called them to their purpose, the leader makes opening remarks. It is important that these be sufficiently informative, climate setting, stimulating, and inviting.

The leader faces four test-points in these opening minutes: (1) immediately after the invitation to the group to begin; (2) immediately after the first member contribution; (3) making the first synthesis; and (4) handling the first member challenge.

When the leader senses that the group members have begun to take up their task together, the leader knows that the *discussion proper* has begun.

FOOTNOTES — CHAPTER 6

1. Herbert A. Thelen, *Dynamics of Groups at Work* (Chicago: University of Chicago Press, 1963 Phoenix Edition), pp. 277–279, asserts: "Control is also exerted in the opening remarks; in fact, some research workers have felt that the whole course of a meeting is determined by the events of the first few minutes."

2. In his *Dynamics of Groups at Work*, pp. 319–320, Thelen discusses one aspect of this delicate balance:

   > In general, there are two opposite sorts of traps into which anxious leaders fall: seduction and dictation. Thus, when a leader cannot see the group's hostility toward him objectively, he is likely to punish himself or to punish them. In the former case, he does so by accepting the notion that trouble *really* is his own fault, and he may begin to try to win the group over with blandishments, gold stars, outside conversation with group members, etc. He spends all his energy trying to be seen as a "nice guy"; in effect, he attempts to seduce the group. The trouble is, of course, first, that he is likely to be unsuccessful because he is overanxious, and this overanxiety is what he will communicate. Second, he has no energy left to lead the group toward the solution of its problem. Third, he makes it hard for the group to express its hostility toward him because it will feel guilty at kicking a man when he is down; the group members either have to suppress their hostility or direct it at some even sillier target.
   >
   > The other trap, dictation, is even more familiar; particularly in situations where the status hierarchies are well defined. As soon as the leader feels the group members are hostile, he begins to blame them and, in effect, treat them like wayward children. This does not work, because the group now has to spend its energy in an undercover effort to placate or sabotage the leader. It has nothing left with which to do its work.

3. James J. Cribbin, *Effective Managerial Leadership* (New York: American Management Association, Inc., 1972), p. 76.

4. Irvin D. Yalom, in *The Theory and Practice of Group Psychotherapy* (New York: Basic Books, Inc., 1970), p. 105, quotes Ferenczi as suggesting that the analyst "must not admit his flaws and uncertainty too early. First the patient must feel sufficiently secure in his own abilities before he is called upon to face the defect in the one on whom he leans." Although the group discussion setting is quite different, this communication principle regarding one who leads would seem to apply generally.

5. Jack R. Gibb, "Defensive Communication," *The Journal of Communication*, **11** (1961): 141–148.

6. Abraham H. Maslow, *Motivation and Personality,* 2d ed. (New York: Harper & Row, Publishers, Inc., 1970), p. 117.

CHAPTER 7
THE DISCUSSION PROPER: DIVERGING PHASE

In the first few minutes of the meeting the members and leader have discovered a great deal about each other, and about what expectations can be held for the group's interaction and final achievement. Thus, the *process* in which they will be engaging together has begun, a process that takes place simultaneously and interactively in two realms—the task realm and the social-emotional or interpersonal realm.

We sometimes overlook this latter process when hazarding a guess as to the productivity of a group; it is easy to think of the group's chance of achieving its purpose as based on two factors: the *demands* of the task before it and the *resources* the members have among themselves to answer those demands. In some groups, those resources would be offered and utilized effectively as the members discuss together. In other groups certain information would not be offered (though someone knew it) for group consideration, or, being offered, would not receive fair consideration. What is being said here? Simply this: that the group's *process* itself is exceedingly important. Ivan D. Steiner says directly: "How well an individual or group performs a task depends upon three classes of variables: task demands, resources, and process."[1] And he casts his thought into a useful formula: "Actual productivity = potential productivity − losses due to faulty process."[2] Steiner's formula can be diagrammed as follows:

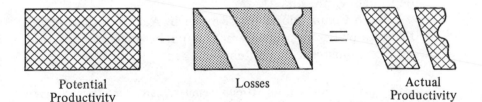

Potential Productivity	Losses	Actual Productivity

This chapter and the following one deal with the discussion process.

7.1   THE PHASE NATURE OF THE PROCESS

Any process has stages—whether clear-cut, as the automated and human activities in successive rooms of a pineapple cannery, or overlapping and almost imperceptible, as the somewhat random activities of children building sand castles on the beach. Similarly, any *discussion* group exhibits phases in its interaction, with phases discernible in both realms—task and interpersonal.

This phasal nature of discussion groups has been widely noted. Schroder and Harvey[3] see system development (of an individual or a group) as evolvement from an undefined state to an integrated one that allows perception of alternatives and resolution of conflicts. They suggest four stages of development and illustrate these stages as follows:

> If the self of a child, for example, is followed in the course of its evolvement, it tends to move in order from a stage of greater undifferentiatedness . . . through a kind of negativism and "self-assertion," to the development of sympathy, role playing, and taking turns, on to a higher state of independence and relativism marked by greater self-sufficiency and adequacy of coping with a complex, changing environment.[4]

Although "tolerance of differences and diversity" appears in the third stage, at the fourth stage the parts can combine for common purposes but still can maintain their unique identity. Schroder and Harvey liken the fourth stage to an orchestra "in which parts may appropriately solo or the totality of components be brought together in one synchronized and interdependent expression."[5]

Speech Communication researcher B. Aubrey Fisher[6] identified four phases in group interaction that he labeled Orientation, Conflict, Emergence, and Reinforcement.

Orientation	Group members search tentatively for ideas and direction; there is much clarification and agreement.
Conflict	Group members begin polarization of attitudes; there is dispute over decision proposals.
Emergence	Group members begin to come to common agreement on the group task; there is less conflict and more movement toward consensus.
Reinforcement	Group members achieve consensus; there is much agreement and positive reinforcement.

Whether applied to the process at large or to the development of a smaller unit within the total process, this sequence of steps seems useful for describing the discussion process.

We might ask a further question: can these stages within the two aspects of the process—task and team—be seen separately as well as in the composite process, that is, the team working on its task? In 1965, Bruce W. Tuckman[7] reviewed fifty articles dealing with stages of group development over time and classified his findings as to whether the behavior being described was *task* or *interpersonal*. He found that four phases tend to occur in both task and interpersonal realms of group interaction. Tuckman named these stages *forming, storming, norming*, and *performing*. He proposes that *storming* might not occur in an unemotional task situation (in contrast to a therapy group situation, for example), and that *norming* would not be so "salient" there.[8] He further suggests that in the fourth stage, "interpersonal structure becomes the tool of task activities. Roles become flexible and functional, and group energy is channeled into the task. Structural issues have been resolved, and structure can now become supportive of task performance."[9] However, even though the same sequence occurs in the interpersonal and the task realms:

1. the group is not necessarily at the same stage at the same time in both realms; and

2. the group's activities in the two realms can be differentiated.

Michael Argyle, reader in Social Psychology at Oxford University, has cast Tuckman's findings into a useful chart:

Table 7-1.

	GROUP STRUCTURE	TASK ACTIVITY
1. *Forming*	There is anxiety, dependency on a leader, testing to find out the nature of the situation and what behavior is acceptable.	Members find out what the task is, what the rules are, what methods are appropriate.
2. *Storming*	Conflict between sub-groups	Emotional resistance to de-

	rebellion against leader, opinions are polarized, resist control by group, conflicts over intimacy.	mands of task.
3. *Norming*	Development of group cohesion, norms emerge, resistance overcome and conflicts patched up, mutual support and development of group feeling.	Open exchange of views and feelings; cooperation developed.
4. *Performing*	Interpersonal problems are resolved, interpersonal structure is the tool of task activity, roles are flexible and functional.	Emergence of solutions to problems, constructive attempts at task completion, energy is now available for effective work; this is major work period.[10]

Not every member in the group may be at the same stage— either interpersonal or task—as the leader or other members; and sometimes a group or an individual member moves back to an earlier stage and needs to come forward again. But these things can be handled if cooperative, integrated relationships have been established.

The phase nature of the discussion seen as a whole is important to understand. The fact that this development from separateness to interdependent/independent participation can be reduced to *two basic phases* is helpful. We see the "storming" stage (Step 2) as a transition between the "forming" stage (Step 1) and the "norming" and "performing" stages (Steps 3 and 4). We see the first two stages as a DIVERGING phase (one of exploration, examination, and testing) and the third and fourth stages as a CONVERGING phase (one of comparison, evaluation, and choice).[11] EXAMINE, then CHOOSE: these two movements occur repeatedly through the interaction of the group; this sequence is descriptive of the activity of the group in its full scope but also in many smaller segments of activity within the whole.[12]

In the task realm the EXAMINE/CHOOSE sequence is the natural movement of thought: the city council may study its transportation problems and examine all possible ways of alleviating them (the DIVERGING phase),[13] then reason through to a choice among these ways (the CONVERGING phase). And this same process may be seen inside the handling of any part of these larger movements: the council may EXAMINE in detail the transportation experiences of another city, then SYNTHESIZE this information to a note of hope or caution for themselves in their efforts. Thus, this movement outward to the bounds of an idea, then inward to a synthesis, describes not only the group's entire thought process but also the handling of any idea *within* the major movement: it is this

same   SWELL COLLAPSE   —the bellows movement,

our own breathing cadence. It is   BUILD REVISE   ;

DEVELOP ADJUST;   ANALYZE SYNTHESIZE.

But the DIVERGING/CONVERGING sequence is also characteristic of the group structure realm, the interpersonal aspect of the group process. Members of the group feel separate at the start, each a product of his or her own experience, personality, expectations, and habits. Each member is aware of the differences between himself or herself and the other group members and may feel challenged and defensive because of these differences. The members try out attitudes, responses, and actions with each other until they can settle into a workable arrangement with each other; from examination to synthesis. Members of a group may note that one person is sitting back, half lost in undisclosed thoughts; they need and want his or her active participation. So the cycle occurs: the members examine (perhaps without speaking of it) why this might be—is the person bored with the line that the discussion has been taking? or is he or she feeling put down by something that has been said or weighed down with external problems of his or her own? And what can be done about this person? Then the members judge among these possibilities as well as they can to handle the situation: SWELL then (to understanding)

COLLAPSE
(to decision
and action). It is EXPLORE RESOLVE; MULLABOUT COALESCE;

DIVERGE   CONVERGE
(as individuals)   (to a team).   It is clear that the sequence
EXAMINE/CHOOSE is relevant not only to the TASK aspect
of discussion but also to the interpersonal, the group structure
or TEAM aspect. It thus seems appropriate to use this outward/
inward model as the basis for organizing our treatment of
these matters.

But we must ask ourselves whether this sequence can really
be divided; are not the two phases tied too closely together?
Have we not said that even within each phase the other occurs
in a subordinate role? Actually, it is important to separate the
two phases because the thought movements differ significantly
and need attention separately for that reason. They need to be
held apart—insofar as that is possible, and it *is* possible on
major thought-movements. Two teachers in the area of creativity in management declared that

> search and appraisal require different mental sets. Search
> requires divergent thinking production with its openness to
> fantasy, experience, and even perceptual inversion and
> distortions. Appraisal requires convergent thinking and
> evaluation, both of which accent rationality, a challenging
> attitude, and the careful weighing of evidence. In a sense,
> combined search-appraisal is a mental exercise almost equiv-
> alent to a physical effort of pushing and pulling at the
> same time.[14]

These teachers report that research studies have shown that
"by extending the search and deferring appraisal it is possible
to improve both the quantity and quality of ideas for solving
problems."[15] We subscribe to this separation.

Thus, the present chapter takes up the DIVERGING phase with an emphasis on creative thinking, and the following chapter takes up the CONVERGING phase with an emphasis on choice making. In each chapter the phase is traced separately within the TASK activity realm and the TEAM activity realm.

7.2   **THE DIVERGING PHASE AS THEATER
                             FOR CREATIVITY**

In the discussion, group members search their minds—seeking new areas of information on the problem; looking at the same thing from new angles; seeing with new perspectives; putting things together in new ways; and finding new relationships in size, shape, texture, and form to suit the group's particular purpose. This raid upon his or her abilities that each member conducts is an active and a creative one.

Since Guilford's hypothesis in 1950, much research has been done on the four factors in creative ability that he suggested: fluency, flexibility, originality, and elaboration.[16] These factors appear repeatedly in the DIVERGING phase of an effective discussion:

Fluency   — the ability to produce many similar ideas. Through a ready flow of words, ideas, and associations the fluent contributor suggests different members of a class (*units*), a second correlate when a first correlate and the relation are known (*relations*), and alternative sequences of steps (*systems*).

Flexibility   — the ability to change to other categories of ideas than the usual ones. The contributor may offer these suggestions spontaneously or may produce them adaptively when the group faces a need. Thus, he or she may move the group to different ways of thinking (*classes*) or actually produce shifts of tactics (*transformations*) in seeking a solution.

> *Originality* — the ability to produce responses that are statistically rare, only remotely related, or clever. Such contributions tend to produce shifts of tactics (*transformations*), and are a form of flexibility.
>
> *Elaboration* — the ability to fill out details. The contributor makes suggestions from the information at hand, then continues with further additions (*implications*).

When creative thinking is taking place in the group situation, the matter of communication of ideas to other thinkers is especially important. C. W. Taylor added a fourth kind of fluency to the Guilford three (word fluency, ideational fluency, associational fluency), "verbal versatility."[17] This factor has come to be called "expressional fluency" since it means the ability to put thoughts readily into words and sentences.

A group of citizens discussing the potential role of individual voters in rendering government more accountable may well demonstrate these factors of creativity as the members move through the DIVERGING phase:

Leader: So we're pointing out the outdatedness of many government agencies?

Fluency

Mary: Yes, a Brookings Institute study showed that of the 175 federal agencies existing in 1923, 123—or 85 percent—were still in existence 50 years later; just 27 agencies had been disbanded, and 246 new ones had come into being.

Flexibility

James: And look at the way the people's interests were drowned on the energy problem in 1975 when the special interest pressures were so great, when millions of dollars were spent to influence legislators, and we—the public—didn't know about it! Our lobby disclosure law is just too weak to handle the problem!

Leader: Shall we list the inadequate lobby disclosure law as a possible cause of the government's separation from us, and come back and give it a look after we've thrashed out our thinking on the once-established-live-forever government agency matter and other symptoms we can think of that indicate that our government is less accountable than we'd wish?

Gordon: Well, it has been good to see that sunset laws have been passed in eleven states . . .

Andy: Help me, will you? What do you mean by "sunset laws?"

Gordon: As I understand it, "sunset laws" are laws that put government agencies—and programs too—on limited life cycles, that is, they have to justify their usefulness or go out of business.

Later in the discussion the group is examining efforts that have been made—unsuccessfully—to make government more accountable, and discusses the Common Cause's lobby in 1975 for a coherent energy policy:

Sue: But that effort by Common Cause just couldn't work; special interests came in with such intense lobbying that Congress just couldn't build a policy. . . .

Andy: Remember what John Gardner said? He was still president of Common Cause then. He said it was like a checkers game with certain players leaning over the board and putting their thumbs on the particular checkers that were important to them and saying: "Go ahead, make any move you want to, but just don't touch this checker." Pretty soon, there were thumbs on all the checkers, and the whole thing stopped. And those thumbs are still on those checkers, and we still don't have an energy policy!

Originality

James: Yes, the special interest lobbies really hit the congressmen. But they hit us citizens back at home too! Grass-roots lobbying, you know. We're getting all sorts of pressure from utilities, oil companies, labor unions, manufacturers, and environmental groups. Think of the advertisements you've seen, the letters to stockholders, the statements by union and company officials! And have you seen that ad about "scrubbers" to clean up the emissions from the smokestacks?

Elaboration

In these portions of the discussion we can see examples of

DIVERGING thinking. The leader exercised careful corrective thinking in recognizing that James's suggestion of the special interest pressures in the energy problem, though demonstrating the flexibility of his thinking, took the group from the line of development they were pursuing together. Thus, James's converging thinking appeared in the midst of the DIVERGING phase; it was used to serve the purpose of maintaining a relatively unbroken thought-line. Certainly the members exercise within their own minds a bit of convergent thinking when they decide what—out of their stock of ideas—will be relevant to the group's thought-line at a given moment. Herein lies the key to the difference between regular discussion processes and brainstorming; whereas the problem-solving discussion processes expect members to police their thoughts to some extent in selecting what they will say so that the others can bring their thoughts to bear upon the same idea at the same time, the brainstorming process expects no such continuity, delighting in wild side excursions even while commending "hitchhiking" ideas. But these small bits of converging thinking only render more useful what is basically a DIVERGING phase, one characterized by fluency, flexibility (including originality), and elaboration that make up creative thinking. The members of the group will not be equal in these traits. But since the purpose of the group in this DIVERGING phase is to suggest and examine ideas together deeply and widely, it is fortunate if at least several of the members are especially strong in one or more of these abilities. Looking ahead to Chapter 8, we should realize that these factors of DIVERGING thinking will appear from time to time in subordinate position within the CONVERGING phase.

7.3   THE DIVERGING PHASE IN TASK ACTIVITY

The group begins its discussion by searching out the nature of its task and the methods by which that task is to be approached. The members and leader are trying to *orient* themselves,[18] as the use of the Bales' Interaction Process Categories revealed to Bales and Strodtbeck[19] in 1951, and to Bales[20] again in 1953. There seems little doubt about the regular occurrence of this *forming* step in problem-management discussions.

In examining this *forming* step in TASK activity we consider

three matters: the use of creative abilities, conditions underlying the use of creative abilities, and the use of patterns
of thought.

7.31   Use of Creative Abilities

Fluency. Members offer their experiences and their perceptions, concrete details from their own years of living and
learning; words to capture what is being said by others, definitions for terms that are confusing to the group. If the group is
discussing the question of how the arts can increase and enliven
the learning process of elementary school pupils and the talk
has been all about painting, the fluent developer can bring in
new facets by adding vivid information about another art, such
as the dance. Or if the group has seen how experiencing the
rhythms of the dance has opened pupils to concepts of mathe-
matics, the highly fluent person can add details of how the
rhythms of sculpture can help with the same mathematical
relationship. If the group has been thinking of steps in artistic
development to be taken individually by the pupils, the person
can propose steps in group work that will yield value in artistic
development. In each case the fluent developer is mining a rich
memory store to bring additional units, relationships, and
systems to the consideration of the group.

Flexibility. Instead of serving the discussion group by thinking along lines similar to those of the fluent developer, the
flexible developer moves off the beaten path, that is, takes a
lateral step. He or she leaves the line of thinking of the group
abruptly, tangentially, but purposefully, with a graphic comparison, a whimsical twist, or a turning of the topic to see it
differently. The unusually flexible person thinks of something
off the subject but with a hidden, possibly rich vein of ore to
examine. If the group is trying to upgrade the morale on a certain project and is talking of bringing in a crew to renovate
the recreation area for the workers, the flexible developer may
suggest giving the workers two weeks off *on pay* during which
they are to renovate the area themselves—the amount to be
spent on the renovations being precisely the same in both plans.

An advisory group could be asked to meet and recommend
whether or not a company should purchase a new piece of
machinery to automate the loading dock of a certain warehouse. The machinery would cost $25,000 but would pay for

itself in three years. The simple question put to the group would be: Should the company buy this machinery for the loading dock of this warehouse? (We have recommended against "yes/no" questions such as this one earlier in the Desk Book, and this example should be seen as illustrating some reasons for our position.) The facts of the matter seem simple enough. Given the question and a relatively short payoff period, most groups would recommend Yes.

But one group discussing this question in a real case came up with a different answer: "The company should not buy the machinery *and* should *sell the warehouse.*" This group followed the "Ideals" system of Gerald Nadler[21] and continued moving to more and more basic levels to ask for the purpose of each proposed action. They began by asking the *purpose* for the loading dock machinery, then moved to asking the *purpose* for the loading dock itself, and then to the *purpose* for the warehouse. It was by this process that the group came to see that the overall purpose of the corporation was not well served by warehousing their products in this location and that the broadest purposes of the company would best be served by ending that practice. So the best answer to the question asked was that the company should *not* buy the machinery *and* *should* sell the warehouse. This answer goes beyond the question asked, illustrating, for one thing, the weakness of the very limited yes/no question when there were broader questions that needed asking. It also shows the need for a group process that permits novelty, creativity, and lateral thinking to work when they are greatly needed and potentially valuable. This is especially true in the DIVERGING phase.

Elaboration. Here a member takes the idea where it is and runs with it; each thing suggested brings to mind a further extension, then another detail from that, and so on. Each piece of information or idea launches the elaborator further, each providing the basis for the next piece. In the morale-building effort mentioned previously, an idea developer could pick up the group's idea of the two-week effort by the workers as members have developed it so far together, and suggest in rapid succession: that the two weeks be a month apart so that equipment ordered in the first week could be on hand the second week; that the final day of each of the workweeks be a gala day as well as a workday, with families present and food being provided for all; that the boss be present in work clothes those last days and work and eat with the others.

This rapid thought run will have to be examined at many points, but the very fact that many new ideas have been introduced is the essence of elaboration. Furthermore, the elaboration could happen with two or more members spurring each other on in spinning out the thought. (For the moment it is an impromptu "hitchhiking" effort *par excellence*.)

7.32 Conditions Underlying the Use of Creative Abilities

What then is needed to foster the use of these creative abilities—fluency, flexibility (including originality), and elaboration? Facilitating conditions are easy to list, but much harder to provide:

1. A continuing openness to speculation, that is, showing the courage to hear half-formed ideas that seem to have little to recommend them at the moment.
2. A wide-open search, that is, holding back restrictions so that unusual departures are invited.
3. An encouragement of ideas from everyone, including those with least experience;[22] maintenance of open lines of communication.
4. A genuine appreciation of differences—of ideas, of viewpoints, of terminology, of interpretation.
5. A careful holding back of evaluation during the idea-producing stage.

These conditions ask that each member look beyond his or her own area of information and ability to elicit and appreciate the suggestions of others. It is to be hoped that the group can move on into the CONVERGING phase in its TEAM activity long before it is able to move out of the DIVERGING phase in its TASK activity; only when the group members have begun to work interdependently can they develop these conditions for creativity to a high degree. Nevertheless much can be done in the divergent phase on the task even if members are still working largely as individuals without yet being able (or willing) to draw upon the resources available to them in the other members. We all have had experiences in groups where there has been a show of spirit before the group settles down to the task: "It's impossible! We don't have the information!" or "Experts ought to be doing this instead of us!" or "This isn't the way to go at it for sure!" Such emotional responses at

some early point are frequently found in the SWELL,

EXPLORE, ANALYZE phase in the TASK realm.

7.33 Use of Patterns of Thought

What relationship does the DIVERGING/CONVERGING movement have to the Problem Management Sequence? To clarify, we consider the first three steps in the PMS—(1) describing the problem; (2) analyzing the problem; and (3) proposing plans for managing the problem—as the DIVERGING phase of the discussion despite the converging nature of certain movements within the phase (as the choice of the direction in Step II). We then consider the fourth step (selecting the "best" plan for managing the problem) as the CONVERGING phase of the whole discussion despite the diverging nature of certain movements within the phase (as the untouched symptoms in Step IV). This designation of certain STEPS as DIVERGING or CONVERGING arises from the major kind of thinking by which they proceed: the DIVERGING phase is characterized chiefly by CREATIVE thinking, whereas the CONVERGING phase is characterized chiefly by EVALUATIVE thinking.

Whether a group's preoccupation with DIVERGING thinking is to achieve the first three steps of a PMS or to fulfill the requirements of a task of lesser scope, its thought-line has one of three characteristic patterns: description, explication, or list making. At times, one of these patterns forms the total task of a discussion group; at other times, these patterns perform their roles within the development of a larger act of thought, such as the problem management inquiry. These patterns of thinking can be illustrated by phrasing questions that would call for their use to handle the overall task of the group:

Description:	What is the Scanlon Plan?
Explication:	What is meant by "going walkabout"?
List making:	What are the causes of the famine situation in Ghana?

These movements of description, explication, and list making will occur repeatedly on a smaller scale within larger movements of whatever kind. Hence, these patterns merit detailed consideration.

Description. The purpose here is to build up an accurate, clear, and sufficiently complete picture of a situation, organization, policy, or the like. Starting from an obscure, confused, or ambiguous notion of the matter at hand, the group moves into a process of data presentation and data grouping that lays the basis for the needed clarification of ideas. What pieces of data are relevant? How can they be grouped? Which of the groups are the most important in the total picture? The first two questions involve what-goes-with-what on aspects that make a difference; the third concerns how much weight each aspect should have in the final picture. The question of relevancy is difficult when appropriate categories are not known and can be discovered only by assembling potentially relevant materials and ordering them systematically, as in describing the work load of an employee. The question of relevancy is much less difficult when suitable categories are rather obvious, as the purpose/structure/procedure/results of the Scanlon Plan.

But the question of the relative significance of the grouped materials in producing the overall picture remains; often the group will have to revert to its original need for the description in order to decide whether the emotional or the physical demands upon the employee are the more important, whether the procedure of the Scanlon Plan is more significant than its results, for example.

No true picture can, of course, result from inaccurate or atypical data. The group must be constantly on the alert to test the dependability of its data. Such descriptions may comprise the full task of a group, but even more often, spontaneous and abbreviated descriptions will need to be produced at many points within all discussions.

Suppose that members of a group had done some reading for a discussion on the question: What is the Synectics method? Clearly they will intend to describe this method to themselves so that all will have a better picture of it.

> *Leader*:   In our series of meetings on specific methods that
> groups may elect to use to upgrade their decisions,
> we've come, as you know, to the method usually
> called *Synectics*. By talking it over together we

hope to have a better understanding of it. Where shall we start in setting out to describe it?

George: The thing I noticed the most in reading about it was the pains the synectics group took to bring things to the surface of their minds that otherwise they'd never have thought of. And some of them were surely strange things!

Alice: Yes, the free speculating that the group did—or got themselves to do—impressed me too. Actually, wouldn't you think that they'd have been embarrassed at some of the things that came out, like getting choked on dry dog food when you were a kid?

Brad: But not getting embarrassed is really part of it. Actually they build in ways to get at ideas that really seem irrelevant but actually might bring out something pretty valuable.

Leader: Could we say that one of the purposes of the Synectics method—maybe there are more?—is to encourage speculation beyond what we would do naturally? And then we began to talk about ways to get this speculating to happen, didn't we. Let's get into that: what *are* the steps that a group goes through when using the Synectics method? Let's be as specific as we can.

After the steps have been suggested and cast into appropriate order by the group if they were suggested in overlapping ways or without concern for what would be done before something else, the leader can again bring up the idea of additional purposes. The group will surely want to set forth the development of the method—its originators and changes that have occurred; the roles of leader, client, and group; possible adaptations of the method; uses made of the method; and so on. The basics would probably be purpose, steps, roles, and adaptations.

Throughout this use of DIVERGING thinking for the purpose of *description*, the leader and group will have to be on the alert for accuracy of information, appropriateness of grouping plus the weighting of the groups if that is relevant, and completeness in all essential matters. All of these are converging factors that must be present to validate the speculations of the diverging thought.

Explication. Here the group is involved with a complex, vague, or otherwise perplexing concept, statement of fact or opinion, proverb, theory, or rule of action—a compacted unit of material whose meaning is not clear or, on the other hand, seems obvious but is thought to have worthwhile depths as yet unplumbed. Thus, the material presents difficulties in being grasped, interpreted, applied, and enjoyed. Whether the obscurities stem from individual *terms* within a statement whose meanings must be examined or from *relationships-among-terms* whose significances must be probed, these materials warrant careful explication, that is, *unfolding*. Sometimes the obscurities arise from a lack of familiarity with the *context* of the statement or its *implications*.

DIVERGENT thinking by the group provides the unlocking of the meanings; attention to terms, idea relationships, context, and possible implications may supply the entry. But the key must suit the lock. How would a group explicate "going walkabout"? No amount of speculation about the terms themselves will supply the richness of the true context; indeed the group may have to separate its thinking from inaccurate leads before it can succeed:

> *Leader*: This phrase, "go walkabout": what do you make of it?
>
> *Betty*: Well, I remember that Queen Elizabeth called her trips to the mill-towns and certain streets in London and other cities in Britain "walkabouts," or at least the television reporters said: "The Queen is taking another 'walkabout' today. . . ." It was part of the Jubilee.
>
> *Robert*: Yes, we kept hearing that phrase "taking a walkabout." But I seem to remember—vaguely, and help me, if you can—words something like that some years ago when Evonne Goolagong lost an important tennis match; I remember the announcers saying something about her having "gone walkabout" right during the match.
>
> *Amy*: One time it was "take a walkabout" and the other time it was "go walkabout"—is that right? They said Evonne Goolagong had "gone walkabout?" Not much difference, *take* or *go*, but maybe it's important?
>
> *Jack*: You know, I think maybe that word *go—go walkabout*—is the key. When I was in Alice Springs, Australia—out in the center of the continent where it's awfully dry—there was a family of aboriginals sitting there together, squatted down in a dry riverbed. I asked the bus driver what they

could be doing, and he said they had probably "gone walkabout." He said it was a tribal custom for an individual—or a family—when the world got too much for them, to just stop whatever they were doing, maybe take a few provisions, maybe not, and go wandering a bit, no destination, no time limit, no plan, just wandering.

Betty: Now I remember! There was a movie called "Walkabout." It was a marvelous story about the wanderings of a young aboriginal boy in the desert of Australia. It was wonderful; I'd like to see it again.

Amy: If it's that deep in the aboriginals, maybe Evonne Goolagong was wandering *in her mind* since she couldn't leave the court?

Robert: And that was probably it! Anyway, that moment or two of inattention lost her the tennis match. But I've just been thinking what I heard a sister of mine say once long ago; she said, "Let me alone for a minute; I've just *got* to go inside myself and rest."

Leader: "And *rest*!" Wasn't that interesting.

Robert: Yes, I guess she just didn't want anything more going on around her for a bit; she didn't want to have to respond.

Leader: Maybe the separation from activity and routine, etc., can be *in the mind* if you can't manage being separated *in the body*! Separation, freedom, rest—we've said. Well, I guess "going walkabout" is pretty different from Queen Elizabeth's "doing a walkabout!" She surely wasn't separated, or free, or resting! Both terms have their interesting connotations, don't they?

Sometimes it is a statement instead of a term that the group needs to explicate. In a group examination at the New School of Speech and Drama at Hampstead, England, the members were given the problem of explicating the familiar old quotation from Samuel Johnson: "When a man is tired of London, he is tired of life." Sitting there in London as they talked, the students described the many-sidedness of life in London, the opportunities for all types of people, and one remembered the remainder of the quotation: "for there is in London all that life can afford." Then they returned to speculate about the nature of the tiredness that would lead a person to miss or not savor these opportunities.

As was true of description, so it is with explication: this

DIVERGING thought-pattern can be used not only as the entire tool of a discussion group but also at many points within the fabric of other inquiries. These descriptions and explications are enlargements of understanding; they supply grist for the mill of thought. They are truly characteristic thought-patterns of the DIVERGING type.

List Making. A group may utilize the DIVERGING function of list making either as *means* or *end*.

The group employs list making as a MEANS when it builds a sequence of items by which to organize discussion (as criteria for use in discussing a question such as: How effective is our city park system?) or as items of an agenda to be taken up subsequently, one by one, as the use of torture as political method of (1) Chile, (2) Iran, or (3) Russia.

or when it builds a sequence of items to further its work somewhere within a discussion (as in a problem-management inquiry when it must *list the causes* before selecting the direction of its attack).

The group employs list making as an END when it produces a listing of items as the intended result of its whole discussion (as on the question: What characteristics should a teacher possess?)

In addition to the special ease with which a group can fall from developmental thinking into argumentative thinking while using the list-making procedure, a group should seek to avoid at least three other frequent errors. All three are CONVERGENT in nature:

1. Poor entitlement of the idea listed

When the *naming* of the item or criterion in the list is inadequately done so that the name does not pick up the idea by the handle, it often follows that the group cannot thereafter decide appropriately on the inclusion or exclusion of borderline information; the scope of the category is left ambiguous. And categories may overlap.

2. Faulty proportioning of significance among the items

When the group gives a minor item a major emphasis (or vice versa), it invites itself to apportion its time poorly and, more importantly perhaps, to make its list unreliable whether that list acts as MEANS or END.

3. Incompleteness of the list

When items are omitted from the list—items that are significant in serving the purpose for which the list is being built—the group operates from a faulty base whether it is using the list as MEANS or END. No matter how well the work is done on the items that *are* listed, the group *cannot* obtain a reliable result.

If a citizen's group that was concerned with the erosion of public confidence in elected officials set out to discuss qualities to be expected in these officials, the members would need to build a list-as-agenda for their discussion:

Leader: We've been talking briefly about our belief that the public has a right to be represented by officials we can trust; we want so desperately to believe in the people we have put in office. My small nephew was reciting the Preamble to the Constitution just the other day—he had had to learn it for a program in his school—and I was thrilled all over again by those magnificent phrases that tell the purposes of the Constitution—to establish justice, insure domestic tranquility, provide for the common defense, promote the general welfare, and secure the blessings of liberty to ourselves and our posterity. That really says it, doesn't it? But what kind of persons will our officials have to be in order to make these promises real? What idea shall we start with?

Tom: I'd like to rattle off half a dozen, but that wouldn't work, would it? Well, maybe we'd like to talk about *integrity*, just plain honesty, holding to principle.

Claris: Could I ask? Are we just making a list now, or should we discuss each one as we go?

Leader: Yes, why don't we clarify that? See any reason why we should do it one way or the other?

Peter: Do you suppose we could pace ourselves better during the time we have if we knew how many items we had yet to take up? On the other hand, if we make our list without any discussion, might we not have quite a bit of overlapping in our items?

Gloria: What if—when someone suggests an idea—we talk about it just enough to be sure we're pretty close in our thinking as to what we mean? And enough to get a good heading for it. But not a lot, because we'll do that later.

Joe: Back to that idea of honesty. I'd surely like to have that on our list. When I think how one senator—one I've always respected highly--joined as a co-sponsor of Senate Bill 926 for public financing of congressional campaigns, pledged himself to vote for "cloture" to stop any filibuster, and then voted repeatedly against stopping the filibuster, I'm just plain discouraged!

Marian: And another senator, after personally pledging to John Gardner of Common Cause that he would vote for cloture to shut off the debate, voted against it twice and left Washington before the third vote!

Leader: Could we hold up just a minute? We've been discussing the matter of honest keeping to commitments, haven't we? Let's make a decision as a group as to whether we want to make our list first, then use it as an agenda, or take up one item, discuss it, and state it for our list, then take up another, and so on. What shall we do? [speaking to the whole group]

Several: Let's make the list first. List them first. See how many we have so we can judge our time better.

Leader: So, make our list first? OK with everyone? [all seem to agree] Well, let's put down this first one then—how shall we term it—honesty, integrity?

Joe: Integrity sounds fine!

Leader: So, *integrity*? Fine. What shall we move into next?

Claris: I've been thinking of something President Kennedy

> said to the Massachusetts Legislature; he said each person in office would be measured on certain qualities and one was—"Were they men of courage, courage to stand up against both one's enemies and one's associates, and courage to resist both public pressure and private pressure." That sounds good to me.

Tom: Yes! Yes! Let's put *courage* down.

Getting the list made is basically a DIVERGING phase, but the group holds itself to the thought-line by certain converging moves: deciding on a way of proceeding and taking pains that the term chosen for the list suits the idea intended. Later the members will have to *iron out overlapping* if there seems to be some, consider whether their list is *reasonably complete*, and *decide on the relative importance* of the items. All of these acts are converging in nature although certain diverging elements prepare for the decision.

Throughout the expanding/exploring/DIVERGING phase of development, the group thought-line will have been produced by using in its cooperative advance at least three thought-patterns: description, explication, and list making. It is in the nature of thought, however, that the corrective/adjustive/CONVERGING phase (which is the focus of Chapter 8) cannot be entirely held back in the DIVERGING phase; choices have to be made, and choices—unless they are to be arbitrary ones—necessarily involve that selection among alternatives that is truly the essence of the CONVERGING phase. Despite the necessary occurrence of the CONVERGING movement within the smaller segments as the group has moved through this inductive phase (the forming phase and, often, the storming phase, in Tuckman's phraseology), the major movement working here has been the DIVERGING movement in the TASK realm.

7.4 THE DIVERGING PHASE IN THE TEAM REALM

By the team or group structure realm we mean the interpersonal feelings, the social-emotional relationships, present in the group. The matters in the TEAM realm are functioning at the same time as those in the TASK realm, though the two realms do not stay in step-by-step cadence; obviously, both start with the orienting step. Tuckman points out that the stages in these two realms tend to go in a similar sequence; he says, "While the two realms differ in content . . . their underlying dynamics are similar."[23] That is, the group moves through the four steps: we see the first (*forming*) as of DIVERGING type and the second (*storming*) as a transition, and we see the final two steps as of CONVERGING type.

The DIVERGING phase as it takes place in the interpersonal or TEAM realm is the period before the group of individuals become an actual *team*. It is not true that once a team always a team; every now and then the group or individual members will fall back to these DIVERGING steps in the midst of a generally CONVERGING movement and will need to be brought forward again into CONVERGING behaviors. On the other hand—with the possible exception of an emergency situation—were the group to move too quickly at the outset into CONVERGING behaviors, a somewhat superficial, false *modus vivendi* might be produced, one that they could probably not sustain. The necessity of moving through the DIVERGING stage would then be likely to strike them subsequently with unusual power and emotion. Each of these phases has its own place in the life of the group; its relative length, its complexity, and its frequency of repetition will depend upon the group, its task, and the characteristics of its specific situation.

In the *forming* stage, each member of the group is trying to find out how things are going to be for him or her; feelings are characterized by high awareness of the self and concern for the self, including concern about others *in their potential influence upon the self*. Each member asks himself or herself questions such as:

What are they like, especially the leader?

Will I [thinking of education, experience, clothing, life-style, and the like] fit here?

Am I prepared for this?

Will they listen to me, that is, respect what I say?

Are they going to want what I've got to contribute?

Uncertainty is always present for each member at the outset. Even if this meeting is one of a series of meetings, and the "cast of the play" is the same for this meeting as it was for the previous ones, there is an element still of uncertainty, though it is, of course, usually much smaller. Will Ken and Gordon take over again—with neither the leader nor any of the rest of us being able to stop them? Will we really settle down to work together this time, the whole group, so we can finally get somewhere? Well, we won't know until it happens, I guess.

Two experts on group interaction at Temple University have described this beginning period as a "time for waiting, for observing what lies ahead, for sorting out potential dangers and acting with discretion." They say:

> Like a child on the first day of school, we tend to:
>> Feel inadequate, but afraid to show it.
>> Feel tentative, but often need to appear fairly certain.
>> Be watchful.
>> Lack a feeling of potency or sense of control over our environment.
>> Act superficially and reveal only what is appropriate.
>> Scan the environment for clues of what is proper: clothes, tone of voice, vocabulary, who speaks to whom.
>> Be nice, certainly not hostile.
>> Try to place other participants in pigeon-holes so that they become comfortable to us, able to be coped with in our own minds.
>> Worry about who "we" should try to be in "this" group.
>> Desire structure and order to reduce our own pressure to perform.
>> Wonder what price it will take to be "in" and whether the rewards are worth the effort.
>> Find it difficult to listen and look beyond our own immediate needs.[24]

The members see these feelings of uncertainty and self-concern manifested in each other in both nonverbal and verbal behavior. They see Joe lean forward a bit anxiously, watching the leader; they see Frank look quickly from speaker to speaker, ready to second anything that sounds good to him or anything that the most vigorous person says; they see Carl lean back in a relaxed, pipe-puffing way, avoiding the eyes of everyone as though the problem was being made far too large and complex. And the sound of each others' voices tells a lot, although the listeners probably don't trace down the source of the impressions they are receiving.

What is said is, of course, highly revealing of what the members are feeling in this orientation phase of their interaction; perhaps this initial period of testing and jockeying when each member feels independence rather than interdependence should be called a phase of preinteraction. How the members handle this unsettledness varies much from one individual to another:

Some begin at once to contribute and respond, wanting to be in on the shaping of the situation from the very start or to be recognized as persons who will take an active part.

Some align themselves with the leader, or with a person who comes to the group with high status, or with some other strong or attractive individual.

And others adopt a wait-and-see policy, delaying their entrance into the interchange until they can see what to expect or until they can sketch out their "opposition."

The preliminary behaviors that members display in orienting themselves in the group depend largely upon two sets of factors: (1) what the individual brings to the group-personality structure, experience in discussion groups, confidence in personal abilities, and knowledge on this particular task; and (2) what the individual perceives as to the others—that is, an on-the-spot interpretation of the attitudes, abilities, and purposes of the others, and of some others in particular, a reading of the initial reactions of others to himself or herself, and the like. The first set of factors may have been considered to some extent in the arranging of the group. It is this second set of factors, however, that is of particular concern here.

Whether this initial period shows the members as amiable, giving the leader a "honeymoon" time, or whether it shows them jockeying a bit with each other for recognition in the group—there is still an attitude of uncertainty. Schroder and Harvey,[25] pointing to the findings of researchers in a number of areas, conclude that the members have a wish *to get the situation pinned down.*

7.41 Use of Creative Abilities

How do the creative abilities work in the DIVERGING phase in the TEAM activities? We may remind ourselves that *fluency* means facility in producing more of the same thing, that *flexibility* means facility in producing a different type of thing (perhaps even original), and that *elaboration* means facility in filling in the details. All of these abilities can find employment in this stage of group development.

Fluency. A fluent developer in the TEAM area is one who is busily engaged in creating membership in the group: interacting vigorously with many others, testing the boundaries of the allowable, trying out behaviors to see what will happen, and giving everyone the benefit of the doubt.

Suppose that an important issue in the mayor's race is that of improving the city center. One candidate, John Hopkins, plans to stress that issue in his campaign and asks his campaign manager to assemble a small group to make suggestions as to what the citizens themselves would like. The candidate and manager decide to ask Peter Harris, director of the program for the disadvantaged at the local community college; Susan Dowland, president of the senior class at the nearby high school; Gordon Collins, youth director at the YMCA; Sam Johnson, outstanding black athlete and freshman at the university; and Mary Gleeson, leader for many years in the local PTA. The campaign manager, a sporting goods store owner and Rotary Club president, chairs the meeting. After the welcoming minutes the group gets down to business:

Chairman:　Mr. Hopkins and I want you to know that we chose you people carefully to help us think out what kind of city center we really would like. We are very much interested in your ideas; when we get them together, I'll be taking them back to Mr. Hopkins and I'm sure he'll get a lot of help out of them. What suggestion shall we talk about first?

(All look at Peter Harris, but he smiles and indicates with a gesture that anyone at all could speak first.)

Mary Gleeson:　What an opportunity this really is! For many years I've thought that our city has a wonderful spot for a center just south of the interchange there on Adams St.

Susan Dowland:　Oh, that is a lovely place!

Gordon Collins:　But I guess we were going to talk about what we'd like the center to be *like*, weren't we?

Chairman:　Yes, we were, actually.

Gordon Collins:　So I'd like to suggest something that has been a long-time dream of mine! I'd like a park area—oh, with galleries and shops and restaurants around, of course—but a park area with fountains, little waterfalls, and small green lawns *to be sat upon* with shrubbery that makes little enclosures. Water splashing and green grass—it would be a quieter, more gracious place than most of us could imagine in the center of a city. But—it *could* happen! It *could* happen!

Fluency of different kinds can be seen in this excerpt: Mary's quick, affirmative characterization of the meeting as an "opportunity"; Gordon's testing to see whether the leader will let a member help in the business end of running the meeting; Gordon's sharing his "long-time dream" with the group. Mary's comment affirms the occasion—and that is valuable for the group to hear—but her immediate speculation of a place reveals that she is thinking strongly as a separate individual. Gordon's use of the pronoun "we" is helpful in declaring the *group* nature of the enterprise; when looked at alone, this comment seems to show Gordon's hope for group interaction, but when he comes right back in after the leader's response with a lengthy, rather personal sharing, it can be seen that Gordon is—perhaps without realizing it—setting the group up by his question and then reaping the reward; an individualistic move. Let us not miss, however, that Gordon's openness is a bid for openness in the group, and thus can be seen as an advance toward groupness.

Flexibility. Flexibility can be seen when a member moves off the *immediate* thought-line; of course this means a tangent but it is a tangent of a good sort. Whether the addition to the group's line of thinking is a valuable one in terms of its overall purpose is the key to whether the shift introduced is a mere tangent or a significant contribution from a flexible developer. In the campaign manager's meeting, Gordon's comment that his longtime dream "could happen!" brings other comments:

> *Susan Dowland:*   I'd really like that!
>
> *Peter Harris:*   Well, I just have to come in at this point. A park is a fine idea all right, but the key to the whole thing is what there is around it. If the buildings around it are ramshackle, and the streets not safe around it, and the traffic on the freeways makes more noise than the fountains, what would the park be then?

There is no doubt that Peter's suggestion has an important thought; it is a move away from the line of thinking, for sure. His flexibility, however, lies in the TASK realm, rather than in the TEAM realm. And its abruptness would probably have a detrimental effect upon both realms: directly upon the task, since it introduces a new idea before the group had had time to handle the earlier one; indirectly upon the team, since it as much as declares the group ineffective and badly in need of himself as the rescuer.

> *Chairman:*   Yes, the environment will be important for us

to consider. But let's turn back to the idea of the park itself for a bit first, shall we?

Mary: Would it help if we asked ourselves who the people are that we'd like to have use the park? If we knew who they would be, maybe we'd have some guidelines in planning what the park should be like—

Gordon: I like that idea. But, on the other hand, how can we tell who would come until we know what we would have there for them? It seems to me if we had big areas with a baseball field, and the like, that would be one thing; if we just had picnic areas—

Mary's suggestion seems to be helping the group take another tack together, and thus might be considered to be an example of *flexibility* in developing more group behavior and less individual-as-individual behavior.

Peter: Let's just figure for a minute. Suppose Sam and I were asked by the community to find out what they felt was lacking now; suppose Sam and I canvassed every family with children living within a mile of our park, think how much more we'd know to begin with—

Sam: Maybe we ought to go to see *every* family, though, I mean even the ones without children; isn't it the senior citizens sometimes who need the parks the most?

Peter's hypothetical illustration seemed to involve Sam, who had said nothing up to this point, and drew a suggestion from him. This action of Peter's could be labeled a creative act of flexibility in the TEAM realm.

Elaboration. If we think of elaboration as filling in the details of something seen vaguely before, we can point to Mary's use of pronouns: picking up the "we" from the chairman's question, she says: "... we ... ourselves ... we'd ... we ... we'd ...." Furthermore, Mary suggests asking, liking, knowing, and having *together*; she is spelling out the details of the cooperative action the group might take. This is elaborative action in moving from individual work in the group toward a team relationship.

7.42 Conditions Underlying the Use of Creative Abilities

Under what conditions will the members be fluent, flexible, and elaborative in the DIVERGING phase in the *team* realm? One underlying, all-important condition needs thorough examination, that of *defensiveness*. In this uncertain orientation period of the group meeting, when members do not yet identify themselves with the group, it is very easy for them to feel on guard, vigilant against threat.

Jack R. Gibb, who was quoted in Chapter 6 on *climate*, pointed out that defensiveness may arise in a person when he or she perceives someone who exhibits these characteristics:

1. Evaluation   If by expression, manner of speech, tone of voice, or verbal content the sender seems to be evaluating or judging the listener, then the receiver goes on guard.

2. Control   Speech that is used to control the listener evokes resistance. That the speaker secretly views the listener as ignorant, unable to make his own decisions, uninformed, immature, unwise, or possessed of wrong or inadequate attitudes is a subconscious perception that gives the latter a valid base for defensive reactions.

3. Strategy   Group members who are seen as "taking a role," as feigning emotion, as toying with their colleagues, as withholding information, or as having special sources of data are especially resented. Particularly violent reactions occur when it appears that someone is trying to make a stratagem appear spontaneous.

4. Neutrality   When neutrality in speech appears to the listener to indicate a lack of concern for his welfare, he becomes defensive.

5. Superiority   When a person communicates to another that he feels superior in position, power, wealth, intellectual ability, physical characteristics, or other ways, he arouses defensiveness.

6. Certainty   Those who seem to know the answers, to require no additional data, and to regard themselves as teachers rather than as co-workers tend to put others on guard.[26]

To restate Gibb's list: conditions that would allow members to exercise their creative abilities in helping move from the self-protective frame of this initial period are withholding judgment, that is, nonevaluative behavior; open rather than derogatory behavior; genuine rather than devious response; concern rather than disregard; equality rather than superiority; tentativeness rather than certainty. These attitudes are *freeing* ones; they allow the members to begin to feel safe in the hands of the group.

7.43 Use of Patterns of Feeling

At the outset of the group meeting, no member knows what this particular group will be like and what will be his or her place in the group. This generalized, undifferentiated situation— where almost everything is still uncertain—is the first stage in system development. Unless development of the group (as a system) is arrested at an early point it will proceed through differentiation to integration, but in the end it will be characterized both by independence and by interdependence. Harvey and Schroder[27] have diagrammed these intra system relationships in this way:

Undifferentiated   Differentiated   Integrated

Gross stages of system development from undifferentiation, through differentiation, to integration.

The member joins the group with an ambiguous perception of the situation; he or she does not know the potentialities of the others nor of himself or herself in interaction with them. Reactions are generalized; if there is threat, the member knows little of where it lies but feels on guard in a condition of separateness. As the DIVERGING phase proceeds, each member will see the others, the group task, and group procedures more clearly; when differentiation has really occurred for the members, the group will have passed over into the first part of the CONVERGING phase and will only be fully in that phase when integration accompanies separateness, when the participants are functioning as TEAM-members as well as individuals.

But growth can begin to occur within the undifferentiated, DIVERGING phase. Members can begin to see beyond themselves, to hear different ideas and begin to be able to look at them. In the presence of others who seem to see things differently, however, they tend to move from the first inquiring/observing part of the shakedown cruise, as it were, into a second stage, one that Tuckman characterized as "intragroup hostility."[28] We tend to see this occurrence more as a transition than an actual stage[29] but regard it as a frequent part of group-as-TEAM development. Members often show belligerence, competitiveness, and perhaps jealousy in this transitional period in group life. They fall into conflict with each other, challenge the leader, and polarize themselves on tender issues as they elbow each other, as it were, for their own place in the group and for a clear-cut view of the situation in which they find themselves. They are rebelling against the way the situation had seemed to them or had seemed at first to be defined. By this rebellion, the members prepare themselves for involvement together on their task, for working on it as a TEAM. They are discovering themselves so that they can work together, independent yet interdependent. Napier and Gershenfeld have explained:

> For change to occur, those involved must see the problem as "their own." It cannot be imposed upon them. Thus, the diagnostic process is vital for involving those who will eventually be responsible for implementing the solutions.[30]

This transition that leads from the self-isolation and self-dependence of the first stage to a beginning of a TEAM relationship shows the move from the DIVERGING phase at its widest stretch to the entrance into the CONVERGING phase of TEAM-activity.

7.5   **CONCLUSION**

In the DIVERGING phase of group growth, the members exercise creative thinking in moving from a singleness of approach to a many-sided one. In the task realm, the group searches out ideas that may describe, or explicate, or produce a list. In the team realm, the group struggles to form itself into a working unit and closes the DIVERGING phase with members as conflicting parts whose very conflicts press them toward developing a better organization. Chapter 8 focuses upon the

CONVERGING phase as it occurs in both the task and the team realms of group interaction.

FOOTNOTES — CHAPTER 7

1. Ivan D. Steiner, *Group Process and Productivity* (New York: Academic Press, 1972), p. 6.
2. Steiner, *Group Process and Productivity*, p. 9.
3. Harold M. Schroder and O. J. Harvey, "Conceptual Organization and Group Structure," in *Motivation and Social Interaction: Cognitive Determinants*, O. J. Harvey, ed. (New York: The Ronald Press Company, 1963), pp. 136–137.
4. O. J. Harvey and Harold M. Schroder, "Cognitive Aspects of Self and Motivation," in *Motivation and Social Interaction*, p. 117.
5. Schroder and Harvey, "Conceptual Organization and Group Structure," p. 149.
6. B. Aubrey Fisher, *Small Group Decision Making: Communication and the Group Process* (New York: McGraw-Hill Book Company, 1974), pp. 140–145.
7. Bruce W. Tuckman, "Developmental Sequence in Small Groups," *Psychological Bulletin*, 63 (1965): 396.
8. Tuckman, "Developmental Sequence in Small Groups," p. 398.
9. Tuckman, "Developmental Sequence in Small Groups," p. 396.
10. Michael Argyle, *Social Interaction* (Chicago: Aldine Publishing Company, 1969), p. 218.
11. J. P. Guilford, the renowned psychologist, uses the terms *divergent production* and *convergent production* to name two of the five operation categories in his structure-of-intellect model. His use of the term *production* refers to retrieval of information from the individual's memory; divergent production means that the retrieval brings a more or less fluent, flexible, and elaborative set of products, and convergent production means that the retrieval brings the one answer required by the given restrictions. He also names *evaluation* as a separate category of operation in his model, defining evaluation as movement by comparison to decision on the basis of satisfaction of relevant criteria.—*The Nature of Human Intelligence* (New York: McGraw-Hill Book Company, 1967), pp. 152, 171, 183.

    Our term *diverging phase* coincides with Guilford's divergent production category in its use of creative thinking abilities and the nature of its products. We use the word *converging* in a broader sense, however, than Guilford does in his term *convergent production*. It is Guilford's concept of evaluation-to-decision-through-comparison that we mean by the *converging phase* of group interaction.

    Guilford explains (page 183) that when the choices among which the individual selects are furnished to him, his activity then is *evaluation*, and when that individual has to provide the alternatives himself, his activity is convergent production as well as evaluation and that the two activities are hard to separate. Guilford sees evaluation as occurring throughout a line of thinking and suggests that, although evaluation appears in the creative process at early points, it probably appears at "higher levels near the end." (page 329) We see this evaluative aspect as the core activity of the *converging phase*. Guilford seems to recognize evaluation as the natural partner to the diverging movement without making his recognition fully explicit. (pages 184, 188, 189, 214–215) Hence, our theory of the diverging phase as the building up phase and the converging phase as the evaluative choice-making phase does not seem alien to Guilford's thinking.
12. Guilford sees the interlacing nature of problem solving; he says: "The memory store makes itself felt all along the way. Evaluation, as a process of self-checking, also makes frequent contributions. Within a main linear trend, behavior also loops and, in the total operation, loops within loops." (page 467). Elsewhere he says: "Evaluation is a persistent operation, but fluency of production is facilitated by the injection of moments of suspended judgments." (page 345). Thus, it is clear that evaluation should sometimes be resisted while in the diverging phase; it will perhaps occur even there at a "lower level" but "a more restrictive evaluative filter" will be at work in convergent production. (page 316).

13. J. P. Guilford in "Potential for Creativity," *Gifted Child Quarterly*, 6 (1962): 87, defines *divergent production* as "multiple responses, all of which are more or less appropriate, in response to a stimulus."

14. William Emory and Powell Niland, *Making Management Decisions* (Boston: Houghton Mifflin Company, 1968), p. 73.

15. Powell and Niland, *Making Management Decisions*, p. 74.

16. J. P. Guilford, *The Nature of Human Intelligence* (New York: McGraw-Hill Book Company, 1967), p. 138.

17. C. W. Taylor, "A Factorial Study of Fluency in Writing," *Psychometrika*, 12 (1947): 251.

18. Tuckman says: "The first stage of task-activity development is labeled as *orientation to the task*, in which group members attempt to identify the task in terms of its relevant parameters and the manner in which the group experience will be used to accomplish the task. . . . In orienting to the task, one is essentially defining it by discovering its 'ground rules.' "–"Developmental Sequence in Small Groups," p. 386.

19. R. F. Bales and F. L. Strodtbeck, "Phases in Group Problem-Solving," *Journal of Abnormal and Social Psychology*, 46 (1961): 485–495.

20. R. F. Bales, "The Equilibrium Problem in Small Groups," in T. Parsons, R. F. Bales, and E. A. Shils, *Working Papers in the Theory of Action* (Glencoe, Ill: The Free Press, 1953), pp. 111–161.

21. Gerald Nadler, *Work Design: A Systems Concept*, rev. ed. (Homewood, Ill.: Richard D. Irwin, Inc., 1970). Especially Chapters 18 and 19.

22. J. P. Guilford, *The Nature of Human Intelligence*, p. 326, declared: "It has also been reported that when a group is engaged in generation of ideas to solve a problem, it is sometimes the tyro or amateur who comes up with the key to the adopted solution. Experts in the field sometimes develop what has been called a 'disease' of hardening of the categories. Flexibility with respect to classifications is an important asset for the creative thinker."

23. Bruce Tuckman, "Developmental Sequence in Small Groups," p. 386.

24. Rodney W. Napier and Matti K. Gershenfeld, *Groups: Theory and Experience* (Boston: Houghton Mifflin Company, 1973), pp. 248–249.

25. Schroder and Harvey, "Conceptual Organization and Group Structure," p. 145.

26. Excerpted from Jack R. Gibb, "Defensive Communication," *The Journal of Communication*, 11 (Sept. 1961): 141–148.

27. Harvey and Schroder, "Cognitive Aspects of Self and Motivation," p. 114.

28. Tuckman, "Developmental Sequence in Small Groups," p. 394.

29. So also do Harvey and Schroder, "Cognitive Aspects of Self and Motivation," p. 136.

30. Napier and Gershenfeld, *Groups: Theory and Experience*, p. 205.

CHAPTER 8
THE DISCUSSION PROPER: CONVERGING PHASE

The movement of a group from the listing of ideas and marshaling of thoughts to the evaluation, paring down, and synthesis of ideas represents a qualitative change in the group process. A gathering of ideas is distinctly different from the shaping of ideas: the *diverging phase* differs from the *converging phase*. Group members must be aware of the different functions of each of these phases and assess what is required at any moment.

The DIVERGING phase is opening and expanding. Evaluation, for example, could be harmful if it is overused in that time. When the group is exploring a problem and the goal is to arrive at as many possible insights as time will permit, it would be better for the group to suspend evaluation. A tentative thought, when presented seriously by a group member, deserves to be developed and explored. Premature evaluation that points out some apparent weakness that could be remedied as the thought is developed by the group could squash the idea. Just as a baby robin requires some nurturance before facing the full environment, so an idea needs some time for development before the group makes the necessary vigorous appraisal. The diverging and converging processes differ in intent, procedure, and in the mental sets required (as was pointed out in Chapter 7) and should be kept separate, insofar as that is possible.

8.1   THE PHASE NATURE OF THE PROCESS

As the term DIVERGING PHASE can characterize the beginning portion of the discussion-as-a-whole as well as many subordinate parts within that whole, so the term CONVERGING PHASE can characterize the subsequent closure phase of both whole and parts. Thus, the phase of the discussion-as-a-whole may be viewed as:

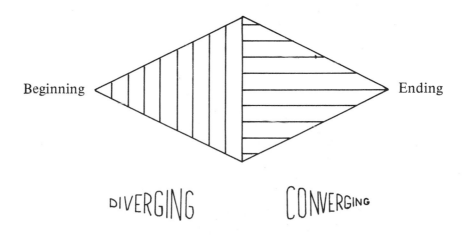

But within the discussion-as-a-whole there are smaller diverging-converging movements.

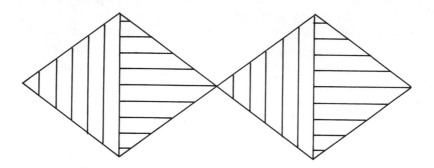

And still smaller movements.

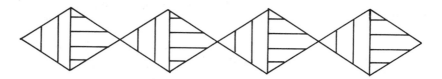

A full discussion-as-a-whole would see these smaller diverging-converging phases occurring within the larger movements. A series of group meetings devoted to discussions of juvenile crime might be encompassed by one large diverging-converging development that begins with the exploration of the problem and ends with a final group consensus on a specific course of action to be recommended. Within this series of meetings there could be smaller diverging-converging units as, for example, when the group discusses possible causes and settles on one direction of attack, or when the group lists many criteria and narrows and selects a few to be applied later in the meetings. There could even be smaller diverging-converging units when, for example, the group considers several possible definitions of "juvenile" and decides on one common definition. This last unit may require only a few minutes, whereas the discussion-as-a-whole may cover many hours over several meetings.

The examples thus far given have pertained to task matters. In our research with task groups[1] we have found this alternating "reach-test" development to be a common occurrence. The group "collects" data and then "selects" data. The group advances and then consolidates its position. We suggested the image of a *spiral*, since the group, as it goes from one level to another, is constantly moving forward.

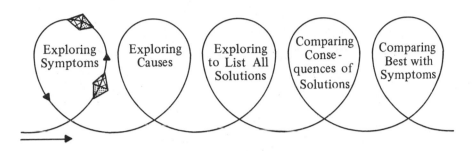

The group effort is not work-pause-work-pause. Diverging and converging represents different types of work, so the better description is as follows.

WORK WORK WORK WORK

These phases apply to the task work and relate to the following general problem management sequence:

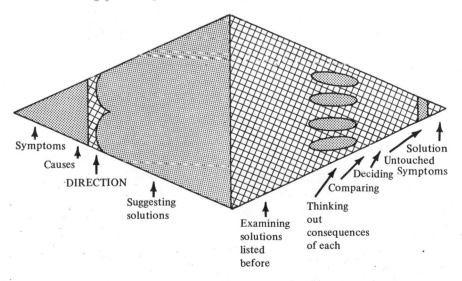

The diverging-converging sequence also applies to the team development in a group. This application might be viewed as follows:

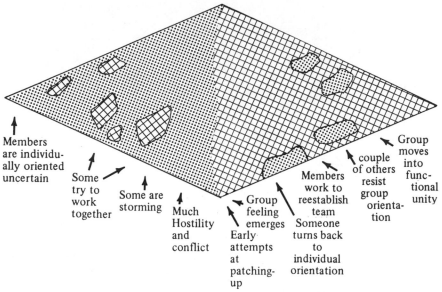

Members are individually oriented uncertain

Some try to work together

Some are storming

Much Hostility and conflict

Group feeling emerges

Early attempts at patching-up

Members work to reestablish team

Someone turns back to individual orientation

couple of others resist group orientation

Group moves into functional unity

The group effort begins with expanding uncertainty of who will do what and how the interaction will be patterned. Then norms begin to develop and patterns and interpersonal relations become clearer as the group coalesces to become a team. The movement over a discussion-as-a-whole may take the following form:

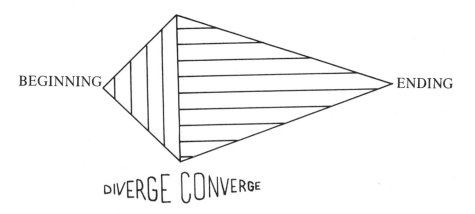

BEGINNING

ENDING

DIVERGE CONVERGE

As with task matters, smaller occurrences of diverging-converging may appear within the larger movement. Although the group follows the pattern illustrated over the full series of meetings, it may also follow the pattern in smaller time periods. Each separate meeting may see the consolidating of the team. Such developments in the growth of the team will sometimes occur as a group moves from topic to topic within a meeting.

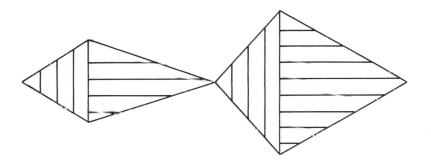

Tuckman's description, as explained in the preceding chapter, seems to fit this analysis for team development. It seems appropriate to refer to Tuckman's first category of *forming* as composing the DIVERGING phase in group structure, and the *norming* and *performing* stages as descriptive of the CONVERGING phase. We see this second category, *storming*, as transitional between the DIVERGING and CONVERGING phases.

When the group begins to find its characteristic way of doing things so that mutual expectations are established and a team-like relationship exists, it is clearly in the team CONVERGING phase. This is not to say that no variations from the expected will occur, but rather that these variations will occur less often and will be authored by fewer of the members. In the CONVERGING phase any such deviations will be more quickly discerned and appropriately handled. (These deviations are, in a sense, returns to the DIVERGING phase so that a return to the CONVERGING phase must then be accomplished.)

In the CONVERGING phase the main tendency is a settling into a pattern of relationships, into characteristic ways of interacting with other members and the leader. The group participants have established a pattern of norms; they talk a common language.

We cannot assume, of course, that these norms are the ones best adapted to handling the group's purpose. Tuckman has postulated the closure upon "flexible, functional roles," but we hold that closure could have occurred otherwise: the group could have converged into a relationship where:

> Only a few take major responsibilities and the others do not participate or merely acquiesce;
> Communication seems expected of only a few;
> Contributions of some are routinely given more attention and weight than those of others;
> The leader is held responsible for all specific preparations and decisions;
> Changes of procedure or relationships are not welcomed;
> The members exhibit a slightly wary, uneasy attitude with little team feeling.

When relationships such as these characterize the CONVERGING phase, the "group structure" will offer less than a first-rate instrument for conducting the task work of the group. All of these relationships would suggest the need for preventive action by the members and leader while still in the DIVERGING phase, before norms are clearly established, as well as alert, remedial action by members and leader during the CONVERGING phase.

The illustrations given suggest that the CONVERGING phase is relatively larger than the DIVERGING phase in team development. We believe that this is generally the case. For most groups the diverging aspects relevant to team work occur quickly, and most of the group time is spent converging to a true team. It is different with the task aspects, where the topic and situation will largely determine the relative lengths of the DIVERGING and CONVERGING phases. Sometimes one will be larger; sometimes the other. There is *no strict parallelism of task work and team work as they develop in diverging-converging phases*. They each follow the pattern of alternating phases but do so independently and at differing paces.

8.2   **THE CONVERGING PHASE AS THEATER FOR CONFLICT MANAGEMENT**

As the DIVERGING phase is characterized by *creativity*,

the CONVERGING phase is characterized by acts of judgment and the *management of conflicts*. In the CONVERGING phase the thought-line involves the relating of terms and concepts, the sifting of ideas by comparison and evaluation, and employs the full powers of discernment. A narrowing selection and consolidation and shaping of ideas is the essence of the converging movement. In this phase the mass of data gathered must be funneled to a meaningful resolution, and some friction inevitably results when all these ideas are brought together for the group's task work. Converging action also occurs for the individuals in the group as they are called upon increasingly to think *together* as a team. People as well as ideas are rubbed together in this narrowing converging process and the resultant pressures often lead to conflicts both on task and team matters. Productive group effort requires the effective management of these conflicts.

Professor Morton Deutsch has suggested that conflict exists whenever incompatible actions occur and that an "action that is incompatible with another action prevents, obstructs, interferes, injures, or in some way makes the latter less likely or less effective."[2] We would suggest that the essential steps of comparison and judgment make some degree of conflict *inevitable* in this phase of the discussion process. But it must also be apparent that conflict in group interaction has many constructive aspects: it keeps group members alert, it is motivating, and it requires judicious thinking. It is difficult to imagine a group resolving any significant question without experiencing conflicting views. The important point is that conflict should be managed so that its positive values can be tapped without encouraging too many negative elements. Group members will want to know something about conflict and be aware of some practical means of channeling its potential.

8.21   The Nature of Conflict

Deutsch[3] suggests that conflicts are usually about one or another of several types of issues:

1. Control over resources (space, money, property, power).
2. Preferences and nuisances.
3. Values (what "should be").
4. Beliefs (what "is").
5. Nature of relationship between parties.

Each of these issues could lead to conflict over task work or team work.

Deutsch provides further aid to the group participant by indicating the various *types* of conflicts that may occur. He lists six different types and emphasizes that they should not be considered to be mutually exclusive; any moment of conflict could involve one or more of these types simultaneously.[4]

TYPES OF CONFLICT

1. Veridical   —This type of conflict "exists objectively and is perceived accurately." This is open and clear conflict. One wants prisons to punish whereas another wants them to rehabilitate. Each understands the position of the other and they disagree.

2. Contingent   —In this case the "existence of the conflict is dependent upon readily rearranged circumstances." The parties perceive themselves to be in conflict, but it is not necessary for circumstances could be easily changed to eliminate the "need" for the conflict. The conflict is apparent but not veridical.

3. Displaced   —The parties in conflict in this instance argue about the wrong thing, displacing the real issue. Two members may argue over an issue relevant to the task, whereas the "true" conflict concerns which one of them will lead the team.

4. Misattributed   —This is a conflict between the wrong parties and usually over the wrong issues. A shortage of jobs may cause white and black workers to feel antagonism between themselves rather than against factors that have led to the shortage of jobs. It is an interesting fact of psychology that we usually take personal credit for our successes but blame others for our failures.

5. Latent   —This is conflict "that should be occurring but is not." A group can be made up of members who do not want to rock the boat. So they fail to recognize genuine differences and issues. As a group they can hardly be productive for they have failed to understand the positive need for and values of "managed conflict" in group work. This often can reveal a group experiencing *groupthink*.

6. False   —This is the "occurrence of conflict when there is no objective basis for it." Deutsch says that such conflict always indicates misperception or misunderstanding.

This system for the analysis of conflict can be helpful for group leaders and members. It provides some verbal handles for identifying and describing the various components of an instance of group conflict.

Another useful analytical tool is provided by Louis R. Pondy[5] who describes conflict as a dynamic process with a sequence of five steps which may be phrased thus:

1. Antecedent conditions	—There must be some underlying causes if conflict occurs. Different group members may have differing views about appropriate group goals, procedures, norms, or needed roles. There may be sets of incompatible values. So long as these underlying causes exist the potential for conflict will remain and it may break out at any moment
2. Perception of conflict conditions	—In this step the parties become aware of the difficulty. The underlying causes have finally resulted in open conflict.
3. Affective impact of conflict	—The parties involved now "feel" or experience the emotional symptoms of conflict. There are feelings of tension, stress, anxiety, and hostility.
4 Manifest conflict behavior	—At this point the feelings lead to action. The conflict becomes open, observable, and obvious to all.
5. Conflict aftermath	—At this stage the fruits of the conflict are seen. If the issues have been well managed and resolved, cooperative group action may occur. If the parties have withdrawn and have suppressed the conflict, but without resolving it, the group returns to step 1 and the causes may mean a recurrence of the conflict at any moment. In this case there is always the danger that the conflict will grow and become increasingly more disruptive. It is possible then that the group will be disbanded.

With this scheme a member or leader can assess the point in the ongoing process of conflict at which the group finds itself. This can be helpful in suggesting where the conflict may go in the near future and indicate steps for management that are specifically appropriate at this time.

8.22 Conflict in Group Decision Making

A review of a classic study of conflict in decision-making groups will be useful in adding meaning to the analytical systems just described. Several years ago, Harold Guetzkow and John Gyr[6] conducted a significant piece of research on the occurrence and the management of conflict. They had three trained observers study the face-to-face operation of over one hundred business and governmental groups (a total of about seven hundred persons were observed). Their aim was to study the types of conflicts that arise in groups and the ways in which conflict was successfully managed so that the groups could better reach positions of consensus (defined as the degree to which the final opinions of the group members as individuals were in agreement with the final position taken by the group). Their findings are instructive to any person concerned with the conflicts occurring in the CONVERGING phases of group work and these are now considered here in some detail. More specific suggestions about managing these conflicts are made in the sections that follow.

In the first place, Guetzkow and Gyr distinguished two primary dimensions of group conflict—*substantive conflict*, which is rooted in matters of task, and *affective conflict*, which is based in emotional and interpersonal relationships. These dimensions are clearly the *task* and *team* elements that are discussed throughout this book. These two aspects of conflict are different from one another but are not mutually exclusive. In some groups both aspects may occur; in others neither aspect will be present. But in most groups there will be some degree of both.

How do groups in which one of these dimensions is dominant best achieve consensus? These researchers found that for the business and governmental groups they studied:

> A group in substantive conflict tends to achieve consensus by emphasizing those factors that positively promote consensus. A group in affective conflict tends to achieve consensus by

reducing those forces that hinder the achievement of consensus. This reduction is largely achieved by withdrawing from a situation in which these forces are present.[7]

Different actions worked best for the two types of conflict. For substantive conflict, positive straightforward action on the task was needed, whereas affective conflict was best handled by avoidance procedures. It appeared better to avoid negative socio-emotional situations, or to withdraw from them when they occur, if possible, rather than to try to meet them head-on with specific positive action.

The following are some specific findings from this research: *Factors related to successful task work* (consensus from substantive conflict)

1. A degree of conflict is necessary and helpful when related to the task.

> In a productive discussion there must be issues and differences to be resolved. There must be a willingness to "give and take." And the "give and take" that occurs must be thorough and efficient.

2. Facts and expert judgments help resolve substantive conflict.

> The facts must be examined carefully and evaluated. The expert's credibility must also be assessed by the group members.

3. An orderly treatment of topics is helpful.

> This supports our heavy emphasis on planning agenda items carefully. But it was also found that "formal" procedures such as formal votes and the use of motions as in formal parliamentary procedures were not of special help. A flexible, planned structure is essential. An inflexible, authoritarian or rigid procedure should be avoided in most cases.

4. Members should discuss one issue at a time rather than discuss several simultaneously with frequent references to previously discussed issues.

> This is much like the matter of the collective monologue discussed earlier. Group members, especially in the CONVERGING phase, should take up an issue and stick with it until they have reached a closure on it before moving to another point. This is not always or totally possible but it should always be the goal.

5. Members must understand what is being said.

Clear, concise statements are needed, and do not occur often' enough in group meetings. Leaders and members should do all possible to be clear throughout. All participants need to work on their listening skills. Feedback should be used to check understanding.

6. Chairmen of groups with substantive conflict should do much more direct seeking for information of an objective, factual nature, largely by questioning, and should offer more solutions than usual and do so tentatively.

In short, it was found that in groups with substantive conflict, more effective group work will result when the leader plays a more central, stronger leadership role. Clearly the leader needs to possess control in such a situation and to use it firmly when it is needed in the situation.

7. When group members seem to like each other personally, substantive conflict is more easily resolved.

This makes clear the interdependency of task and team work. Good productive task work can be better with good team work. And good team work cannot be an end in itself when the group's major interest is in handling an external task.

Guetzkow and Gyr summarize:

The special conditions which served to terminate substantive conflict in consensus were largely intellectual in nature: availability and utilization of facts and efficient problem-solving procedures. These intellectual techniques were given full opportunity to operate when the personal interrelationships existing among the participants were warm, friendly, and nonrestrictive.[8]

Factors related to successful team work (consensus from affective conflict)

1. The expression of many self-oriented or personal needs is detrimental to achieving group consensus.

Some persons need to argue or to dominate (to play center stage); others need to have a group go their way; others use groups as audiences for special pleadings on topics other than that for which this group meets. All these self-oriented behaviors can slow or derail a moving group.

2. It was found that groups experiencing affective conflict that finally did reach consensus often had some members withdraw from the problem situation (engage in side conversations, become inattentive) or decided as a group to postpone certain agenda items.

It can easily be observed that neither of these practices, even if useful in ending affective conflict, contributes to an efficient and productive work group.

Guetzkow and Gyr summarize:

In groups in high affective conflict, there were no *unique* conditions reinforcing the tendencies within the group toward reaching consensus. Instead, the analysis disclosed only factors that could be interpreted as reducing the force of the tendencies hindering the achievement of consensus.[9]

The findings of Guetzkow and Gyr show that these natural groups in business and government were able to handle task difficulty better than team difficulty. Whereas they found more or less regular ways of handling substantive conflict, they found no *unique* ways of successfully handling affective conflict. We believe, however, that members can use certain plans and practices to help prevent both affective and substantive conflict and to handle these conflicts with some effectiveness when they occur.

8.3   THE CONVERGING PHASE IN TASK WORK

After the broad and systematic examination of ideas performed in the DIVERGING phase is completed, the members turn to the sorting out process that enables them to move to the completion of their task. Consideration must be given here to two factors: the *use of patterns of thinking* and the *handling of conflict*.

8.31   Use of Patterns of Thinking

In the CONVERGING phase, the group builds its task thought-line with characteristic thought patterns such as: *classification, evaluation, comparison*, and *synthesis*. By these movements alone or in combination (and not necessarily in this order), the group achieves the selective, synthesizing, and narrowing function of convergence. These patterns of thought may be illustrated by phrasing questions that might occur within a group meeting (or be the total purpose of a session), which would entail their use:

Classification: Is *In Cold Blood* a novel?

Evaluation: How effective is the *New York Review of Books* as a literary journal?

Comparison: Which is preferable: a conscripted or a voluntary army?

Synthesis: How can we summarize these obstacles to the implementation of the plan?

Classification. A group faces the task of deciding whether a particular item belongs to a certain class, that is, whether it can be accurately characterized by a certain descriptive or evaluative label. The mere *possession* of particular traits or elements will meet some standards; on others a particular *degree* of excellence or appropriateness must be reached to meet the requirements inherent in the question.

The crime of burglary, for example, is widely defined in law as (1) the forcible entry of (2) a dwelling in (3) the nighttime with (4) an intent to commit a felony therein. A jury might be asked to decide whether the actions of a particular person could be classified as burglary. The jury would have to be satisfied that the actions taken met all four of the criteria for that specific crime. If not, the actions might fit the definition of some other crime, but could not be classified as an instance of burglary.

In the typical group decision-making or policy-determining meeting, the "appropriate criteria" for classification are not so ready for use by the group as a legal definition, such as the one given. When such identifying marks and accepted standards are not at hand for the task, the group will have to engage in a list-making thought movement (a small *diverging* movement) to prepare an acceptable set of criteria on which to test the item being considered. Truman Capote said, for example, that his *In Cold Blood* was not a novel. If a group were to discuss the topic mentioned, the members would have to begin by drawing up a definition of a "novel." The standards would have to be listed and the book would then have to be analyzed to see how well it met these standards and, therefore, whether it fit within the classification of "novel."

A group discussing an experience with fluoridation may deem it acceptable to give a qualified answer (for example, "Yes, fluoridation was a success, given the dental practices of that day," or "No, fluoridation was not a success, but we view it as having been a worthy expedient."), thus providing enough of a resolution that the group can move the thought-line forward.

An example of this thought movement would be as follows:

A group of citizens interested in the livability of their city decided to use the standards employed by Ronald Gelatt and others[10] to make an assessment on the question: Is Seattle a livable city? The leader listed the Gelatt criteria in brief topical form on the chalkboard before the group:

overall cost of living

climate

population mix

effectiveness of local government

education

transportation

general environment

safety on streets

cultural life

recreational opportunities

economic prospects for future

After spending a few minutes on each criterion to clarify its scope and meaning, the group agreed as to which of the criteria are most important and had the leader put a star next to the especially important ones on the chalkboard list. So the members are ready to begin their consideration:

Leader: Let's see. We've agreed that the overall cost of living is especially important, that education is of the highest importance, and that cultural life and recreational opportunities are very important. Since we're asking ourselves how Seattle stacks up on these criteria in order to decide for ourselves whether we want to classify Seattle as *a livable city*, let's begin with one criterion at a time; how about beginning with "cost of living?"

James: Good idea! Actually, that IS the place to begin, isn't it?

Charles: Where else?

Ron: We said we meant housing, utilities, food costs, clothing—

Standard reviewed

Paul: And taxes!

Facts first

> Mary: Transportation—
>
> Leader: Yes. Now what about these costs in Seattle? Anyone have some facts here?
>
> Janice: We all know costs are going up for sure, but it's still pretty reasonable. Federal statistics show Seattle as ranking sixteenth in cost of living—that is, for a middle-class family—
>
> James: Property costs, for one thing, are shooting up. If you want to buy a house now, you have to put out at least a third more—

· ·

Summary of
substance

Judgment

> Leader: So we've found that each of the major living costs is high—some more so than others—but that as an overall estimate, we're not too badly off—
>
> Ron: And remember that federal comparison—sixteenth in the country—
>
> Leader: Do we give Seattle the nod then on this standard, *cost of living*?
>
> Paul: Despite the flatness of my bank account, yes!
>
> Others: Yes. Yes.

Evaluation. In the evaluation movement, as in the classification movement, the group must have a set of standards or criteria that represent the expectations held for all individual items in that class of items. These expectation standards are not simply matters of the presence or absence of features or traits (as is true of the most common forms of the classification movement), but each evaluation standard is a *range* or a *continuum*, the question thus being at what point the item stands within that range and along that continuum.

Before attempting the evaluation, it is essential that the investigators understand clearly the scope and intent of each criterion and whether any one of the criteria is more important than the others for providing a fair assessment of the item. Then, with their framework for evaluation ready and commonly understood by all, the members look critically at the item *on each criterion* in turn.

For example, in bringing information about the *New York Review* on a particular criterion they would have to bring data from many issues of the magazine so that what is *typical* becomes clear to the group. Once they have found what is typical, the group gives attention to *atypical* pieces of information, asking themselves how frequently such atypical instances occur and how different those atypical ones are from what the group has agreed upon as being typical.[11]

Their judgment of the item on this criterion must reflect their decision on what is typical, appropriately modified by due consideration of these variations from the typical. They move from this substantive judgment into a characterization of the item as good, excellent, poor, and so on. Then, if a scale is being used, the group agrees upon a number on the scale that indicates this characterization. From substantive judgment—to evaluation in words—to numerical rating: these are workable steps in synthesizing the group's evaluation of the item.

The group must use a scale with an appropriate number of intervals. Often a scale of 1–7 or 1–9 will allow all the gradations a group will need and can use, as well as provide a midpoint number (4,5). When an overall picture is desired—instead of just concluding with a profile of evaluations—account must be taken of any variations in importance of the different criteria.

After a judgment has been made on each individual criterion, the members of the group will need to pull the separate assessments together into a composite judgment that takes into account any differences in the importance of the various criteria. It may be useful for the members, after they have gone through this converging thought-movement, to say not only that the *New York Review* does "very well" but that its particular strengths or weaknesses "lie along these certain lines,—and—." The value of such a concluding comment would depend, of course, upon the larger framework of thought of which this *evaluation* is a part; at times the additional information would be more helpful than just the degree of approbation or derogation they have assigned to the item.

One of the undesired tendencies here is for the group to *pair off extremes*, that is, when one *plus* extreme is suggested, a *negative* extreme is immediately mentioned to offset, as it were, the effect of the plus extreme on the group's assessment. This tendency has two harmful effects. First, it tends, by putting extremes against one another, to make the group thought become disputative and persuasive rather than investigatory and inquiring. Second, it seems to be averaging the extremes (one plus against one minus) and thus can obscure the effect of the extremes. There is a real difference, for example, between two items when one has four positive, eight moderate, and four negative aspects, and when the other has sixteen moderate aspects. If averaged, the two items may be judged alike. But the difference in their full profiles must be considered. It may be helpful to consider all the plus extremes first, then turn to all the minus extremes (or vice versa) to keep the profiles clear and to keep the movement an inquiry rather than allow it to become a debate.

An example of this thought movement would be as follows:

Members of a study group interested in effective government decided to discuss the career of Thomas Jefferson; they decided to narrow their question and make it an evaluative one: How good a president was Jefferson? They elected to use the five criteria that Henry Steele Commager,[12] who has written some forty books on American history, says that Americans tend to look for in their presidents. Out of Commager's remarks they have drawn these five standards: (1) strength, (2) vision, (3) integrity, (4) intelligence, (5) fortitude. They decided to use a 1 to 7 scale with 7 being the highest. After these preliminary agreements they take up Jefferson's attitudes and actions under each criterion, in turn, moving from information to reasoning about the information, from that reasoning to judgment, and then to a number rating. As to the first criterion, *strength*, they decided that, despite Jefferson's failure to work actively to push his programs through Congress, his building of a party that was strong enough to paralyze the Federalists and his fighting of a naval war against the Barbary pirates entitled him to a claim of great strength; the group rated Jefferson "6" in *strength*.

	Leader:	Let's move on, then, to the second criterion, *vision*. Weren't we thinking of things like farsightedness, the long view, seeing the good of the country in the future—when we listed the criterion *vision*?
Standard reviewed	*Mel*:	Yes, a sort of correct sense of the future, borne out by history, I guess.
Facts first	*Alice*:	Of course, we all think right away of the Louisiana Purchase. Jefferson realized—even before he knew how big a piece of territory we were actually going to get—how important it was; he wrote to James Monroe, who was our envoy in Paris: "The future destinies of our country hang on the event of this negotiation."
	Paul:	The man *loved land*. Remember how happy he always was at Monticello? He was always experi-

menting with what he could grow! After he came back from his five years of representing us in France, every year for twenty-three years he received a box of seeds from a friend he'd made there, a superintendent of some public gardens.

Dorcas: And the size of that purchase! Our negotiators were extremely lucky—they came off with over 500,000,000 acres (counting land and water), an area five times as large as France itself! And this was some of the richest farmland in the world!

Gary: And for about four cents an acre! What an achievement!

Mel: And then Jefferson got to do what he had wanted to do for twenty years—send an expeditionary force across the continent to the Pacific! We've all studied about the Lewis and Clark Expedition, but I didn't know until just the other day that Captain Meriwether Lewis had been private secretary to Jefferson for two years before that.

Gary: Jefferson was thinking of expansion, with land for everyone. What a dream of the future.

. . . .

Summary of
substance

Leader: Now, to sum up a bit. We've said that Jefferson really understood what westward expansion could mean to the country; that he had a deep faith in the honesty and common sense of the people, as the basis for governing themselves; that education for the people would wipe out ignorance—

Howard: Opportunity—self-government—education. He really was holding out a future for America, wasn't he?

Alice: He saw it, and he helped to shape it in a very significant way.

Evaluation
in words

Leader: Are we saying, then, that he had a very good sense of the future? That his vision for the country was really excellent?

Several: Yes. There's no doubt about it. Excellent, for sure.

Rating in
numbers

Leader: Let's see. On our scale of 1 to 7, where would excellent be, 6 or 7 probably?

Many: 7. 6? Probably 7. Let's say 7.

Comparison. Comparing two alternatives is a thought movement used by a group at many points in its deliberations. In all except the most obvious or unimportant issues it is prudent to avoid merely posing the claims of one alternative against another in a random fashion as the means of making the choice. Such a procedure is likely to be both incomplete and faulty—incomplete because less immediately visible issues may not be considered at all, faulty because those issues that are considered usually have exaggerated coloration given them out of the intense feelings of their proponents or attackers.

In *comparison* (as in *evaluation*), appropriate criteria are needed with added weight given for the considerations of special importance. Taking each criterion in turn, the group needs to proceed through a sequence of steps: bringing relevant, sufficient, and dependable information on each alternative; reasoning from these data to decide which alternative is superior to the other on that criterion and to decide also how great the degree of superiority is.

When the superiority (and the degree of superiority) has been decided on each criterion separately, the group can gather up the pattern for each of the alternatives and can then decide, taking into account the varying importance of the criteria, which combination of ratings is to be preferred. For example, suppose Item A had a significant superiority on an extremely important criterion as compared to Item B, and two relatively small superiorities on criteria of lesser importance. These two patterns of superiorities would have to be weighed against each other by the group.

sss

Sss

ITEM A   ITEM B

Which would be chosen? Probably Item A.

One of the frequent weaknesses in *comparison* is that of letting the alternative that is superior to the other on the first criterion gain an advantage, a presumption of the likelihood of further superiority. The group should rather start afresh with each new criterion in turn, the winner of the preceding analysis getting no advantage in the next juxtaposition. All group participants must guard against this natural tendency.

A related error that is likely to creep in is bringing in the item's excellence on one criterion to bolster its case on a different criterion where it seems to be losing out to the other alternative. For example, if *conscription* had been judged as highly superior to *volunteering* on the criterion of "affording national security," that same information must not be inserted into the discussion as evidence on another standard such as "reflecting popular opinions." Each decision must be made on the merits of the two alternatives on the single standard under consideration at that moment. When *all* the judgments of superiority have been made, it is time to discover how the alternatives compare in full, taking all the criteria into account. The comparisons might look as follows:

Table 8-1.

RATINGS ON THREE CRITERIA			
	ITEM A	ITEM B	ITEM C
On Most Important Criterion	s	S	s
On Next Most Important Criterion	S	s	s
On Least Important Criterion	S	s	S

Each item has a large, medium, and small superiority on the three criteria, but, on balance, Item B would probably be chosen.

An example of this thought movement would be as follows:

A committee has been formed to decide upon its college department's handling of the problem of the use of sexist language in professional publications. The five members have studied the problem as it would most likely apply in their situation and have decided to recommend a set of guidelines for departmental adoption. They have agreed upon four criteria upon which to base their choice among alternative sets of guidelines.

1. accurate representation of meaning.
2. easy application.
3. wide coverage of situations.
4. grammatical integrity.

Having completed their work on the use of the word *man* to indicate either a man or a woman, they have now turned their attention to the use of masculine pronouns. Their research has turned up four alternative approaches and they are about to make comparisons.

Leader: How about comparing the first two on our list: the

National Council of Teachers of English plan and the Symbol Modification plan?

Rodney: Could we hear each of them again—just the gist of each, I mean?

Leader: Yes, let's do that. the NCTE plan has five points: [pointing to chart before them] (1) recasting into plural: (2) rewording to eliminate gender problems; (3) replacing with *one, you,* or (sparingly) *she or he*; (4) alternating male and female examples; (5) substituting plural pronouns after *everybody, everyone, anybody, anyone.* Do we have these in mind, or shall we give ourselves some examples?

Information reviewed

. . . .

Leader: Now, let's get the Symbol Modification plan before us. Let's put up our chart. This is quite a different approach. Shall we run through it? [points and reads]

$$Se\ -\textit{He or She}\qquad\qquad \text{ɟe}\ -\textit{he or she}$$

$$\text{H}'\ {-\textit{His or Her (Hers)}\atop \textit{Him or Her}}\qquad \text{h}'\ {-\textit{his or her (hers)}\atop \textit{him or her}}$$

Joe: We just come upon these modified symbols in our reading and pick up the appropriate one of the possible meanings, is that it?

Leader: Here's a sentence [writes on board: The driver put on h' brakes.] —how would that read?

Several: The driver put on *his or her* brakes. Not bad: Let's try another.

Leader: How about this? [writes: When the nurse came, he opened the window.]

All: When the nurse came, *he or she* opened the window.

Madge: In this plan, we don't change sentences or words; we leave it to the reader to do the interpretation, don't we?

Bert: I think I'd like that. It's simple and you can do it right on your typewriter!

Leader: That's true! Probably we'd better take one criterion at a time and look at both plans on it—so we can see which is superior on each criterion separately. Our first one is *accurate representation of meaning.* Well, let's see how the NCTE plan—we listed it first, should we just take it first?—fits here.

Discussion focused

Bert: *Recasting into the plural*—let's see: "Hand each student his paper. Hand the students their papers." In general that's the same, but I feel a little difference; a little loss of individual action, I wonder?

Chris: Yes, I visualize the separateness of the action more in the "hand each student his paper" but I'm not sure that matters—

Joe: I hear that little loss of specificity, and I'm not sure I like it.

Discussion focused

Leader: Does this slight loss of specificity reduce the accuracy? I guess that's the question we have to ask.

Madge: If we judge accuracy at the point of the receiver, I suppose we'd have to admit that the statement is accurate in a casual sense—the students did get their papers—but as a representation of the action of giving the papers to them, it falls a little short?

Several: Yes. That's it.

[The group goes on similarly through the other aspects of the NCTE plan]

Leader: Now we're ready to look at the Symbol Modification plan, aren't we? This plan changes the symbol that our eye picks up [pointing to the chart]; what does that change of symbols do to accuracy of meaning?

Discussion focused

Rodney: As I get it, the reader says "he or she" as he—or she!—sees the first symbol: *He or She* will be home soon. I don't think it will take us long to learn the symbols. I guess I'm saying that because I don't want anything to stand between us and the meaning. I suppose the worrisome part would be our thinking of the alternatives—he or she, him or her, etc.—all the time. Might that reduce the accuracy of our reception of the meaning?

Chris: It would—at least for a while—take part of our attention and to that extent, I suppose, it would reduce the fullest perception of the meaning of the sentence somewhat—

Madge: I suppose we have to wonder whether it brings in an intrusive element—the sex of the student wasn't important in getting the paper back. But if we are now alerted to "sexist" language, we know that saying "Hand each student his paper" brings in—unnecessarily—the student's sex. So what this Symbol Modification plan does is admit the intrusion but avoid the slur that comes with the omission of the other sex—

Bert: That's a comparison between the Symbol Modification plan and our present usage, isn't it? But it tends to clarify the Symbol Modification plan, I think. So *would* the SM plan reduce accuracy by just bringing our attention to this matter—even though it would do so in a nonsexist way?

Joe: Maybe it would just make us work a little harder but not really disturb the meaning?

Chris: Yes, that's probably the case—

Others: Yes. Probably so.

Leader: Well then, let's compare the NCTE and the SM! We found that the *recasting to plural—rewording to eliminate gender—replacing with indefinite pronouns* of the NCTE plan does reduce the accuracy—the sharp image—of the sentence a little. We found that the SM plan diverts our attention a little but probably doesn't touch the meaning.

Discussion focused

Summary

Bert: It is interesting to notice that the NCTE plan actually allows us to say he or she once in a while!

Superiority

Chris: Yes. Actually, isn't the SM plan superior here?

Several: Yes.

Degree of superiority

Leader: A little or a lot?

Several: A little. Probably not a lot.

Summary

Leader: So we'd say the SM plan has a small superiority here.

Synthesis. In the characteristic lines of thought described thus far, the group is working on particular ideas and concepts, taking these items *as structured* and cooperating to make their decisions. They ask and work together to answer: Is X a ——?, or How successful was X?, or Is X preferable to Y, or Z?

Another line of thought that occurs frequently in the CONVERGING phase is *synthesis*, that is, the restructuring that results in a different idea or plan from those previously considered. Rather than starting with ⟨A⟩ , B , and C as possible alternatives, and choosing, perhaps, B , the group may, by *synthesizing*, end instead with B/A .

Such an action would be the result of combining, blending,

and substituting ideas from the alternatives (plus further changes suggested by these modifications) into a better product than any one of the alternatives *taken singly* would have been. Synthesis, then, may be the major thought movement by which a problem-management group moves through the CONVERGING phase to a decision as to its recommendation or action. But the process of synthesizing takes place on a much smaller scale throughout the group's cooperative building of ideas; from the suggestions made and developed the members adjust, modify, and create their group thought-line.[13]

Synthesis is a narrowing down of the field of possibilities to one choice, but *not* a narrowing down that has been restricted to the alternatives as offered; the final choice may contain elements taken from, or suggested by, alternatives that were *not chosen*. The goal is to obtain the optimum product, and this purpose is sometimes best served by refusing to think of ideas as watertight packages. If the plan, as thus modified, begins to look "like a camel" (as jokers are fond of saying about a horse produced by a committee), it is pleasant to remember that camels can handle routes that horses dare not venture upon.

Synthesizing differs from mere summarizing, which is a concise listing or restating of the major ideas that the group has built cooperatively. A summary is useful at many points within a discussion and can be done by any member or by the leader for the benefit of the entire group. Synthesizing is a modifying of the ideas that have preceded it—omitting some, stressing others, assembling them differently, piecing some together—thus producing something that was not present before. A synthesis may take place within an individual member's contribution or through the interacting work of several members at many points within either the DIVERGING or CONVERGING phases; that is, it is a suitable thought movement wherever the "best" of the possibilities seems to be some combination rather than an outright selection.

The participant who "summarizes what we have said so far" and gets it wrong is all too frequently found in discussion groups. Too often this member summarizes what he or she wishes had been said or includes only those parts of what has been contributed that he or she especially agrees with. A biased *synthesis* is probably even more harmful than a biased *summary*. A summary is essentially a repeating and can be fairly well checked by the other group members (although not always easily). A synthesis, on the other hand, is produced by changes and additions, and is thus much more difficult to check. Members and leader will want to work together toward "appropriate syntheses" in the CONVERGING phase: "syntheses" in that the synthesizing statements converge and recast ideas of the group, and "appropriate" in that they truly represent the recasting done by the *group*. Few things can be worse than to lose or mutilate a part of the product of the group effort by making a faulty final statement of that product.

A significant use of *synthesis* is shown in the work of the committee comparing the NCTE plan and the Modified Symbols plan for nonsexist use of language in their professional publications:

> *Leader*: Now we're ready to compare these plans on the fourth criterion; let's see—how did we say it?— *grammatical integrity*—
>
> *Joe*: So we're asking ourselves how the plans square with the principles of correct usage, aren't we—
>
> *Rodney*: OK to start again with the NCTE plan? Well, here goes, then. Isn't the fifth item of the NCTE plan the one that's really relevant here—substituting plural pronouns after *everybody*, *everyone*, *anybody*, *anyone*?
>
> *Chris*: Yes, the fifth; the other changes don't affect the grammar.
>
> *Bert*: Let's see, I've got the place here; I'll read it: "Using the masculine pronouns to refer to an indefinite pronoun (*everybody*, *everyone*, *anybody*, *anyone*) also has the effect of excluding women. In all but strictly formal usage, plural pronouns have become acceptable substitutes for the masculine singular."—Here's their example of so-called sexist usage: "Anyone who wants to go to the game should bring his money tomorrow."—And here's the alternative they suggest: "Anyone who wants to go to the game should bring their money tomorrow."
>
> *Rodney*: "Acceptable substitute" except in "formal" writing! NOT TO ME! "Anyone—bring *their* money!" It hurts my ears!
>
> *Madge*: Mine too, actually. I wonder how they can say it's accepted—it isn't in Follett's *Modern American Usage*; of course, that was published too long ago, 1960—

Facts given

Chris: Yes, this concern about eliminating sexist language has come up since then—

Joe: The NCTE leaflet says that the directors contacted members of the Committee on the Role and Image of Women in the Council and the Profession, editors of journals published by the Council, and from professional staff members at NCTE.

Rodney: If I remember correctly, Thomas Middleton, who writes that "Light Refractions" page in the *Saturday Review*, suggested this same use of the word *their*, and got hit with a barrage of mail. And then he admitted that *he* wasn't going to use it!

Madge: Maybe that's the point! What kind of writing are we talking about? The NCTE guidelines don't say they consider *their* acceptable in *formal usage*; what about the professional papers we publish— which is what we're really meeting about, of course—would *they* require "strictly formal usage?" If so, this suggestion wouldn't apply to us; we'd still write, "He does *his* part"—

Discussion focused

Leader: Yes, let's think about that. The letters we write to colleagues probably *wouldn't* demand "strictly formal usage" and the bylaws we write for our department probably *would*; but what about the professional papers we write?

Chris: Since what we write- if we're lucky enough to get it published!—will be on permanent display in our journals, I tend to think we ought to use the more careful rather than the less careful form—

Several: Yes. That's right.

Joe: That would mean, then, that we'd write, as we've written in the past: "Every person should know his own strengths."

Leader: Yes. Our classifying our papers as needing "strictly formal usage" means that the NCTE guidelines won't help us out on pronouns in this *each* or *any* usage—

Modification

Rodney: Could I make a suggestion? I'm thinking of that earlier NCTE suggestion—that we alternate male and female examples and expressions—how does their alternative example go—[reads] "Let each student participate. Has she had a chance to talk? Could he feel left out?" Could we extend that principle of alternation to the each/any problem?

Bert: How would that be, Rodney?

Rodney: We would write in our articles: "Every person should know her own strengths" and then follow it with "Each person should examine his own life to see where his strengths lie."—And, of course, the *her* part wouldn't always have to come first.

Madge: That would save the grammar *and* avoid the sexist language! But—one thing—it makes us double everything; would that be bad?

Joe: Oh, the situation really wouldn't come up often enough to be too troublesome, would it? And, anyway, I find myself liking the rhythm of the double form; it's like the pulsation you hear in Hebrew poetry, in the Psalms, for instance: "Lord, who shall abide in thy tabernacle? who shall dwell in thy holy hill?" That gains—instead of loses—by being double!

Chris: Joe, you convinced me!

Leader: Are we saying, then, that the NCTE suggestion on plural pronouns after *each/any* constructions doesn't apply to us? And that we ourselves suggest adding the principle of *alteration* in the pronouns that follow the *each/any* words?

Restatement of Synthesis

Bert: Yes, let's modify the NCTE guidelines to this extent—of course, we haven't chosen them yet as our plan, but I mean in our consideration—what we are suggesting is that we apply the rule they've given just above here too—

Rodney: Then—in our case—there's no problem of affecting grammar adversely, is there?

Madge: And the doubling wouldn't affect the grammar.

Leader: We're saying then—are we—that we see no harm brought to grammatical integrity by the NCTE plan modified as we've suggested? Well, now let's turn to the Symbol Modification plan to see how it stands on this grammar criterion. Then we'll see which—the NCTE plan modified or the SM plan—is superior on this fourth criterion. So, what about the SM plan?

Discussion focused

With the use of these four thought movements—classification, evaluation, comparison, and synthesis—whenever and wherever any one of them is appropriate and needed, the group will move to its final position, fulfilling its task. Thus, the group will complete the CONVERGING phase. When the group ends the DIVERGING phase, it has much of the necessary material in hand for its later work—descriptions and definitions, explications, and listings—but when it ends the CONVERGING phase, it has narrowed its thinking down to a particular resolution out of the alternative possibilities. The bellowslike move-

ment—   OUTWARD INWARD   —has been completed.

Doubtless some of the most difficult decisions in the whole sequence go on in the converging phase. What was loose and possible and tentative has been shaken out; now judgments and choices will have to be made. Conflicts are inevitable and will have to be managed carefully so that the group can fulfill its task in the best way it can. If *abundance* could be said to be the chief mark of the DIVERGING phase, *accountability* is the mark of the CONVERGING phase.

8.32   Handling Conflict in the CONVERGING Phase: Task Work

We now consider some practical suggestions that may help with conflict as it occurs on matters of task.

1. *Attempt to manage, and do not suppress, task conflict.* The leader and members would want to be certain in the first place that the conflict noted is what Deutsch would label *veridical* rather than one of the other types. Finding out the nature of the conflict would require the process of classification. But if the conflict is veridical, it should not be suppressed or be permitted to remain latent. Latent conflict would, in Pondy's terms, hold a group continuously in the initial, uncertain step, with conflict likely to break out at any moment. Every effort should be made to (1) be sure task conflict is veridical; (2) give it a clear analysis, looking to causes and type; and (3) find a strategy to control it, while realizing its positive values. One could use the procedures for moving to different levels of conflict—assertions, reasons, evidence, values, and group goal—as described on pages 21-23 in Chapter 2. Other actions are also possible, the following being of especial importance.

2. *Keep any developing conflicts at the task level rather than permitting them to become interpersonal.* The Guetzkow and Gyr research seems to emphasize that substantive conflict can be more easily managed than can interpersonal conflict. What can a leader do to keep the conflict at a substantive level? Alan C. Filley presents one useful suggestion in his recent book, *Interpersonal Conflict Resolution*.[14] Suppose a father

and son were at the dinner table. The father says, "Eat your spinach," and the son replies, "I don't like spinach." This conflict could easily develop into a highly charged emotional confrontation with hostile comments back and forth, or grudging withdrawal and bitterness on the part of one of the participants, or even physical aggression. Filley suggests that both parties should keep the matter substantive and ask: What is it that each desires—what is the goal or underlying value behind the surface conflict. It may be found that the father wants "nourishing food" for the son, and the son wants "food that tastes good." Given these standards, both could then think together on the question, "Is there nourishing food that also tastes good?" This gets them to a cooperative, substantive *thinking together* rather than a hostile, interpersonal, and emotional conflict. This is an example of what Deutsch would label *contingent conflict*.

Filley also provides a case that occurred in a Wisconsin prison in which this technique was used to good advantage. A meeting was held to discuss possible prison reforms. One issue that developed concerned the advisability of eliminating the uniforms that were traditionally worn by the prison guards. The discussion became heated and a vote was taken. The result was six to three against the wearing of uniforms. The vote didn't end the issue because the three on the losing side were angry. A group consultant who was present at the time suggested another look at the situation and probed for the underlying goals and values: *Why* did a person want or not want uniforms for guards. Those in favor of uniforms said that prisons are attempting to rehabilitate persons and to teach them to deal constructively with authority; they saw uniforms as a means of achieving that goal. Those against uniforms said that uniforms created such a stigma that guards could not deal with inmates on a one-to-one basis. The consultant asked whether there was a solution that would incorporate the desires of both groups. Finally it was agreed by group consensus that guard supervisors would wear uniforms but that guards in constant contact with prisoners would not. By keeping the issues at the substantive level, it was possible for the group to think together and to come to a decision that was agreeable to all.

All knew that the one clear purpose of the discussion was to find the fair answer. As Kenneth Boulding pointed out: "It is the process of conflict toward some kind of resolution which gives it meaning and which makes it good."[15] In this example, the conflict was contingent, correctly assessed, and managed. The conflict was not permitted to escalate to the *personal* team level, nor to remain latent and potentially disruptive.

Another analysis of this instance of genuine conflict in a group is possible. Conflict between two parties is often viewed by analogy as a "game." From this viewpoint, three types of outcome are possible. In the usual case one party will win and the other will lose (win-lose). In some games it is possible for both parties to lose (lose-lose) or for both to win (win-win). Applying this classification to group behavior, we can see occurrences of each of these outcomes.

Examples of lose-lose situations abound. If a group ends in compromise where each side has given up on issues that were important to it, then it may be that no one is pleased with the outcome. If group members grudgingly give acquiescence to an unpopular compromise and middle ground, the matter may be "settled" (and sometimes this is the most that is possible) but this conclusion can hardly be very desirable. Again, we would expect great foot dragging during the implementation stages.

It is, of course, much more desirable if everyone can win (win-win). This is possible in group decision-making processes but it usually requires a search for additional, newer proposals that can better satisfy the differing goals of the parties in conflict. An example would be the conflict between the father and son about eating spinach, a conflict that might end with a mutual decision to have more broccoli in the future.

In every group process the participants would do well to ask whether their present procedures are leading to a group action that would best be characterized as one of

Win-Lose

or

Lose-Lose

OR

Win-Win

3. *Increase the leader's central, direct role if the task conflict intensifies.* The Guetzkow and Gyr findings make this point clear. Formal procedures such as parliamentary procedures were not helpful, nor was a dictatorial style of leadership. But

a clearly understood plan of action was helpful. And the leader must be more active in getting the facts out before the group, largely by asking probing questions and establishing an open atmosphere. The leader probably will also offer (*tentatively*) more solutions than usual, an action that is much more appropriate for a leader in the CONVERGING phase with conflict present than in the DIVERGING phase where such action may stifle the creativity of others in the group. Sometimes a conflict over alternative programs can be resolved by a careful look at technologically-made forecasts of consequences. John M. Allderige, who sees information technology as a way of extending a group's thought processes, declared:

> An even simple on-line computing arrangement at aldermanic council meetings might do very much toward illuminating various proposals—the most quarrelsome malcontent might well rapidly be shown to be just that, or quite possibly an innovative genius whose concepts of action when projected turn out to be very appealing indeed.[16]

4. *Increase the quality of listening done in the group.* Particularly in the CONVERGING phase the members must "put their heads together." No insight that anyone has, no flicker of warning that anyone feels must be withheld from the group. And no insight that is offered or warning that is voiced must go *unheard*. Listening to each other is nowhere more important than here in the CONVERGING phase when some of the group's hardest work must be done.

Distant possible consequences have to be analyzed and assessed for each alternative "action" including the taking of "no action" at all; matters of likely response of individuals and the public have to be estimated as reasonably as possible. Where data seem contradictory and where reputed experts differ in their interpretations and viewpoints, the group has to struggle to its best interactive judgment. The members may have to face hard questions of timing: should they opt for lesser, short-range results or hold out for potentially greater, long-range ones? These are but a few of their difficult choices; resolution by cooperative reasoning in this CONVERGING phase will not be easy.

There is simply no way of accomplishing the task work of the CONVERGING phase with any degree of success without a high quality of listening. This means the alert, evaluative, and supportive listening that was recommended in Chapter 3. But two applications of listening are especially important in the management of conflict: (1) listening to locate the core of the difference and (2) listening to be able to link the new thought with the group thought-line. Locating the core of the conflict starts the converging action, for what is agreed can be written off and what is seen differently can have the spotlight turned upon it. And being able to link the new contribution with what has gone before keeps the group's efforts concentrated rather than disconnected. Indeed, the successful groups that Guetzkow and Gyr studied tended to discuss and resolve one issue at a time before moving on to others. Linkage *that works* means more than a Yes, and a swift movement on to the speaker's own thought; linkage *that works* picks up the gist of the preceding thought with a swift, apt phrase, "*Such social concern* is seen at many levels. . . ." *Locate* and *link* are two important functions of listening in the management of conflict.

5. *Facilitate the management of task conflict by clear statement.* Altogether too much of the language used in group meetings tends to be overly informal, overly casual, and rambling. People often speak faster than they think and fail to discipline in any effective way the flow of their words. Spontaneity can be of great value in groups; if poorly handled, it can also be a potential source of conflict and a sure hindrance to the resolution of conflict. When ideas are stated generally and loosely, they cover a broad area and permit the listener to make all sorts of interpretations that may differ from those held by the speaker. And when the speaker breaks his or her remarks by repeated use of trite phrases such as "I mean," "you know," "well, it's like this," and "if you know what I mean," it is impossible to know what he or she really does mean. Repeated use of such expressions is a clear indication of the sketchiness of the speaker's thinking as well as the disturbing hold of a language habit.

The example of clear speech by the leader and other members may invite the unclear, rambling member to try for more effective presentation of his or her ideas. But whenever communication is ambiguous, listeners have the continuing responsibility to request clarification and to check understanding by rephrasing tentatively: "Could you give us an example of what you mean here?" "Is this what we're saying . . .?" Unless group members understand pretty much in the same way what is being said, there is no such thing as a group thought-line, no such thing as convergence on the task by working out conflict.

8.4 **THE CONVERGING PHASE IN TEAM WORK**

People are brought together, just as are ideas, in the converging movement of group work. For effective group work to occur, the various members must come together as a *team*, as that feeling and activity were discussed in Chapter 3. From the separateness and groping of the DIVERGING phase the group has moved—often through a period of somewhat active hostility and rebellion—into the more cooperative CONVERGING phase. But the participants do not immediately achieve full cooperation and harmony nor, once they have developed such a relationship, do they sustain it continuously. There are regressions to less effective team relationships, but now the damage can be repaired more quickly and the group can again become a full-fledged team. Some groups, however, become fixated at one of the earlier stages—self-assertiveness or leader-dependency, defensiveness and hostility, reluctant and intermittent cooperation—and never reach the level of mutual interaction and confidence a true team displays. James Cribbin points out that "Historically, there has been far too much talk about dealing with individuals, but relatively little stress has been given to the importance of team building."[17] Consideration is, therefore, given to two factors: aspects of teamness and handling conflict in the converging phase of teamness.

8.41 **Aspects of Teamness**

There seem to be two basic aspects of *teamness*: feeling like a team and acting like a team. *Feeling like a team* is a matter of "we-ness," to use the term coined by the early sociologist C. H. Cooley. And *acting like a team* is a matter of integration, the putting together of independent forces interdependently. Which comes first—feeling or acting? These factors interact too closely for such a question to be answered clearly. One can say that the group members could *feel* themselves a unit without acting effectively upon their feeling; one can also say that the quality of their team action will be conditioned by their degree of we-feeling. These two factors are now taken up in turn.

1. Feeling like a team: WE-NESS

Feeling like a team describes how each individual in the group feels: individual→group; individual→other members; and individual→self as member. In other words: cohesiveness, trust, and involvement.

Cohesiveness in a group is generally considered to be the overall attractiveness of the group to its members. It is the force that keeps a member willingly in the group and wins his or her loyalty. Reasons for feeling initially attracted to the group vary somewhat from member to member:

Concern with the task the group is undertaking.

Enjoyment of people in groups.

Friendship with a particular member.

Prestige of being in this particular group.

But the responsibilities shared within the group are also significant in developing cohesiveness. Chris Argyris,[18] with his long experience in human relationships in management, considers these "shared responsibilities" more of a basis of cohesiveness in a group than "the compulsion to like or be liked." The point here is that groups can work themselves into cohesiveness by their cooperative interaction. Nevertheless, the feelings of safety and freedom within which members interact must not be undervalued. Alexander Mikalachki, professor of Organizational Behavior at the University of Western Ontario, from his study of blue-collar work groups, adds the factor of "members' concern for others." He explains:

> If group members do not accept individual differences, are not concerned with each other's well-being, and do not mediate antagonisms among group members, then the interdependence of members' roles and the opportunity for member interaction, which force the members to remain in contact with each other, will make the group less rather than more cohesive.[19]

Even in groups in which membership is not compulsory, this factor of how members treat each other is crucial in the degree of cohesion felt in the group.

As cohesiveness develops in the CONVERGING phase, we need to ask: how high a degree of cohesiveness in a group is desirable? We have already pointed out that extremely cohesive groups may fall into GROUPTHINK, in which members incapacitate themselves for effective work by wanting above everything else to preserve their group relationships. Consequently, wrong decisions are often made in such situations.

As for productivity of groups with varying degrees of cohesiveness, Fisher presents the following diagram:

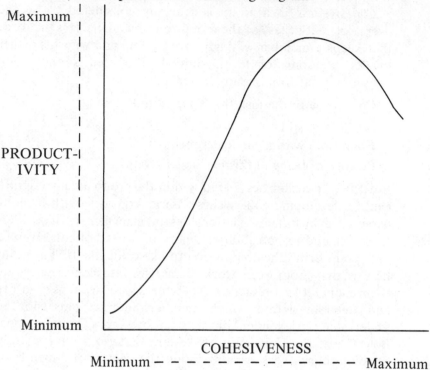

Fisher, long a student of small group functioning, explains the curvilinear relationship between cohesiveness and productivity thus:

> As groups raise their level of cohesiveness, the more likely they will raise their level of productivity. Conversely, the more productive the group, the greater the likelihood that they will be more cohesive. However, the relationship breaks down toward the upper end of the two continuums. . . . According to this illustrative diagram, extremely cohesive groups are more likely to have moderate to low productivity. Although the productivity of highly cohesive groups probably doesn't sink to the level of extremely low cohesive groups, they are not nearly as likely to be productive as groups with moderately high cohesiveness.[20]

Cohesiveness is desired in groups, and leaders and members should actively seek to build to a high level during the CONVERGING phase as the group becomes the team. But too much cohesiveness may lead to GROUPTHINK symptoms and diminish the group product.

Trust grows in the CONVERGING phase. As the group relationships converge into TEAM relationships, the members become more sure of the situation, more confident of the actions of others in the group. They are building a supportive atmosphere in which they find it possible to accept whatever criticism of their ideas or their behaviors is made and to use it constructively. Rensis Likert, director of the Institute for Social Research and professor of Psychology and Sociology at the University of Michigan, explains how this feeling of security works:

> whatever their content, the member feels sufficiently secure in the supportive atmosphere of the group to be able to accept, test, examine, and benefit from the criticism offered. Also, he is able to be frank and candid, irrespective of the content of the discussion. . . . The supportive atmosphere of the group, with the feeling of security it provides, contributes to a cooperative relationship between the members.[21]

Where the group develops high interpersonal trust, the members feel free to use their best abilities rather than hold back in fear. Where an environment is trustworthy, the members can be at their best. The social psychologist J. R. Gibb pointed out: "The barriers to person potential are all variants of fear, derivatives of distrust: alienation, hostility, impotence, psychological distance, indifference, loneliness, and competitiveness."[22]

Involvement. Whereas in the DIVERGING phase of team development the member was asking himself, Do I want to be a part of all this? What has this to do with me? now In the CONVERGING phase he or she is part of a going concern, no longer fearing the loss of his or her individuality by becoming a working member of the group. The member has seen that it is not necessary to give *up* oneself in order to give *of* oneself.[23] The member feels that the goal sought by the group is his or her goal, and has come to see that seeking this goal will not do violence to one's personal goals. Likert has described this feeling:

> The members of the group are highly motivated to abide by the major values and to achieve the important goals of the group. Each member will do all he reasonably can—and at times all in his power—to help the group achieve its central objectives. He expects every other member to do the same. This high motivation springs, in part, from the basic motive to achieve and maintain a sense of personal worth and importance. Being valued by a group whose values he shares,

and deriving a sense of significance and importance from this relationship, leads each member to do his best. He is eager not to let the other members down. He strives hard to do what he believes is expected of him.[24]

As the CONVERGING phase proceeds, it is increasingly more clear that the members have thrown in their lot with their colleagues and intend to see the matter through. They see each other not as rivals, but as teammates, coworkers on a common task.

This excerpt shows a feeling of We-ness in the group:

Seven women are discussing the question: How can women prepare themselves to be better members of nonprofit boards? They are getting ready to set up a noncredit course for board members in the private sector.

	Leader:	Yes, the replies to our questionnaires seem very good; they will surely be helpful to us in setting up our course. We have studied them all now and are ready to report. It was really interesting that so many of them had extra comments and suggestions at the end!
Involvement	*May*:	I guess they understand that *we mean this*!
Trust	*Esther*:	This sounds wonderful! But I'm a little at a loss—I'm just back, you know, and—what is this about questionnaires?
	Leader:	That's right—I'm sorry—you were in the East when we sent them out. They went to executive directors and board members of nonprofit organizations here in Seattle. Mainly we were asking what they thought the major weaknesses in women's participation on boards of nonprofit organizations and agencies are.
	Grace:	We sent them both to director *and* to members so we'd have viewpoints from both sides.
	Jane:	On Monday we had had 65 percent returned. Did we get any more?
Cohesiveness	*Leader*:	Yes, several yesterday—enough to bring our percentage of return up to 75 percent! Frankly, that's very good—but we all thought it *would* be good, didn't we? Now, let's see—the executive directors were pretty much in agreement that the major deficiency in board members is their lack of knowledge of finance.
	May:	Yes, and I know that's true of myself! I go to a meeting and they hand me a budget and cash flow

statement, and all I can do is watch John Abell, our accountant, to see how *he* seems to be responding to the idea!

2. Acting like a team: INTEGRATION

As the group converges in becoming a team, integration will occur. Some of Maier's early studies considered the integrative function needed for individual problem solving. Just as the behaviors of an individual must be coordinated, so must be the behaviors of members of a group.

As group members narrow their activities to become a team, they must come, as a group, to see what functions are needed, and must fill those needs. They must first be correct about *what is needed*, and then they can act. These needs may lie in either the TEAM realm or the TASK realm. A member may see that another participant is baffled, or frustrated, or angry: he or she then acts to remove the source of the trouble if possible. A member may see that the whole group is lagging or momentarily at odds, and seek to change whatever has made them so. Or some member may observe the group's difficulty in the task work, reason that an example is needed, and supply one. Seeing that the group is bypassing some angle of the problem, a perceptive member introduces it. A synthesis needs to be made: some member makes one and tests it with the group.

All these functions must be accomplished efficiently by the members of the team. No needed action can be omitted nor can any action be repeated needlessly. Where *integration* exists, all members are spontaneously active to maintain the working effectiveness of the team and to accomplish the group task.

Integration has two aspects: independence and interdependence. These aspects must and can exist together in members during the CONVERGING phase. Lippitt and Whitfield see this coexistence of independence and interdependence as made possible by cohesiveness: "Perhaps the most effective cohesiveness is that which enables members to work together in an *interdependent* way, where each member feels free to invest himself and to make his contribution toward the work of the group, while retaining his individuality."[25]

No matter how drawn a member is to the group, no matter how much he or she believes in the goal the group is seeking, the member must not forget that the group needs that member's *differences* as much as his or her affirmations—perhaps even more. To be *accountable*—as every member must be to keep a team healthy—the observant member will bring these contradictory items and speculations to the attention of the others. Of course, independence flaunted is a handicap to the team, but independence appropriately monitored and manifested is of great value to the team.

There are times when a person's viewpoint is so different from those held by the group in general that that person is seen as a deviant, as out of step with the group. At this point the group shows clearly how far the members have moved in their CONVERGING phase; if they turn to these discordant ideas as possible sources of group benefit instead of as sure stumbling blocks in the group's progress—stumbling blocks to be dealt with as quickly as possible so that the group can get back to the important matters—they show their integration. If they manage to resist rejecting the deviant and the deviant's ideas, they are valuing his or her independence. Dentler and Erickson say:

> From the point of view of the deviant, then, the testing of limits is an exercise of his role in the group; from the point of view of the group, pressures are set into motion which secure the deviant in his "testing" role, yet try to assure that his deviation will not become pronounced enough to make his rejection necessary.[26]

Groups that are well integrated realize that deviants—unless they are too markedly disruptive—help the members to clarify their boundaries of what is acceptable, to know better what they really mean. It has been found that groups who reject a deviant and thereby lose their boundary-testing agent, may soon have another member assume a somewhat similar deviant position. An integrated group helps each member to mine his or her information and abilities to serve the common purpose.

Members of a group in the CONVERGING phase in the team realm are at work coordinating their efforts; they are mutually responsive. They use what others offer; they offer and suggest and speculate so that others can use their ideas and intuitions. Perhaps interdependence can be seen from two angles: *seeking needs and filling them*, as previously explained; and *using substitutability*. If a second member gives the thought that a first was ready to add, or suggests an example that clarifies the matter before the group, or removes a tangled thought that was baffling the group, or welcomes the suggestion of a deviant—momentary needs in the group—the first member should let the matter drop; the work has been done. That the need may have been answered by another member makes no difference; *each member's action serves for all the others.*

Saying that each member restrains himself or herself from duplicating what has already been done sufficiently well does *not* mean that there is not merit at times in speaking up to agree that the idea is accurate or valuable, for this is a supportive act. Nor does it mean that the next speaker should avoid picking up the relevant part as a bridge into the forthcoming comment, for this is a valuable linking act.

Both fulfilling discovered needs and using substitutability are hallmarks of a group whose integration has developed well as it moves along through the CONVERGING phase.

Both independence and interdependence can be seen in the following excerpt:

Maybelle:	We all know how it feels to sit on a board where all you are is a rubber stamp for the director!
Grace:	You feel as though he is the authority—and who are you to question what he says—
Esther:	But if all the board acts that way, how does the policy get made? The executive director can't make it—he doesn't have the perspective; the staff can't, of course. It's the board's JOB to make policy!

Independence

Jane:	If I really thought that, I wouldn't sit on a board! Here I am—college graduate, homemaker, two years in voluntary work—what do I know about million-dollar budgets? It scares me to think about it! I think we're going too far when we suggest that we should be in on making the budget policy!

Deviant
contribution
used

Delores:	Jane, it scares me too, actually! But I look around the board—and the others are as scared as I am. So we let the director do it, and where's the input that lets him know what he needs to know?
Maybelle:	Scared is the word for it! And I'm just scared enough that I'm going to take this course we're planning myself! I'm going to sit in the front row and take notes! And I'm going to lay out my pencils in front of me—all sharpened—and when the one I'm using begins to smoke, I'll grab up another one!
Jane:	Maybelle! Well, maybe you can afford to lend *me* a pencil!

	Leader:	Another aspect of finances mentioned is lobbying for funds. The questionnaires referred to the fact that most of the nonprofit organization funds come from government—
	Jane:	Or United Way—or private foundations.
Substituta-bility	*Leader*:	Yes! So board members need to understand that lobbying for funds is legal.
Special knowledge	*Betty*:	How odd! But one of the attorneys in our office has just put out a pamphlet entitled What Citizens Need to Know About Lobbying. We've heard him about it over coffee for weeks!
Inter-dependence	*Esther*:	We're lucky you know about it! We should all have copies!

8.42 Handling Conflict in the CONVERGING Phase: Team Work

When conflict occurs in the CONVERGING phase in the team work, it means that some member or several members have slipped back from *integration* to separateness. Often the regression seems a severe check to the group, for the members will have come to expect their harmonious, secure atmosphere to continue unbroken. Fortunately for the group, however, in the CONVERGING phase the members have more tools with which to handle the conflict, tools derived from their inter-personal trust and from their experiences of successful cooper-ation. As was pointed out earlier, affective conflict can be handled better by removing or reducing its causes than by addressing the conflict directly. Nevertheless, such handling is not always possible, and a more direct approach is necessary. Again, in the CONVERGING phase, it may well be that the cooperative momentum of the group will allow successful efforts in managing the conflict to be made. If a member who has virtually left the team after attacking somewhat sharply the way things were being handled or the plan someone has suggested is given understanding and trust, the conflict brought by this deviating member may be effectively resolved.

Some practical suggestions may help with conflict as it occurs on matters of the team.

1. *Alter an appropriate factor in the task work.* It is wise to think of all conflict as task based as long as possible. More opportunities for working out the difference constructively are available in the task realm. Even a conflict in feelings can often

be construed as an honest difference in information or thought, and the emotion drained off.

Suppose that the group has found itself coming to a dead end in its struggle to work out the task; it is sometimes true that the lack of success will weaken the team's confidence in itself, and allow the interpersonal bonds to weaken. Mutual faultfinding tends to occur. Perhaps the group members need quick, indisputable success on some aspect of their task that matters to them.

2. *Treat an interpersonal problem as a group—not an individual—problem.* The group has struck a roadblock on its way to its goal, and must see all members as being equally involved in the resulting situation. The parties in conflict are not the only ones concerned. Likert suggests:

> At such times, it may be necessary for the group to stop its intellectual activity and in one way or another to look at and deal with the disruptive emotional stresses. After this has been done, the group can then go forward with greater unity....[27]

But looking at and dealing with the stresses do not mean undue "psychologizing," as Thelen says. Though Thelen's words concern *training groups*, his recommendation is valid also for *task groups*, such as we are concerned with in this Desk Book:

> It is not the group's concern to diagnose why individuals feel the way they do. It is its concern to know what feelings people have and use the fact that such feelings exist as symptomatic of conditions in the group that need to be made more explicit and studied.[28]

3. *Strengthen the general feeling of security in the group.* Conflict in the realm of team work is startling to all the members, and especially so in the CONVERGING phase of group interaction. What has been taken for granted has become less sure; security is threatened. At this point the supportiveness of the members should be increased; defensiveness and impatience must not be shown. Lifton has reported from his research with therapy groups that "Individuals (groups) have an innate capacity to heal themselves, *if they are provided a setting where they can feel secure enough to examine their problems*."[29] Self-healing in conflict situations in a task group may also occur if the group offers enough security to allow retreat from deviance.

4. *Expect some conflict in team work.* No group is at its

best at every moment; every group will have fluctuations in the degree of teamness with which they handle themselves. These ups and downs—even within a generally cooperative atmosphere—are not only natural; they are of some value. Actually, too much ease in interpersonal relations is likely to bring a state of euphoria, where everything is taken in stride and approved of. This uncritical mood may well affect adversely the members' work on their task; they may abandon the necessary analysis of ideas because they approve the idea givers so wholeheartedly; they may resist the introduction of contrary suggestions and fall into GROUPTHINK. But if members remain *independent* even while they become *interdependent*, they will provide enough difference to keep the group alert and dependable, though cohesive and congenial.

8.5   CONCLUSION

The CONVERGING thought movement is phasal, as is the DIVERGING thought movement. Whereas the DIVERGING phase is characterized by creativity, the CONVERGING phase is characterized by the management of conflict. Conflict on both the task and the team levels is an inevitable part of the converging action.

Frequent patterns of task work occurring in the CONVERGING phase are classification, evaluation, comparison, and synthesis. Conflicts can be analyzed and, when found to be veridical, they can be managed.

The patterns of development of the team are coming to feel like a team (we-ness) and acting like a team (integration). Conflicts occurring on the team level should be handled by altering an appropriate factor in the task work, treating an interpersonal problem as a group problem, strengthening the general feeling of security in the group, and expecting some conflict in team work.

FOOTNOTES — CHAPTER 8

1. Thomas M. Scheidel and Laura Crowell, "Idea Development in Small Discussion Groups," *Quarterly Journal of Speech*, **50** (1964): 140–145.
2. Morton Deutsch, *The Resolution of Conflict* (New Haven: Yale University Press, 1973), p. 10.
3. Deutsch, *The Resolution of Conflict*, pp. 15–17.

4. Deutsch, *The Resolution of Conflict*, pp. 12–14.

5. Louis R. Pondy, "Organizational Conflict: Concepts and Models," *Administrative Science Quarterly*, 12 (1967): 298–306.

6. Harold Guetzkow and John Gyr, "An Analysis of Conflict in Decision-making Groups," *Human Relations*, 7 (1954): 367–381.

7. Guetzkow and Gyr, "An Analysis of Conflict," p. 373.

8. Guetzkow and Gyr, "An Analysis of Conflict," p. 377.

9. Guetzkow and Gyr, "An Analysis of Conflict," p. 379.

10. Ronald Gelatt et al. Introduction, "America's Most Livable Cities: A Portfolio of Urban Optimism," *Saturday Review*, III (August 21, 1976): 9.

11. Lester R. Bittel emphasizes the use of exceptions in making management decisions. He suggests that, in addition to looking at the exception itself, the decision makers should look at its effects in every direction. "You will also want to seek answers to these questions: How big is the exception? How frequently has it occurred? How delayed is its effect? How broad is its impact? Does it affect policy, planning, organization, staffing, marketing, finance, operations, research, purchasing?"–*Management by Exception* (New York: McGraw-Hill Book Company, 1964), p. 148.

12. Henry Steele Commager, "Our Greatest Presidents," *Parade*, May 8, 1977, p. 16.

13. We should not, of course, assume that every piece of information that is brought before the group will be in an immature stage and thus need to be developed by synthesis. If the proposal, for example, is the result of the work of a task force over a period of months, it is relatively unlikely that the members of the discussion group could bring detailed improvements to the plan. But, even in such a situation, there would be times when nonexperts could examine certain aspects, such as the proposal's probable impact on public welfare in their area, and suggest relevant adaptations.

14. Alan C. Filley, *Interpersonal Conflict Resolution* (Glenview, Ill.: Scott, Foresman and Company, 1975), pp. 120–121.

15. Kenneth Boulding, *Conflict and Defense: A General Theory* (New York: Harper & Row, Publishers, Inc., 1962), p. 307.

16. John M. Allderige, "Decision Aids: Needs and Prospects," in *Decision-Making: Creativity, Judgment, and Systems* (Columbus: Ohio State University Press, 1972), p. 253.

17. James Cribbin, *Effective Managerial Leadership* (New York: American Management Association, Inc., 1972), p. 107.

18. Chris Argyris, "Employee Apathy and Noninvolvement–The House That Management Built?" *Personnel*, 38 (July-August, 1961): 14.

19. Alexander Mikalachki, *Group Cohesion Reconsidered* (London, Canada: School of Business Administration, The University of Western Ontario, 1969), p. 67.

20. B. Aubrey Fisher, *Small Group Decision Making: Communication and the Group Process* (New York: McGraw-Hill Book Company, 1974), p. 33.

21. Rensis Likert, *New Patterns of Management* (New York: McGraw-Hill Book Company, 1961), p. 167.

22. J. R. Gibb, in *Human Potentialities: The Challenge and the Promise*, Herbert A. Otto, comp. and ed. (St. Louis: Warren H. Green, Inc., 1968), p. 167.

23. Chris Argyris, "Employee Apathy and Noninvolvement," p. 12.

24. Rensis Likert, *New Patterns of Management*, p. 166.

25. Gordon L. Lippitt and Edith Whitfield, *The Leader Looks at Group Effectiveness* (Washington, D.C.: Leadership Resources, Inc., 1961), p. 5.

26. Robert A. Dentler and Kai T. Erickson, "The Functions of Deviance in Groups," in *Readings on the Sociology of Small Groups*, Theodore M. Mills, ed. (Englewood Cliffs, N.J.: Prentice-Hall, Inc., 1970), p. 169.

27. Rensis Likert, *New Patterns of Management*, p. 176.

28. Herbert A. Thelen, *Dynamics of Groups at Work* (Chicago: The University of Chicago Press, 1963), p. 317. Phoenix edition.

29. Walter M. Lifton, *GROUPS: Facilitating Individual Growth and Societal Change* (New York: John Wiley & Sons, Inc., 1972), p. 23.

CHAPTER 9
THE FINAL MINUTES

9.44   Acceptable to Group

9.45   Suitable to Purpose

9.46   Effective in Overcoming Difficulties

9.5   Leadership Work after the Final Minutes

9.6   Conclusion

Although the final minutes of a meeting are a part of the general *converging* action of the group, their terminal quality makes them especially important and requires separate consideration in this Desk Book. In the last minutes the group members must see clearly just what they have accomplished in their interaction and what guidelines are necessary for their next step, whatever that may be; they also should feel the sense of having produced these results together. The nature of the *work* to be done in these last minutes depends upon what was purposed for the meeting, what happened during the meeting, and what, if anything, is purposed for the group in the future.

9.1   LENGTH OF THE FINAL MINUTES

How long shall these final minutes last? Like Lincoln's reply to the question of how long a man's legs should be—long enough to reach the ground—these final minutes must be long enough to do their job. They must allow the group's work to be properly rounded off. Often the ending time for the meeting is established in the *preparation* or the *first minutes* stage, and is thus known to all the group members. It would, however, be a waste of the group's energy to have everyone responsible for watching for the approach of the hour set for closing; the members should be concentrating on developing their thought-line with only a minimal awareness of the passage of time to help them monitor the length and elaboration of their contributions. For example, with about an hour remaining for group interaction, a member might take some time to offer helpful specifics of a similar plan used elsewhere; on the other hand, with only fifteen minutes remaining in the meeting, this member would speak only of the most important aspects of the plan. But the leader, throughout the discussion, will have tried to *pace* the discussion so that the group is reaching its decision as the closing time approaches, and thus can initiate the group's move into the work of the final minutes.

At what moment shall the leader move the group into this closing phase? If the group has the guideline of an announced closing time, the problem is lessened, for all the members have a general sense of the time span of the meeting. If no such time has been announced or agreed upon, the leader should suggest that the group will have to conclude in about so-and-so many minutes. Especially if the leader notes signs of restlessness or evidences of growing concern about the closing, he or she should clarify the matter such as by mentioning the approximate period of time left for work.

The leader, then, should move the team members into this final phase early enough to allow them to complete their tasks for that session. There will be times, of course, when no amount of effort by the leader and group members will have brought the group so far along on its task as it should be before moving into the final minutes. In such a case, if the task is truly important, the leader may press onward with the main aspects of the decision-making tasks briefly, and then use the final minutes either to *arrange for another meeting* to complete the task in more favorable circumstances or to *give a highly compressed statement* of the group's thought-line at that point. If extending these final minutes is possible and is agreeable to the members, the leader will not be forced to either of these expedients.

How much time the group will actually need to conclude appropriately cannot, of course, be precisely told. This matter is preferably considered by the leader in the preparation period. A good indication of the time required may be obtained by considering the purposes that must be met in this portion of the total group process; there are at least four common purposes.

9.2 PURPOSES OF THE FINAL MINUTES

9.21 To Close

What the group has been doing with more or less success and with more or less cooperativeness throughout the meeting must now be brought to an end. What has been achieved needs to be stated clearly so that all can feel that they understand their product similarly. They need also to feel the sense of teamness again as they close. William Schutz,[1] eminent consulting and research psychologist, suggests that the three phases by which a group builds integration (inclusion, control, and affection) occur again as a group moves toward its close, but *in reverse order*. The members tend to work out any hard feelings that might remain, then talk about how well they have worked together, and finally wonder whether the group should continue meeting: matters of affection, control, and inclusion. Although Schutz is speaking of groups in a training situation, his suggestions ring true, perhaps with less emotionality, in the task groups about which this Desk Book is concerned.

9.22 To Arrange Another Meeting

If another meeting is to be held on the same problem in the future, the issues resolved in this meeting need to be stated clearly so that they will not be discussed again at the next meeting. The issues to be taken up at the subsequent meeting also need clarification. Members need to know whether special information or materials will be needed for that meeting. If the time of the later meeting is already known, only a confirmation of the day and hour is needed. If a later meeting was expected by the group but its time has not yet been settled upon, possible times need to be suggested and group-wide agreement reached. Norman Maier[2] tells of a group planning a subsequent meeting in which the preference was 19-to-1 to hold that meeting on the coming Friday. The minority person, when questioned, explained that the coming Friday was his daughter's wedding day and that he would like to be present to give her away. His reason for not wanting the coming Friday sounded better to the other members than their reasons for wanting it, and consensus for his preference followed. Meeting times are important matters and should be arrived at, when possible, by *group* decision.

If a group has not expected to meet again but another meeting is later found to be necessary, the group members may feel that they had failed at the first meeting. If this attitude is not dispelled, the members may approach the subsequent meeting with feelings of disappointment that may jeopardize their chances for success at that time.

9.23 To Prepare for Making a Group Report

Some groups make no report, but for those who do, its preparation is an important matter. Whether the report is to be given orally or in written form to another group or person, the final minutes must ensure that all members understand and approve the information to be given as the group's thinking. It is often desirable to report conflicting opinions brought out in the group as well as the general group viewpoint finally reached; such a method is routinely used in unit meetings of the League of Women Voters. A league unit meeting may conclude with a leader's final statement reviewing the progress:

> In answer then to our question, "Who shall be responsible for financing these programs—local, state, or Federal sources?" we are saying that two-thirds of our group feels that the State government should have full responsibility, about one-third believes that State and Federal government should bear the total costs. Is that an accurate summary?

The actual wording of the group's decision will not need, in most cases, to be worked out *by the group*, but the sense and feeling must be clear enough so that the report will represent the team's action accurately. Hal Marckwardt, a training consultant of much experience, gives good advice for written reports: "If a written report is required, see that it is done before the reporter has lost the fine points of the decision."[3]

9.24 To Serve As the Basis for Group Action

When the decision made by the group is to be carried out by the group itself, additional decisions must be made prior to these final minutes: When will the plan go into effect? In what order should the separate actions be taken? Who is to do what? How shall evaluations be made at a later date? When shall that be? Actually, these decisions are another exercise in problem management and work upon them will have to be started some time before the final minutes begin. After these arrangements have been completed, the group will need to hear a brief recapitulation of (1) the plan itself and (2) the arrangements for its implementation; thus, agreement is retested and the participants can feel the satisfaction of having completed the planning stage and will tend to feel strong commitment to the action stage.

9.3   **DIFFICULTIES IN THE FINAL MINUTES**

The actual closing of even a profitable and satisfying session carries its own potential difficulties.

9.31   Prolonging the Discussion Unduly

One of the most frequent difficulties occurs when members prolong the discussion beyond what might seem desirable and necessary: they provide information and opinions (or repeat and elaborate ones already given) or draw out lengthly the point that was most recently before them. They seem to be making a last-ditch stand on their task; there seems to be an unwillingness to close the books. Whether this uneasiness results from a vague dissatisfaction with the decision made (a TASK matter) or from an equally vague wish to remedy a somewhat unsatisfying experience together or to delay terminating a pleasant time together (TEAM matters), they talk on without ostensible profit.

9.32   Relaxing Efforts in Anticipation of the End

Knowing that not much more *can* be done sometimes diminishes the motivation of the group to do what could yet be done. Sometimes this diminution of effort seeps back even into the period before the final minutes begin and weakens the work of the team at the time when that effort should be at its very peak: fewer contributions come freely, modifications do not seem worth making, a near-hit is accepted for a hit in meaning. Members who cooperated willingly before are no longer resilient enough, dedicated enough, or objective enough to seek out a common line of thought.

9.33   Failing to Move to Agreement

Sometimes a group comes into the final minutes with no real chance of finding agreement. The members may have *intended* to agree or sought concurrence vigorously, but they have not discovered a suitable formula for this particular case. After honest attempts to agree, failure to do so may be shattering to all the team members. The members have presented more information, tested different interpretations, and then tried compromise and integration, but no attempt has brought them into agreement on a common resolution of their problem. These true differences of viewpoint (veridical conflict), honestly held and openly set forth, have brought the group to an impasse, and the final minutes are upon them. The group members must realize that if the discussion time ends without their breaking the impasse they are forced to the position of recommending (or taking) *no action* at all. And whether *no action* is an option open to them will depend upon the specific situation.

Or the members may not really have sought consensus wholeheartedly; sometimes members seek to persuade, maneuvering to win their point. This situation is an entirely different matter; this group has also reached an impasse, but one that differs substantially from the impasse fallen into by a group intending—though failing—to agree. This is a TEAM impasse, not a TASK impasse. Again the group's purpose has not been served; *no action* is the group decision (by default) as the Final Minutes run out.

9.34 Making Hasty Decisions

When development of the group thought-line has moved slowly or the discussion period has been entirely too short, members may begin to decide matters in the later phases without subjecting them to careful thinking, and may often make decisions without realizing that their mental sharpness has become a bit dulled by their need to somehow reach a solution. Their decision then is not a product of their highest potentialities but a bending to the pressure of time. This circumstance cannot be genuinely satisfying, even though the members assert their acceptance of the decision.

9.4 LEADERSHIP WORK IN THE FINAL MINUTES

The need for the leader's work has been implicit throughout this analysis of the group's Final Minutes, but the matter is sufficiently important to merit additional attention. The leader's work comes to a climax in these final minutes. As these duties are many and important it is fortunate that the leader at this point in the meeting has the group's *experience together* to build upon. Some degree of mutual confidence will usually have arisen that enables the leader to give the swift, sure guidance the group now needs. The leader is permitted to do now—in handling both task and team—what he or she could not have done before, but the leader must be careful not to abuse this privilege.

9.41 Well-timed

The leader's sense of timing is crucial at this point. *When* should the group be guided into these Final Minutes? Does the leader cut the main work too short, that is, reserve too much of the available time for this wrap-up period? Or too little? Once the final minutes are begun, does the leader move through the necessary matters swiftly enough to capitalize on the momentum of the group? Or so swiftly that the members feel that they are being railroaded into the leader's view of the decision? To answer these questions in any situation, the leader must keep both the TASK and the TEAM in mind, and must utilize this information toward the achievement of the group purpose.

9.42 Suitably Toned

Just as timing takes on special significance in the final minutes of a group meeting, so does the *tone* of the group become of heightened significance. By tone is meant everything from the basic tone of voice to the general tone of the meeting. In working with training workshops over the years we have noted that a higher proportion of the group energy is spent on emotional matters both early and again late in a meeting or series of meetings.

Emotional tone hits one high point early in the DIVERGING phase of team work when the group members are brought together in a new situation and must sort out procedures, norms, and roles to see how they themselves fit together as a team. Interpersonal relations are very important at such a point, and the tone and pace established will condition what occurs throughout the meeting. In the large middle portion of the group effort the accomplishment of the task takes center stage. But then again in the final minutes a return to higher emotional tone seems to occur. The group goal is now in sight and the emphasis turns more to team work as the group members must tie loose ends together and bring their cooperation to a close. Task work can end with a summary but team work seems to end with more emotion felt throughout the group. Just as two persons in a conversation may have finished what they have to say but still have difficulty in leaving each other, a group may have difficulty in ending its team work.

Thus, in this period the leader will attempt to help create and maintain a spirit in which the members feel completeness, resolution, satisfaction, mutual support, friendliness, and warm appreciation of the others. All these feelings would combine as elements of the desired tone with which to conclude the meeting.

9.43 Aptly Phrased

The language of the leader is always important, as stressed in Chapter 4, but it is especially so in the final minutes. The thought movement in the CONVERGING phase is synthesizing and narrowing development; this movement accelerates during the final minutes. The language used by the leader in these minutes must be in tune with that thought movement or else the incongruity between language and thought will be jarring in its effect.

At the same time that the task work is narrowing to decision, the team work is also moving to a close. And the language of the leader must mirror both these events—clear and direct and sure in final shaping of the group's decision, cordial and genuine in appreciation of the kind of team the group has become. Even if the group's product is something less than had been hoped for, or its meshing of effort less smooth than was desirable, the leader must find a way to let the members feel some degree of satisfaction about what they have done together. The leader's vivid, reasonable language reports the group achievement fairly and animatedly, letting the members end the session with a feeling that their joint efforts have been worthwhile.

The language needed to fulfill these purposes will not be the same in every situation. From a bluff and hearty ring to a quiet but reassuring note, the leader's words need to say in effect: "We did it! and it's pretty good, isn't it?" Like the final movement of a great symphony, the whole complex interchange culminates in a fitting close.

9.44 Acceptable to Group

What the leader offers to the group in the way of summary obviously should conform to the members' opinions of what they have agreed upon. If contrary opinions as well as the actual decision made by the group are reported, the leader must make certain that the sense of these differing views is checked with the group. Some of the summarizing ideas will, of course, have been tested with the group at earlier junctures in their thinking. Now the upshot of their thinking is offered in clear, orderly fashion for the consideration of the group, not only in order that any errors, distortions, or omissions can be caught by the group but that the approved product can stand as the basis for a report of the decision or for the group's subsequent action upon it. The resolution of questions as to how the members' own action is to be taken must be produced with strong member participation. This whole careful process of shoring up the group's decision emphasizes the TEAM nature of the activity, thus giving satisfaction and strengthening commitment.

9.45 Suitable to Purpose

The leader must see that the way the Final Minutes in a particular situation are used serves that group's specific purpose:

if merely *to close*:	a usable, correct summary, plus some attention to the team needs for affection, control, and inclusion;

if *to arrange another meeting*:	a clear statement of issues resolved and issues to be taken up in the next meeting, and a time established agreeable to all;
if *to prepare for a report*:	an overall summary, one probably more in detail than for the first two purposes;
if *to serve as a basis for group action*:	an overall summary of the plan, also decisions made on the When, How, By Whom of its implementation, probably followed again by a quick wrap-up of the plan.

9.46 Effective in Overcoming Difficulties

Thus, whatever the major purpose of the group's interaction, the leader needs to present a summary. This summary is generally to be checked with the group, whether by a quick glance or a pointed inquiry will depend upon the situation. Thus, the net result of the LEADERSHIP WORK of these final minutes is a feeling of TEAMSMANSHIP. Nor can the leadership work here be done "to the tune of closing notepads, moving chairs and people standing to leave,"[4] as Marckwardt has phrased it. The expectations of the leader and his or her relationship with the members hold them in their attitude of work until all are ready to take their shoulders from the wheel at the same time. The leader must take pains to counter the difficulties—those detrimental feelings and behaviors that tend to show themselves in these final minutes:

1. *Prolonging discussion*	1. Move in quickly to review decisions and the reasons behind them.
	2. Speed up his or her own presentations.
	3. Make the relevant issue especially clear.
	4. Reiterate warmly the purpose of the group.
2. *Relaxing efforts as the end nears*	1. Increase solicitation of the members' contributions, without calling on anyone personally.

	2. Praise their achievement so far and encourage them to stay with the task.
	3. Add a new value, a new angle that will again engage their efforts on the task.
3. *Failing to move to agreement*	1. Draw out any segments of agreement that the group has achieved.
	2. Suggest giving a particular solution a trial run.[5]
	3. Start through the Problem Management Sequence again.[6]
4. *Making a hasty decision*	1. Introduce a change of pace.
	2. Make the appropriate steps to decision very clear, and give a little more guidance in taking them.
	3. Defer the final judgment, if possible, to another meeting.
	4. Get a second decision.[7]

9.5 **LEADERSHIP WORK AFTER THE FINAL MINUTES**

What the group leader does immediately after the verbal closing of the meeting is more important than most leaders realize. The group begins to break up and members prepare to go their own ways. Whether they feel elation over their successful work together or distress (and perhaps even anger) over their interaction or its product—the break-up moments are significant. The leader cannot feel that his or her work is over when the pencil is laid down and the notes gathered up: the members deserve a more gradual transition to their separateness; the tone the leader has carefully established in the final minutes must now be sustained and sanctioned.

Some members will come up to the leader with questions and comments on their work together; or someone may simply wish to identify with the leader for a moment (or wish to be seen doing so); or no one may come up to the leader but all may walk out in little groups or singly. To each of these situations—and an infinite variety of others—the leader will be responding. By inappropriate remarks, attitudes, or actions the leader can at this point undercut the achievement of the whole session: members may feel that what had seemed genuine is now seen as an act for the moment only; members may feel their commitment dwindling away when they see careless post-meeting behavior replace careful earlier work. The leader can and should show that what the members have done together has been worthwhile.

9.6   **CONCLUSION**

It is not easy for the leader to know *when* to call the group into the Final Minutes nor how best to use these precious moments. But he or she will know that somehow the group's TASK must be brought off as well as the situation allows, the group maintained as a TEAM throughout, and the LEADER-SHIP work conducted so that the group purpose is well served. The best help available lies in the fact that the group members have worked together under the leader's guidance throughout the discussion and have a right to feel pride and satisfaction in concluding their task together.

FOOTNOTES — CHAPTER 9

1. William Schutz, *The Interpersonal Underworld* (Palo Alto, Calif.: Science and Behavior Books, 1966), Chapter 9.
2. Norman Maier, *Problem-Solving Discussions and Conferences: Leadership Methods and Skills* (New York: McGraw-Hill Book Company, 1963), p. 148.
3. Hal Marckwardt, *The Leader Makes the Difference* (Reseda, Calif.: Western Center, Consultants, nd.), p. 6.
4. Marckwardt, *The Leader Makes the Difference*, p. 6.
5. Likert uses the term "pragmatic consensus," and explains that "it represents an agreement to try out a solution for a period of agreement even though some of the members of the group still have reservations concerning it. The solution on trial may deal with only a part of the problem, but, even so, the willingness to agree to try a part often represents an important step toward ultimately achieving a solution to the total conflict."—*New Ways of Managing Conflict* (New York: McGraw-Hill Book Company, 1976), p. 149.
6. Likert calls this method the "backup, recycling technique"; he suggests: "The group starts by reexamining the statement of the problem to be sure that it is considering the real problem and that the problem is stated well and clearly. It would be well to examine the conditions that were originally thought to be essential to see if any of these conditions can be classified as desirable but not essential. Two steps, in particular, need intensive effort when trying to do a better job the second time. These are (1) searching for additional and stronger integrative goals and relevant situational requirements, and

(2) seeking to create or discover an innovative solution which will meet all of the essential conditions, and consequently, be acceptable to all."—*New Ways of Managing Conflict*, p. 150.

7. Norman R. F. Maier is a believer in the power of letting the group work out a second solution when the first one selected is somewhat unsatisfactory; he holds that dissatisfactions with the first one will operate to bring a better second one.—*Problem-Solving Discussions and Conferences*, p. 120.

PART THREE

Materials for Use

CHAPTER 10
RESOURCES AND OTHER SOURCES

10.1 Resources

    10.11 Making Lists
          Brainstorming
          Nominal Group Technique (Part I)

    10.12 Pruning Lists
          Nominal Group Technique (Part II)
          Scanning Strategy (Converging)

    10.13 Creating New Products or Procedures
          Synectics
          Checklists

    10.14 Developing and Handling Ideas
          Incremental Strategy
          Ideals Concept
          Chairman's Privilege

    10.15 Building Involvement/Understanding
          Charrette Planning Process
          Role Playing
          Buzz (or huddle) Groups

    10.16 Handling Conflicts
          System 4T
          Integrative Decision Making

10.17 Planning Implementation
Scanning Strategy
PERT—Program Evaluation and Review Technique

10.2 Other Sources (shelf books)

10.21 William Emory and Powell Niland, *Making Management Decisions,* 1968

10.22 Irving L. Janis and Leon Mann, *Decision Making-A Psychological Analysis of Conflict, Choice, and Commitment,* 1977

10.23 Charles H. Kepner and Benjamin B. Tregoe, *The Rational Manager: A Systematic Approach to Problem Solving and Decision Making,* 1965

10.24 Rensis Likert and Jane G. Likert, *New Ways of Managing Conflict,* 1976

10.25 Norman R. F. Maier, *Problem-Solving Discussions and Conferences: Leadership Methods and Skills,* 1963

10.26 George M. Prince, *The Practice of Creativity: A Manual for Dynamic Group Problem Solving,* 1970

10.27 Tudor Rickards, *Problem-solving Through Creative Analysis,* 1974

10.28 Marvin E. Shaw, *Group Dynamics: The Psychology of Small Group Behavior,* 1976

10.29 Ralph M. Stogdill, *Handbook of Leadership: A Survey of Theory and Research,* 1974

10.1   RESOURCES

10.11   MAKING LISTS

Brainstorming

A group generates ideas on a specific problem as rapidly as possible without making evaluations while the listing is being done.

Recommended Sources	Alex Osborn, *Applied Imagination* (New York: C. Scribner's Sons, 1957) C. H. Clark, *Brainstorming* (New York: Doubleday & Co., 1958) Tudor Rickards, *Problem-solving through Creative Analysis* (New York: John Wiley & Sons, Inc., 1974)

When to use

It is appropriate for a group to use brainstorming when

1. the problem is specific and fairly limited in range.
2. the problem is capable of having *many* answers.
3. the group's immediate purpose is to produce a list of as many items as possible without giving attention to their quality.

Details of use

Composition of group

Invite 6–10 persons; or up to 50 or more.

Include both men and women, drawn from many walks of life.

Avoid including too many experts in the problem field because of the freshness of ideas that persons from outside can produce.

Try to have at least half of the group made up of people who have been in brainstorming sessions before; their familiarity with the process is helpful.

Meeting time

The time can be as short as 15 minutes on occasion, but usually an hour or more is desirable because of the value of the momentum built up.

Conduct of meeting

Two persons in charge are needed: a leader to explain and carry out the rules, and a recorder to write the suggestions on a chalkboard or flipchart.

The leader explains carefully the problem to be brainstormed.

The leader explains the rules:

Freewheel	Members are to call out their ideas freely, not holding back an idea because it might be repetitious, or obvious, or too far out. Actually, the more original the ideas, the better it is. One idea per person at a time.
Postpone Judgment	No one is to characterize or evaluate or shoot down anyone else's idea. No one is to defend his or her own idea or try to explain it.
Hitchhike	All members are urged to build upon ideas already suggested—combine, modify, and go beyond them.
Quantity Breeds Quality	The more ideas the members can suggest in the time allotted the better; quality will take care of iteself if enough ideas are suggested.

The recorder prepares to write down

the suggestions, using the speaker's own key words, and numbering the suggestions as they are made.

A warm-up session of 10–15 minutes is held to help the members learn to hear suggestions without evaluating them and to get into the swing of the rapid-fire outpouring of ideas. Some remarks on creativity or some exercises on originality can be used. Also the problem can be redefined—if that is thought necessary—before the real session begins.

The brainstorming session is held:

The leader and recorder take their places, and the group members sit where they can see the board or flipchart easily.

If the group is over 15 in size, members are asked to raise their hands as they start to speak so that (1) the recorder can spot the speaker and catch the suggestion more easily, and (2) in the case of two persons starting to speak at the same moment, the leader can bring in one and then the other.

If a lull occurs in the suggestion giving, the leader can read every third or fifth idea from those listed to stimulate more thinking; or tell the group how many minutes of time for suggestions remain, and urge them to add a certain number of ideas during that time.

If all the ideas at some point seem to be following along the same line of thinking, the leader can pick out the *wildest* idea proposed up to that time, and suggest that the members brainstorm out from that particular item.

The leader keeps the session lively by his or her own interest and animation; the recorder does not take part in handling the ideas but is efficient in getting them all down in a readable fashion.

Modifications

Trigger sessions: (See Rickards, pp. 69–71)

This is an alternative form of idea listing in which each person in the group works alone for perhaps five minutes to write down a list of suggestions. At the end of that time, each member reads his or her list aloud to the group; after a list is read the group has a brainstorming period, then another list is read, and so on, until all lists have been shared.

A trigger session should be preceded by a warm-up, as in the regular form of brainstorming. It is well adapted for use when groups are very small, say of six or seven people.

Reverse brainstorming: (See Rickards, pp. 74–75)

This form can be used whenever it is necessary to list possible bad consequences quickly, when the group members need to ask themselves: "Yes, this sounds good, but what might go wrong with it?"

Reverse brainstorming is very useful after an idea has been *selected* in the postbrainstorming evaluation session, but members consider that the actions the idea requires are *expensive* and that any mistakes made in carrying it out would be *serious*.

Benefits of use

1. Brainstorming brings a lengthy list of suggestions in a relatively short time; the regular form tends to

bring out more ideas than the *trigger session* form.

2. The sheer length of the list means that some excellent and highly original ideas are included and can be drawn out (and even improved upon) in the *evaluation session* that comes a few days after the brainstorming session, or by an official concerned with the problem.

3. This method produces some feeling of accountability in handling a problem since the members have suggested the ideas themselves.

4. Brainstorming brings ideas from a broad base, not only because of the diverse composition of the group but because the rules (especially the nonevaluative climate and the encouragement given to members to build on what others have said) make free participation safe and interesting.

5. Experience with brainstorming can aid the members to improve their own individual thinking since it shows them clearly how valuable it is to hold back the evaluative process while they are listing the ideas in the first place.

Cautions in use

1. Avoid using the brainstorming method on too vague a subject; it is suited to the kind of topic that can be so clearly stated that all of the members will be putting their minds to the same problem at the same time.

2. Plan to use the warm-up period even though the members are experienced in brainstorming; suit the activities of the period to this condition.

3. Since a brainstorming session puts the members into a highly stimulated, free, and fanciful state of mind, do not expect them to go immediately into a problem-solving, evaluative process. The follow-up, weed-out-the-list process should not be taken the same day not only because it is too hard for the members to shift from the exhilaration of brainstorming to the exacting analysis and synthesis of decision making but because some very good ideas may occur to them in the next day or two and should be added to the list.

Nominal Group Technique (Part I)

The Nominal Group Technique (Part I) can be useful in the Diverging Phase of group work for "list making." It might be described concisely as a silent brainstorming.

Recommended Source	Andre L. Delbecq, Andrew H. Van de Ven, and David H. Gustafson, *Group Techniques for Program Planning: A Guide to Nominal Group and Delphi Processes* (Glenview, Ill.: Scott, Foresman and Company, 1975), especially Chapters 2, 3, and 5.

When to use

When making lists in groups with (1) dominating group members or (2) members who tend to talk overly long on a point before moving on.

In response to the stimulus from the leader, "Could we list the various obstacles as we see them?" a dominant member will likely present a suggestion. The group may then tend to "talk about" that suggestion rather than continue adding items to the list. In a given amount of time less than a desirable number of items are listed. And, with this procedure, the less assertive members will have a lesser voice in making up the developing list.

The aim of the Nominal Group Technique is to overcome these two problems by providing a means for (1) getting more items on the developing list and (2) equalizing the contributions and influence of the various group members.

Details of use

The first two steps (Part I) of the Nominal Group Technique could be summarized as follows:

1. *Silent Generation of Ideas in Writing*
   The group members are asked to list individually, in writing, the major obstacles seen to be applicable to the problem at hand. A five-minute time period may be allowed for this silent listing. Members tend to be stimulated by seeing others working nearby on their lists.

2. *Round-robin Feedback from Group Members As Items Are Listed for All to See*
   Going around the room, and taking one item per member each time, the recorder lists each item in a terse phrase on a flipchart or chalkboard. The round-robin listing prevents any person from having all of his or her items listed together and it prevents the first person asked from having his or her items all listed first. It thus helps to prevent the close association of an idea and the person presenting that idea. Hitchhiking is encouraged as items are listed: if an item mentioned by one member encourages another to come up with a

new item not already listed, it can be presented at the end of the round-robin procedure.

These first two steps of the Nominal Group Technique could be used for list making. The other steps (Part II) would be useful for pruning a list.

Benefits of use

A group using the Nominal Group Technique should come up with more items on a list than it would by using any other group technique.

All group members have an equal voice and vote in the developing list.

The use of this technique can add a novel element to the group proceedings, which can serve to rekindle interest and involvement. We have seen it used productively in a conflict situation to change the pace and depersonalize the work for a time.

Cautions

As with all other group procedures, the NGT should be viewed as a tool that can be helpful but can also be misused. It should be seen to be a flexible procedure that must be adapted (amount of time, manner of listing items) to the specific situation.

The NGT has a potential problem in common with Brainstorming. With both procedures the group members may become carefree and less vigorous in their thinking during the free-wheeling period. But, once such a list is developed, work must continue with it in what will become a converging thought-line. The relatively carefree attitudes of the earlier stage may work against the necessary serious efforts of the later stage.

10.12   **PRUNING LISTS**

Nominal Group Technique (Part II)

The Nominal Group Technique (Part II) can be useful in the Converging Phases of group work for "pruning a list." It is a means for reducing the size of a list of items to those that will receive full evaluation.

Recommended Source	Andre L. Delbecq, Andrew H. Van de Ven, and David H. Gustafson, *Group Techniques for Program Planning: A Guide to Nominal Group and Delphi Processes* (Glenview, Ill.: Scott, Foresman and Company, 1975), especially Chapters 2, 3, and 5.

When to use	When a list has been developed by the first two steps of the Nominal Group Technique (Part I), these next steps could be taken. Or when a list has been developed by some other procedure (such as Brainstorming, for example) the Nominal Technique (Part II) could be used. When a group desires to reduce any list to a few items for especially careful evaluation and comparison.
Details of use	Beginning with an initial list of items a group employing the Nominal Group Technique (Part II) would follow these steps: 1. *Discussion of Each Idea for Clarification and Understanding* With items listed on a flipchart or chalkboard, the group members would take each in turn and make certain that there was common agreement and understanding of what the item means and entails.

The aim at this step is to clarify each item so that all group members will be evaluating the same things.

2. *Individual Voting on Priority of Items*

Rather than discussing the list to consensus, a group following the Nominal approach will vote to reduce an initial list to a rank-ordered smaller list that they then may or may not discuss as a group. Suppose a list of fifteen items was generated. This could, for example, be a list of obstacles to the solution of a problem. Each member of the group would rank-order the five obstacles he or she feels to be most important. (The most important obstacle receives a 5, the next most important a 4, and so on. Unranked items, of course, receive a zero or no weighting.)

	Group Members				Totals For Each Item
Items	A	B	C	D	
1					
2	2	1	3	2	8
3					
4		2	2	1	5
5					
6	5	3	5	5	18
7					

Items	Group Members				Totals For Each Item
	A	B	C	D	
8	4	5		3	12
9					
10					
11	3	4	4	4	15
12					
13					
14	1		1		2
15					

In this example the group decision would be a rank-ordering of obstacles with the order 6, 11, 8, 2, 4, 14. The group might decide to take the top three (6, 11, 8) and evaluate and compare them, one with the other, in deciding which they will work on. This example also shows the need to have the higher ranked items receive the higher values, for the unranked items implicitly receive the lowest possible (zero) rankings.

Benefits of use

This procedure can be useful in the Converging phase. It is a quick and easy way to reduce the length of a list. It also gives every member an equal voice in the outcome for the votes count equally. This prevents the strong voice of a few members from dominating the meeting at this point.

Cautions

If used to reduce a list to a manageable size for further discussion, this approach may be a useful aid. But it must be realized that most of the advantages of group interaction are lost. The narrowing here is based on individual votes only and not on idea development. It is possible, however, to use this method as a means of cutting the list to a manageable size and then have the group members interact fully in developing and evaluating the items remaining.

Scanning Strategy (Converging)

The Mixed-Scanning Strategy is useful as an early part of Converging thought development. Alternatives are scanned to eliminate those with "crippling" weaknesses.

Recommended Source	Amitai Etzioni, *The Active Society: A Theory of Societal and Political Processes* (New York: The Free Press, 1968), especially Chapter 12.

When to use

This approach could be considered for possible use to prune a list to a few alternatives.

Details of use

When a group has listed all relevant alternatives that come to mind, including those not usually considered feasible, they can employ the following steps of mixed scanning:

1. *Briefly Examine the Alternatives one by one, rejecting those found to have a "Crippling Objection."*
   Crippling objections could be any of the following:
   a. *Utilitarian Objections.* The means required are simply not available.
   b. *Normative Objections.* The alter-

native would violate the basic values of the decision makers.

c. *Political Objections*. The alternative would violate the basic values or interests of other persons whose support is essential for implementing the decision and making it work.

2. *For the remaining alternatives go back through steps a–c in greater detail.*

3. *Repeat the process again in still greater detail.*

On each scanning of the alternatives the same criteria are applied in increasingly greater detail.

Benefits of use

The scanning strategy could be incorporated into the Problem Management Sequence as presented in Chapter 2. This strategy applies standards or criteria to alternatives by group interaction. The uniqueness of the approach is the series of scannings with increasingly greater detail.

Cautions

Group members must work with special care during the first scanning. Once rejected, an alternative will not have a second chance. So it is essential that items that are dropped early do indeed have crippling weaknesses.

10.13   **CREATING NEW PRODUCTS OR PROCEDURES**

Synectics

A method used by a group to produce a solution to a practical problem by bringing previously unrelated elements together.

Recommended Sources	W. J. J. Gordon, *Synectics: The Development of Creative Capacity* (New York: Harper & Row, Publishers, Inc., 1961) George M. Prince, *The Practice of Creativity* (New York: Harper & Row, Publishers, Inc., 1970) Tudor Rickards, *Problem-solving through Creative Analysis* (New York: John Wiley & Sons, Inc., 1974) S. J. Parnes and H. Harding, eds., *A Source Book for Creative Thinking* (New York: Charles Scribner's Sons, 1962)

When to use

In its detailed form this method is best used by an experienced group of persons representing a variety of professions or hobbies and of a variety of casts of mind—some analytical and some synthetical, some concrete and some abstract. The group should work together over a period of time to use the Synectics process most effectively.

Various parts of the method can be used with profit by any problem-management group at any time.

Details of use

Members with a high diversity of interests and experiences are gathered for a three-hour session.

The leader introduces a general problem. The members discuss randomly, using up their first ideas. Then the leader specifies the problem a bit more, adding facts to narrow the problem down a little. Discussion continues, with the leader assisting the members to:

(1) separate the problem from its customary context so that it can be seen differently, and thus to

become highly involved with it in this new frame;

(2) to avoid settling on the first solution that comes up, rather to work onward to a better one;

(3) to think freely and unguardedly;

(4) to let the problem take over, as it were, and produce solutions on its own.

If the members are not sufficiently speculative in their thinking, the leader may suggest taking an *excursion*, that is, moving over into analogies in order to stimulate new ideas. The leader's questions can invite the members into different kinds of analogies:

personal—"How would one feel if one were a clamp?"

direct —"What is there in nature that would work like this?"

symbolic—"What is something entirely different that somehow makes you think of this?"

fantasy —"If you had all power—over nature and time and all— what would you dream up to manage this?"

When the group seems to be closing in on the problem, the leader describes its exact nature, and the members move in to choose the most useful, appropriate analogy.

Using this chosen analogy as their springboard, members try to work out their idea into the finished product, which must pass tests of novelty, feasibility, and testability.

If the problem attacked by the group is a problem of *things*, one solution is probably enough; if the problem is one of *people*, several solutions should be developed in detail.

Benefits of use   Elements of the Synectics methods can be used by any problem-management group without using the full structure: *feedback* (showing that the listener understands), *paraphrase* (relating to one's own experience), *redefinition* (looking at the problem in a new way), *itemization of response* (recognizing valuable parts of an idea and seeing others as ones to be modified rather than immediately characterizing an idea as satisfactory or unsatisfactory).

Using the full structure with an experienced leader and a trained group can produce and has produced solutions of great originality and high effectiveness, for example, the *"stitching" with steel* metaphor, which brought the closure for vapor-proof suits. (See John W. Lincoln, pp. 274–275 in Parnes and Harding.)

Cautions   Self-taught practitioners of the formal Synectics procedure should probably seek out professional instruction, then build skill through experience.

Do not think that the Synectics group must include a large number of very creative persons; a few are needed but other persons with good ability in listening and supporting can help in the production of significant results.

If the Synectics group is relatively inexperienced in the method, the leader will probably invite only *direct* analogies. On later occasions he or she may introduce the other types.

Checklists

A group uses a detailed series of questions to increase the range of its speculations for improving a product or procedure.

| Recommended Source | Alex Osborn, *Applied Imagination* (New York: Charles Scribner's Sons, 1957) |

When to use

It is appropriate for a group to use the Osborn Checklist when:

1. A plan under serious consideration by the group has possibilities but does not fully fit the purposes and needs of the group in solving the problem.
2. The group wants to give itself an organized experience in creative thinking.

Details of use

The leader opens the session by clarifying the problem for which the members will be trying to create a solution by changing a product or procedure that is before them.

The leader helps the members to familiarize themselves with the important features of the product or procedure that they will be trying to change. When all questions and comments about the product or procedure have been handled in the group (but keeping away from making suggestions for its change), the group is ready to try the checklist.

The leader places the checklist before

them on a flipchart or chalkboard or on individual sheets of paper:

Osborn Checklist

Put To Other Uses?
New ways to use as is? Other uses if modified?

Adapt?
What else is like this? What other idea does this suggest? Does past offer a parallel? What could I copy? Whom could I emulate?

Modify?
New twist? Change meaning, color, motion, sound, odor, form, shape? Other changes?

Magnify?
What to add? More time? Greater frequency? Stronger? Higher? Longer? Thicker? Extra value? Plus ingredient? Duplicate? Multiply? Exaggerate?

Minify?
What to subtract? Smaller? Condensed? Miniature? Lower? Shorter? Lighter? Omit? Streamline? Split up? Understate?

Substitute?
Who else instead? What else instead? Other ingredient? Other material? Other process? Other power? Other place? Other approach? Other tone of voice?

Rearrange?
Interchange components? Other pattern? Other layout? Other sequence? Transpose cause and effect? Change pace? Change schedule?

Reverse?
Transpose positive and negative? How about opposites? Turn it backward? Turn it upside down? Reverse roles? Change shoes? Turn tables?

Combine?
How about a blend, an alloy, an assortment, an ensemble? Combine units? Combine purposes? Combine appeals? Combine ideas?

The leader reads one heading plus the subquestions. He or she encourages suggestions and records those given where all participants can see them. No objections or evaluations are permitted. The leader does this for each of the nine headings. The suggestions make up *one list* of items and are numbered consecutively.

The leader asks each member to select three suggestions to be pursued by the group. Any that is named by more than two persons will remain in the shortened list, but all other suggestions will be kept in reserve so that the members can return to them later if they wish.

The group takes up each of the most favored suggestions in turn, developing it further, then listing advantages and disadvantages it would have if it were applied to the problem.

The group again polls itself to discover the three suggestions that are considered the best. Two are compared carefully as to effectiveness, cost, and promptness, and the better of the two is compared with the third. Having thus determined the "best suggestion," the group picks a "second best."

Benefits of use

1. Although many of the checklist

questions will bring no suggestion from the group, in responding to the whole list ideas will be produced that would not otherwise be thought of.

2. The members will have built a habit of looking together at ideas before they move to compare them; such cooperative consideration builds a basis of mutual effort instead of a feeling of defeatism or advocacy.

Cautions

1. Do not employ the checklist method in cases where the suggested product or procedure is too complex to be kept in mind.

2. Avoid letting the members feel that every subquestion will start a flow of suggestions.

10.14   DEVELOPING AND HANDLING IDEAS

Incremental Strategy

The Incremental Strategy is a quick, easy, and low-risk alternative approach for group decision making.

Recommended Source	David Braybrooke and Charles E. Lindblom, *A Strategy of Decision: Policy Evaluation As a Social Process* (New York: The Free Press, 1963)

When to use

If, in a particular situation, the Problem Management Sequence seems inappropriate because

1. There is too little time available to pursue it,

2. The problem seems hopelessly complex with too many unknown aspects,

3. The problem seems relatively less significant and not demanding of the group's fullest efforts,

4. The participants are not sufficiently skilled to follow the PMS.

Details of use
The Incremental Strategy represents more of an attitude toward problem solving than a series of required steps. Its major goals are few in number.

1. Move *away from the problem* rather than *toward a goal*. The agenda for the Incremental approach in its simplest form would be (a) Describe the problem, (b) List alternative incremental solutions, and (c) Agree upon one. The group attempts to check the symptoms of the problem without identifying and agreeing upon a long-range goal. The viewpoint is that it is easier to "suppress vice than to define virtue."

2. Move in *incremental* (*small*) *steps* away from present actions. Making small changes in the system involves minimal risk for, if the change doesn't work, the group can recommend movement back to the previous policies. If the small step taken seems to help only partially, it is possible to add another small step. A series of small steps can result in significant changes.

Benefits of use
1. This approach takes very little time. It focuses attention upon the symptoms and seeks group consensus on a course of action to follow.

2. It does not ask group members to agree on values, standards, criteria, or on problem causes.

3. It involves minimal risk because the

effects of incremental changes are assessed before further steps are taken.

Cautions

Because this approach takes no long-range vision, the solutions derived from it are usually limited in scope, conservative in direction, and represent only small variations from the status quo. It has, therefore, been termed by some as a strategy of "muddling through."

Ideals Concept

Based upon the view that group decision making is often more of a matter of *designing a solution* rather than of *researching a problem*, this strategy attempts to provide an alternative group approach that is efficient and creative.

Recommended Source	Gerald Nadler, *Work Design: A Systems Concept*, rev. ed. (Homewood, Ill.: Richard D. Irwin, Inc., 1970), especially Chapters 18 and 19.

When to use

When the situation is clear enough to permit solution-mindedness earlier than usual in the group process.

When relatively more time needs to be devoted to the designing of the solution.

Details of use

The ten-step strategy is as follows:

1. *Determine the function.* For just what function or purpose is the solution to be designed? What are the broadest possible purposes underlying the solution?

2. *Develop the ideal system target.* Describe the most ideal goal or target to serve as a guide.

3. *Gather information.* With the spe-

cific and pertinent questions raised by the previous steps in mind, gather only that information that is needed.

4. *Suggest alternatives.* Where information gathered indicates the need, develop alternative solution components that stay as close as possible to the ideal target goal.

5. *Select a workable system.* Select a system by this process that is workable and as close as possible to ideal.

6. *Formulate the system.* Detail the specifications and requirements of the selected plan.

7. *Review the system.* Review the total system or plan as now completely detailed for feasibility and practicality.

8. *Test the system.* Make any pilot tests possible on the various components of the plan.

9. *Install the system.* Make any changes indicated by the preceding step, provide necessary training and follow-up, and prepare to put total plan into operation.

10. *Establish performance and control measures.* Plan for assessment and further modifications to the plan if and when a need to do so becomes apparent.

Modifications

It is possible to use Step I, "Determine the function," alone for a given problem. A group would ask what is the desired function or purpose sought. They would then ask the purpose behind that purpose, which could lead to new insights.

With a continuing probing for deeper

and deeper levels of purpose, as illustrated by this example, the first step of the Ideals approach could be used without following up with the remaining nine steps.

Cautions
Probing for purposes behind purposes behind purposes can lead a group to a useless level of abstraction far from the original problem. This could become time consuming, frustrating, and unproductive.

With this system a group could move too quickly to design a solution without fully understanding all the ramifications of the problem.

Chairman's Privilege

An orderly way to prepare members who hold strong differences of opinion on an important question to come to agreement on that question.

Recommended Source	Irving J. Lee, "Procedure for 'Coercing' Agreement," *Harvard Business Review*, 32 (January–February 1954): 39–45.

When to use
When the group is at odds on a matter of real importance, when the disagreements are bringing strong tension into the group's deliberations, when everything that is said seems to widen the differences, or when people are contradicting each other.

When the group is bogged down with strong disagreement and a method of settling these disagreements both effectively and agreeably is needed.

Details of use
The leader declares a period of "Chairman's Privilege" and asks some proponent of the view that started the

controversy to state or restate the position. The leader explains that the speaker is not to be interrupted with denials or rebuttals; such comments will be ruled "out of order" during this period.

The leader explains that members *can* ask the speaker *questions* but only of three types during this period. Lee gives these examples:

1. *To clarify*

   What did you mean when you said . . .?

   Did you say . . .?

   You said . . .; did you mean . . .?

   (Information is sought here as to what the speaker actually means as distinguished from what the listener may have assumed was meant. Sometimes, as a consequence of such a question, the speakers corrects his or her own earlier statements.)

2. *To examine uniqueness*

   In what way is this different from other situations or proposals we have faced?

   (Information here may reveal whether the opposed parties are reacting on the basis of experiences in the past that differ from the conditions of the present; such a discovery can lay the background for reanalysis in the present.)

3. *To find means of testing*

   Can you tell us any way of testing your assumptions or predictions?

   (Information is sought on a way by which listeners may check these claims with reality, as, for example, by a trial run or a test with a small sample. This type of question is not applicable in a purely theoretical discussion since it presumes a *specific* problem.)

The leader must watch carefully for questions or comments that are evaluative or combative and rule them out of order. Such a strong ruling is highly desirable in the early part of the procedure.

When the opponents of the idea have no more questions, the leader puts aside the "Chairman's Privilege," and the group continues in its regular procedures of problem-management.

Benefits of use

1. Imposition of the questioning rules causes the opponents of the idea to seek understanding rather than give arguments during this preliminary period. Thus, the arguments given later will be based upon a clearer view of the idea.

2. The questioning sometimes causes a proponent to re-examine and modify or withdraw the proposal.

3. Tensions are reduced as members become aware that they are fighting common problems rather than each other.

4. These cooperative efforts toward *understanding* the proposal give the members experience in agreement and make other subsequent agreements more possible.

Cautions

Neither the leader nor the members must deceive themselves into thinking that these efforts at understanding will *eliminate the differences.* But this procedure will have ironed out those false differences that arise from misunderstanding, and prepared them to work together on the real differences that remain.

This method is time consuming and must not be used on trivial differences; it is to be considered a method for emergency use.

The group should have spent a meeting or two in getting to understand the procedure and the reasons for its use. Lee suggests that each member should have a copy of the rules, and that the rules be explained carefully to the members.

The leader must not feel defeated if the group cannot always move quickly to agreement when the members return to the actual discussion; the leader must realize that the "Chairman's Privilege" period will likely have dispelled at least some of the tension and will have set the stage for the most cooperative work possible in that situation.

10.15   BUILDING INVOLVEMENT/UNDERSTANDING

Charrette Planning Process

A procedure for conducting a series of intensive meetings, with carefully prepared resources available, involving participants who will be implementing and who must live with the plans adopted.

Recommended Source	Rodney W. Napier and Matti K. Gershenfeld, *Groups: Theory and Experience* (Boston: Houghton Mifflin Company, 1973), pp. 195–202.

When to use	1. When views of the persons directly involved are most necessary.

2. When information and experts are needed as resources.

3. When deadline pressures are severe.

Details of use

The Charrette steps are as follows:

1. Steering committee prepares for series of intensive Charrette meetings.

   a. Participants are sought from those directly involved with the problem. Wide representation is highly desirable.

   b. Task forces collect a data base about all the significant issues of the problem. This necessary information is available at the later meetings.

   c. Appropriate experts and authorities are selected and arrangements are made to have the needed experts available (*as resource persons only*) at the Charrette meetings.

   d. Necessary supplies and materials—flipcharts, paper, tape recorders, overhead projectors—are planned for so that the work of participants will be facilitated.

2. The series of intensive Charrette meetings is held. A typical case might involve meetings from 9 A.M. to 9 P.M. beginning on Monday and ending on Friday. Participants meet in a large total group (plenary sessions) and often in small subgroups as well. The subgroups often follow steps such as those in the Problem Management Sequence. The agenda is flexible within a tight framework of guidelines and deadlines. The Charrette meetings end

with a public presentation of the conclusions at which the participants have arrived.

Modifications

Charrette is a French word meaning "small cart." Such small carts were used in the 1800s to carry the exercises of architecture students in Paris to school for final evaluation. Students who had not completed their projects jumped on the cart to complete their work before the deadline while the cart rolled along.

A Charrette policy planning process thus uses the same principle of a final effort by the persons involved to meet a deadline. Of course, all materials must be available and at hand if the final push is to have any chance of success.

The idea of the Charrette could be used in a much abbreviated form. For example, a church group might conduct a Charrette with the entire congregation on one or two long evening meetings. It would only be necessary for many of the congregation to take part and for all necessary information, authorities, and materials to be available at the meetings. A predetermined time to conclude and summarize a final report would impose the necessary time pressures on the group.

Benefits of use

1. Leadership can surface and be trained within the Charrette process.
2. Participants are involved directly in making the decisions that will affect them. Their commitment should be enhanced by such participation.

Cautions

As with all group activity, careful

preparation is essential. One observer of several completed Charrettes asserted that "their productivity was more dependent upon the quality of the leadership than any other factor."

Role Playing

A structured experience in which participants play specified roles in a designated situation in order to see how such an event would *feel* to those taking part in it.

Recommended Sources	N. R. F. Maier, A. Solem, and A. Maier, *Supervisory and Executive Development: A Manual for Role Playing* (New York: John Wiley & Sons, Inc., 1957) M. Chester and R. Fox, *Role-Playing Methods in the Classroom* (Chicago: Science Research Associates, Inc., 1966) A. F. Klein, *How to Use Role Playing Effectively* (New York: Association Press, 1959)

When to use	In a training session for leaders, members, employees, management personnel, and the like. In a series of discussion meetings in which TASK problems arise because members do not sense the values in the situation vividly enough or ones in which TEAM problems are preventing satisfactory work on the task. To get a situation more clearly before the participants as a basis for a realistic and vigorous discussion.
Details of use	A facilitator states the problem clearly and specifically, and announces the situation that is to be role-played. The description of the situation must give enough content so that it seems

real to the players but must avoid complexities that would take attention off the problem they are working on.

A facilitator assigns the roles to persons who can play them well and will probably not feel threatened by them. He or she must take care not to overurge anyone to play a role.

The role takers are briefed privately or before the whole group. The briefing must not include structuring exactly what the role takers are going to say and do.

The facilitator gets the role play started and lets it proceed uninterruptedly; or cuts it (calls it to a halt) when

1. enough behavior has occurred to make the point;

2. the group doesn't know how to go on; or

3. the group has carried the situation to a natural ending.

The role players and remainder of the group are engaged in a discussion of the problem under study, with the players themselves commenting first.

The situation may be replayed by the same or different players as the basis for further discussion.

Modifications

1. *Role reversal*

When the role-play situation is a confrontation, it is sometimes valuable to replay the situation with the key roles directly reversed, that is, whoever played the employer now plays the employee and vice versa.

2. *Alter ego*

This modification of role playing is useful when it is important to show the conflicts going on within a person in a situation. One (or more) of the role takers will have two or three others who stand in a semicircle behind the person and respond to represent other specified aspects of his or her personality. Each of the alter egos must understand his or her role and know the purpose of the interaction but speak and act spontaneously. Again, the facilitator must *cut* the action at the appropriate time, and lead the group in the ensuing discussion.

3. *Multiple Role playing*

Maier and Zerfoss have suggested that role playing can work in larger groups if all present are divided into small groups, with each of these subgroups playing out the same role-play situation at the same time. The subgroups are of a size that each member has a specified role. When the facilitator has called the role playing to a close and reassembled the whole group, the reports from the subgroups are used as the basis of the group's discussion.

Benefits of use

1. The experience of discovering how something *feels* helps the group to appreciate factors that might otherwise have remained hidden; in the case of interpersonal relationships (either within the group or outside) feelings can be portrayed and analyzed.

2. The group members can discuss the problem more pointedly because their attention has been centered on the essentials of that problem in a graphic way.

3. Role-play situations are intrinsically interesting; the role players step into a different scene and can lose themselves in portraying their roles.

Cautions

1. The facilitator must make sure that all the role players move into the role play at the same time; if one or more of the players is talking as himself or herself whereas others have already taken on their roles, the opening is ragged and the spirit of the activity is lost.

2. The facilitator needs to "cut" the role play in the time that exciting work is still being done by the players; if discussion is started after the role play has lost its "steam," the group's interaction starts at a lower level of interested participation than was necessary.

3. Avoid the overuse of role playing. Keep it for problems in human relations.

4. Allow enough time for the discussion afterward so that the role playing will give real insight on the problem.

Buzz (or Huddle) Groups

Division of the discussion group into a number of smaller groups working concurrently, with members given a decision to make or suggestions to be assembled within a stated time; the members are expected to report their findings to the larger group at the end of the allotted time.

Recommended Source	George M. Beal, Joe M. Bohlen, and J. Neil Raudabaugh, *Leadership and Dynamic Group Action* (Ames, Iowa: The Iowa State University Press, 1962), pp. 191–196.

When to use	When wide participation is needed in a group that is too large to make vigorous interchange possible or likely.
	In a group as small as 12, if deep involvement and clear understanding are essential to the group task.
Details of use	The leader presents a clear, limited, and specific task to the whole group; tells how long the subgroups will have to accomplish this task; and asks that someone be ready to report from each subgroup at the close of the "buzz" period.
	The leader suggests how the group is to be divided, or actually makes the division. Division of the group may be by choice (find five other people to work with), or by designation (three persons in alternate rows turn around to the three behind them; or count off so that there will be six one's to sit together, six two's, and so on).
	The leader tells when the allotted time is up, calls the whole group together again, and obtains reports from all the groups. The leader lists the suggestions on the board, asking each group to present its list even if it has duplications of items that are already listed.
Benefits of use	Use of the buzz group technique tends to get more personal involvement in the topic, and more participation by those who are less likely to speak in the larger group.
	The buzz session allows each member to ask questions and voice interpretations.
	Members are more likely to speak up in the larger group, once they have talked in the smaller groups.

	Used during a long problem-management meeting, the buzz session provides variety and renews participation.
Cautions	Avoid use of buzz groups for purposes where detailed, careful weighing of ideas is needed.
	Be sure to tell the members the question and the time allotment before assigning the people to the groups; and stay within the time limitation announced.
	Make the shift into buzz groups physically easy and quickly accomplished.

10.16   HANDLING CONFLICTS

System 4T

System 4 Total model organization (System 4T) is intended to help improve productivity by managing conflict in large organizations.

| Recommended Source | Rensis Likert and Jane Gibson Likert, *New Ways of Managing Conflict* (New York: McGraw-Hill Book Company, 1976). |

| When to use | When there is a desire to reduce conflict and improve productivity in organizations. |
| Details of use | A brief description by Likert of the System 4 organization is as follows: |

> The human organization of a System 4 firm is made up of interlocking work groups with a high degree of group loyalty among the members and favorable attitudes and trust among peers, superiors, and subordinates. Consideration for others and relatively high levels of skill in personal interaction, group problem solving, and other group func-

tions also are present. These skills permit effective participation in decisions on common problems. Participation is used, for example, to establish organizational objectives which are a satisfactory integration of the needs and desires of all the members of the organization and of persons functionally related to it. Members of the organization are highly motivated to achieve the organization's goals. High levels of reciprocal influence occur, and high levels of total coordinated influence are achieved and effective. There is a flow from one part of the organization to another of all the relevant information important for each decision and action. The leadership in the organization has developed a highly effective social system for interaction, problem solving, mutual influence, and organizational achievement. This leadership is technically competent and holds high performance goals.

A quantitative description of an organization's *interaction-influence network* is completed for this analysis. A full description of the method is available in the recommended source and in Rensis Likert, *New Patterns of Management* (New York: McGraw-Hill, Inc., 1961). Part of the analysis looks to the manner in which the organization copes with conflict. The most desirable (System 4) procedure would include the following:

1. The opposing parties try to understand the points of view, needs, objectives, and preferred solutions of the others.

2. Each party seeks to use joint problem solving to develop innovative solutions that are satisfactory to both parties.

3. Communication between the op-

posing parties is open, candid, and unguarded.

4. Opposing parties try not to deceive but rather to inform the other correctly.

5. There are many open channels of communication for the flow of information and influence between virtually all leaders and many of the rank and file.

6. The channels for the flow of interaction and influence between opposing parties are highly effective.

7. Extensive efforts are made to build, rather than to restrict channels of communication.

8. Innovative, mutually acceptable solutions are sought without each party striving to impose a preferred solution on the other.

9. Each party strives to discover and state explicitly the integrating goals and common interests they share.

10. Each party can state clearly the points of view, needs, objectives, and preferred solution of the others.

11. Opposing parties seek mutually satisfactory solutions *with* the other party rather than try to gain power *over* the other party.

12. Creative problem solving using consensus is attempted.

13. A third party is often used to assist opposing parties find mutually acceptable solutions.

14. When solutions are reached, opposing parties give overt and

covert acceptance and seek full implementation.

15. Solutions reached result in favorable cooperative attitudes among the opposing parties.

Benefits of use

Groups moving toward System 4T approaches have experienced improvements in productivity ranging from 10 to 40 per cent. The system seems applicable to a wide range of organizations, such as schools, hospitals, and governmental agencies.

Integrative Decision Making

Integration Decision Making (IDM) is an analytical approach intended to help in the assessment and management of conflict.

Recommended Source	Alan C. Filley, *Interpersonal Conflict Resolution* (Glenview, Ill.: Scott, Foresman and Company, 1975).

When to use

When the aim is to analyze and manage conflict in a specific organizational or interpersonal setting.

Details of use

The stages of IDM are outlined as follows by Filley:

1. *Review and adjustment of relational conditions*—the comparison of the objective conditions in which parties are related with conditions known to promote cooperation rather than conflict and the possible adjustment of those conditions.

2. *Review and adjustment of perceptions*—the use of reality testing to determine facts regarding the parties.

3. *Review and adjustment of attitudes*—the use of reality testing of feelings and attitudes between the parties.

4. *Problem definitions*—the mutual determination of the depersonalized problem.

5. *Search for solutions*—the nonjudgmental generation of possible solutions to the problem.

6. *Consensus decision*—the evaluation of alternative solutions and the agreement on a single solution.

The first three stages call for a depersonalizing of the situation and ask the parties in conflict to assess their adjustment to one another and to the reality of the situation. The latter three stages turn to the problem definition and solution.

Six useful guidelines proposed for problem definitions are

1. Conduct a problem analysis to determine the basic issues.

2. Avoid stating goals in the form of individual priorities.

3. State the problem as a goal or as an obstacle rather than as a solution.

4. Identify obstacles to goal attainment.

5. Depersonalize the problem.

6. Separate the process of problem definition from the search for solutions and the evaluation of alternatives.

Guidelines for the evaluation of possible solutions and consensus upon the best solution are

1. The range of solutions should be narrowed.

2. Solutions should be evaluated in terms of both their quality and acceptability.

3. Avoid the requirement that parties justify their personal feelings or preferences.

4. The parties should agree on criteria for evaluation that may be dealt with individually and specifically.

5. Consensus is most likely where there is little expression of self-oriented needs.

6. Parties should periodically review members' evaluations of alternatives.

7. Parties should avoid using agreement mechanisms that prevent open discussion of alternatives.

8. Where the evaluation problem can be divided into parts, it may be helpful to establish smaller subgroups to deal with the parts.

9. Feelings of conflict should be resolved before continuing with the evaluation process.

Benefits of use

The IDM approach can help parties in conflict seek new alternatives that may be satisfying to the values of both, thus creating a win-win situation in conflict management.

10.17   PLANNING IMPLEMENTATION

Scanning Strategy

The Mixed-Scanning Strategy is useful for planning the steps by which to implement a chosen group solution.

Recommended Source	Amitai Etzioni, *The Active Society: A Theory of Societal and Political Processes* (New York: The Free Press, 1968), especially Chapter 12.

When to use

Once a group has arrived at a single chosen solution, the members must consider whether they will be responsible for planning the implementation steps for that solution.

Details of use

The following are the planning steps for implementation with mixed scanning:

1. *When possible, fragment the implementation into several serial steps.*

   It will be easier to monitor and evaluate the progress of implementation when it can be viewed in smaller steps rather than as one total act.

2. *When possible, divide the commitment to implement into several serial steps.*

   This is a political rule. If persons must give full and complete commitment to a proposed project before it is even started, there may be greater hesitation about beginning. It, therefore, may be useful to require only partial commitment prior to instituting a program with increasing support required in successive stages.

3. *When possible, divide the commitment of assets into several serial steps and maintain a strategic reserve.*

   This is simply the old rule that we should not put all our eggs in one basket.

4. *If possible, arrange implementation so that costly and less reversible decisions will appear later in the process than those that are more reversible and less costly.*

   Again, this step is calculated to prevent waste if the plan fails or is dropped along the line as it is being put into action.

5. *Provide a time schedule for additional collection and processing of information so that information will be available at key turning points between steps of the implementation schedule.*

This is to have the needed information available so group members can assess whether to move from one step to the next, whether to modify the steps of implementation, or whether to abandon the program.

Benefits of use

This approach to program implementation requires that implementation be accomplished as a *planned series* of *small steps*. This procedure permits continuous evaluation and opportunity for modification as the plan is installed. It also helps to control risk and expense for the installing group is never required to risk all, or expend all, of its available resources.

PERT—PROGRAM EVALUATION AND REVIEW TECHNIQUE

With a proposed group solution at hand, PERT provides a method with which a group can develop a workable operations plan.

Recommended Sources	Gerald M. Phillips, *Communication and the Small Group* (Indianapolis: The Bobbs-Merrill Co., Inc., 1966), especially pages 88–108. William Emory and Powell Niland, *Making Management Decisions* (Boston: Houghton Mifflin Co., 1966), especially pages 183–202.

When to use

When the group arrives at a program to be implemented, PERT will provide some mathematical estimate of the time required and the probabilities of meeting deadlines. It helps to detect probable bottlenecks, allocate personnel appropriately, estimate reasonable deadlines, and determine necessary starting times. A computer may be needed for *very* complex operations, but pencil and paper tabulations will suffice for most problems.

Details of use

The major steps of PERT planning are as follows:

1. *Stipulate the final event* or occurrence marking the completion of the program. The group is asked here to stipulate an act that, when it has occurred, will signal the end of its work.

2. *List events* that must happen before the final event can happen. What steps or events must occur before the final event?

3. *Determine necessary, immediate, and preceding events.* This step calls for an *ordering* of the *necessary* events over time: which events are necessary to which other events.

4. *Develop a diagram* showing the connection of events. The ordering of events could be laid out as follows:

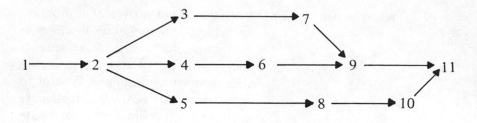

5. *Enumerate activities* to take place between events. What must happen between each two of the steps?

6. *Estimate the times required.* The group attempts to estimate some likely time requirements for the activities occurring between each two events. Three estimates are made: the most optimistic; the most likely; and the most pessimistic.

7. *Compare expected completion times with necessary completion time.* Detailed formulas are provided in the recommended sources for making these comparisons.

8. *Calculate the probabilities* of satisfactory completion based on the "critical path" from start to final event. The critical path is that single series of connected events from first to last with the least total slack time.

Modifications   The PERT approach could be followed less formally with simple commonsense estimates of timing and likelihood of meeting deadlines. The analysis of steps to be taken and timing needed on each in diagram form would still be helpful. A related "network technique"—the Critical Path Method (CPM)—is also presented in the Emory and Niland source.

Benefits of use

The use of PERT alerts a group to the need to think of all necessary steps so that no essential is left out (completeness), to consider the time relationships so that steps are taken in the correct order (sequencing), and to take into account the varying time demands and flexibilities for each step along the way (coordination) so that all separate aspects converge at the correct time.

Cautions

1. There is always a chance the group will overlook some essential steps.
2. Time estimates can only be estimates and may be in error.
3. Uncertainties and the unexpected will often occur in the installation of any new program despite careful use of the PERT technique.

10.2 **OTHER SOURCES (SHELF BOOKS)**

10.21 Making Management Decisions

Authors: William Emory and Powell Niland
Publication Data: Boston: Houghton Mifflin Company, 1968

> Professors Emory and Niland have taught graduate courses in the Business Administration School, Washington University, for many years. William Emory has conducted many seminars for business executives on creativity in management. Powell Niland specializes in production planning, scheduling, and inventory; he is a well-known scholar in operations research and quantitative methods for the analysis of management problems.

Emory and Niland use their first five chapters to explain clearly and interestingly the steps in decision making; they use the next eight chapters to introduce the reader to the newer quantitative techniques that give help in analyzing decision possibilities; they conclude with an integrative chapter that takes up problems in applying these mathematical techniques to decision making in business.

It is noteworthy that these authors have written their book for readers who have had no mathematical training beyond a beginning course in algebra; they do not use matrix algebra or calculus, nor do they assume a knowledge of statistics or probability. Thus, *Making Management Decisions* is useful not only for business administration classes and in management training programs but also for any person who wants to lay sturdy groundwork for better decision making by self-instruction.

Although the book is geared to decision making by an *individual*, many of its concepts and techniques are also extremely useful in *group* decision making.

William Emory and Powell Niland, *Making Management Decisions*, 1968

Contents

10.22 Decision Making: A Psychological Analysis of Conflict, Choice, and Commitment

Authors: Irving L. Janis and Leon Mann
Publication Data: New York: The Free Press, 1977

> Irving L. Janis is professor of Psychology at Yale University. He has published significant research reports on persuasion and attitude change as part of the Yale program initiated by Professor Carl Hovland. He has investigated decision making in foreign policy decision groups and his observations were presented in his widely cited *Victims of Groupthink*. Leon Mann received his Ph.D. from Yale and is now professor of Psychology at Flinders University of South Australia.

Decision Making: A Psychological Analysis of Conflict, Choice, and Commitment focuses on patterns of decision making employed by individuals working alone or in groups. The concerns range from very individual and personal decisions, such as with matters of a career choice, to the broadest of problems of governmental foreign policy questions. The aim is to explicate the "causes and consequences of patterns of decision making that interfere with vigilant information processing [the ideal]" and to present techniques which can be practically useful to help individuals avoid defective patterns of coping with problem situations.

The authors integrate a wide body of research findings in their attempt here to present a comprehensive theoretical framework explaining the ways in which we cope with everyday demands for decision making.

Decision Making places an emphasis upon task and upon the strategies for managing decisions. It also emphasizes the emotional element in recognizing the decision maker as a person under stress, with internal doubts and conflicts. Finally, it emphasizes the practical, and presents analytical schemes for assessing the conditions needed for arriving at stable decisions.

Irving L. Janis and Leon Mann, *Decision Making*: *A Psychological Analysis of Conflict, Choice, and Commitment*, 1977

Contents

10.23 **The Rational Manager: A Systematic Approach to Problem Solving and Decision Making**

Authors: Charles H. Kepner and Benjamin B. Tregoe
Publication Data: New York: McGraw-Hill Book Company, 1965

> Kepner is a social psychologist whose research work centers on decision-making processes, large-scale organizations, and small group processes. Tregoe is a sociologist with special interest in human behavior. Both worked at the Rand Corporation, and then formed Kepner-Tregoe and Associates, Inc., in 1958 to hold training courses for executives, managers, and supervisors.

The Rational Manager sets forth the concepts that form the basis of their training methods, a three-part process: study of the concepts, intensive practice of the concepts in a simulated situation, and feedback sessions on actual performance.

Defining a problem as "a deviation from a standard of performance," Kepner and Tregoe emphasize the careful determination of the most likely cause. They follow this problem analysis step with the decision-making step, in which they set objectives, seek out alternatives, test each in relation to the others against the *musts* and the *wants*, decide upon the best, and then explore for future possible adverse consequences. These steps are made very clear with excellent diagrams, and their whole treatment of steps is made realistic with detailed examples. Although concerned with business matters, this book gives valuable explanations for any group concerned with managing problems.

Charles H. Kepner and Benjamin B. Tregoe, *The Rational Manager*: *A Systematic Approach to Problem Solving and Decision Making*, 1965

Contents

10.24 New Ways of Managing Conflict

Author: Rensis Likert and Jane G. Likert
Publication Data: New York: McGraw-Hill Book Company,
1976

R. Likert is emeritus professor of psychology and sociology at the University of Michigan. He directed the morale division of the U.S. Strategic Bombing Survey at the Survey Research Center, University of Michigan, 1946–49. He served as director of the Institute for Social Research 1949–70, and is now director emeritus. Likert received the Outstanding Achievement Award of the American Association for Public Opinion Research in 1973.

J. Likert is a writer and editor, a former teacher, and former vice-president of the League of Women Voters. Jane Likert is project director and counselor at the Center for Continuing Education of Women, University of Michigan.

New Ways of Managing Conflict brings major research findings on organizational effectiveness to the problem of managing conflict. The authors recommend System 4 T as the best method now available for handling substantive conflict, including those more difficult situations in which affective conflict is happening at the same time. They state: "The basic proposition of this volume . . . is that the management of conflict can be improved substantially by replacing the traditional structure and processes of organizations with those based on a more effective social system, namely System 4 T." The heart of this recommended system is its emphasis upon the use of relationships and processes that allow people to have an appropriate influence in the decisions that affect them.

Whether a problem-solving group is or is not tied into an organizational structure, the principles of motivation, interpersonal relations, and decision making that are explained in this book are valuable for the group's leader and members.

Rensis Likert and Jane G. Likert, *New Ways of Managing Conflict*, 1976

Contents

10.25 Problem-Solving Discussions and Conferences: Leadership Methods and Skills

Author: Norman R. F. Maier
Publication Data: New York: McGraw-Hill Book Company, 1963

Norman Maier is professor of Psychology at the University of Michigan, having joined the faculty there in 1931. His research publications and participation in executive training programs have made him known throughout the world. Dr. Maier acted as consultant for the European Productivity Agency for the year 1959–60, visiting management training centers in eight countries. Dr. Maier received the Society of Humanistic Management award in 1974. His *Who's Who* citation ends with this sentence in italics: *Research motivated by curiosity leads to the greatest satisfaction because it keeps the mind open and the search never ends.*

Out of a lifetime of experience, research, and careful thought on the problems of leading discussions effectively, Maier has written this highly useful book. Its special helpfulness lies in these factors: the analyses and recommendations are realistic and down-to-earth; examples of groups from his own workshops and reports of research from his own laboratories are used to undergird his explanations; the ideas are made clear without recourse to jargon.

The four central chapters move sequentially from "locating the problem" to "reaching the decision" with sound suggestions for the leader at each step of his work. Throughout the book, Maier urges the leader to develop skill in differentiating those problems in the group that arise from feelings from those that arise from facts, and handling each appropriately. He sees both *high quality* in decisions made and *high acceptance* of these decisions as needed for effective group decisions. Maier thinks that these skill requirements will not be difficult for a leader to learn once he or she has broken with old habits that interfere with success.

Another useful volume by Maier, bringing together the details and results of studies on individual and group problem solving that he has conducted and sponsored over the past fifteen years, is *Problem Solving and Creativity in Individuals and Groups* (Belmont, Calif.: Brooks/Cole Publishing Company, 1970).

Norman R. F. Maier, *Problem-Solving Discussions and Conferences: Leadership Methods and Skills*, 1963

Contents

10.26 The Practice of Creativity: A Manual for Dynamic Group Problem Solving

Author: George M. Prince
Publication Data: New York: Harper & Row, Publishers, Inc., 1970

> George Prince worked with W. J. J. Gordon for seven years, the last five of which were in the company they established, Synectics Inc., an organization for invention, research on the invention processes, and teaching. His Problem Laboratories have drawn many clients, from whom Prince learned and for whom his methods have been highly influential.

Prince urges the substitution of Synectics methods for the traditional methods of committee work. He sees the Synectics methods as having two key approaches: fostering normal means of speculating and disciplining responses to speculation so that it is not choked off. Prince offers well-reasoned suggestions to leaders in releasing the creativity of the participants. Chief among his recommendations is the extended use of *analogies*.

The Practice of Creativity has numerous transcripts of discussions that illustrate the points Prince is making; for example, the elusive mechanism called Force Fit in the Synectics vocabulary is very effectively set forth. It would be possible to use the Synectics methods from the explanations and the examples given in this book; furthermore, the excellent advice on good listening and on leadership would help in any problem-solving group.

George M. Prince, *The Practice of Creativity: A Manual for Dynamic Group Problem Solving*, 1970

Contents

10.27 **Problem-solving Through Creative Analysis**

Author: Tudor Rickards
Publication Data: New York: John Wiley & Sons, 1974

Tudor Rickards is a Research Fellow at Manchester (England) Business School. He lectures, conducts research, and directs workshops and seminars on creative and problem-solving techniques. He started the INCA (Innovation through Creative Analysis) research program at Manchester Business School; he is founder and executive director of INCA (Research Consultants) Ltd. Dr. Rickards lectures on creativity, problem solving, and innovation to managers and students throughout Europe, and has prepared program manuals for many industrial companies.

Problem-solving Through Creative Analysis has two basic parts, one explaining techniques for creative problem solving and the other presenting case studies showing the use of these techniques.

Rickards recommends "keeping the creative and analytical stages separate but interacting." His explanations of procedures for producing new ideas by individuals and in groups are clear, detailed, and well illustrated with graphs. He presents twenty-three case studies of actual situations, ranging from a search for new business opportunities to creativity in a biological research project. Rickards suggests that the reader try out the methods suggested and check his or her results with those reported in the second part of the book.

Though written for managers, the book presents a basic philosophy that would help a leader in any task group and techniques that could be adapted to any situation. This book is very well written: it explains steps of a process carefully enough so that they can be tried by the reader; it reports actual case studies with sufficient detail to be understood but with admirable omission of unnecessary particulars.

Tudor Rickards, *Problem-solving Through Creative Analysis,*
1974

Contents

PART ONE   THE TECHNIQUES OF CREATIVE ANALYSIS

PART TWO   CREATIVE ANALYSIS IN PRACTICE

PART THREE   APPENDICES AND BIBLIOGRAPHY

10.28 Group Dynamics: The Psychology of Small Group Behavior

Author: Marvin E. Shaw
Publication Data: New York: McGraw-Hill Book Company,
2d ed., 1976

> Marvin Shaw is professor of Psychology at the University of Florida.
> He has served as consultant for several major American manufac-
> turing firms. Shaw's research interests are in small group processes,
> attitudes, and personal perception.

Group Dynamics: The Psychology of Small Group Behavior
provides an overview of research findings on small groups.
Written primarily for the college student at the senior or beginning graduate student level who has some awareness of social
psychology, the emphasis is upon the results of controlled
"empirical studies rather than on the theoretical or logical
analysis of groups." Each chapter concludes with a list of
"plausible hypotheses" derived from studies reported on in
that chapter.

For the person interested in group discussion in community
settings, several of these research findings have implications
that should be considered for a better understanding of the
group process. For example:

> The best evidence suggests that members of mixed-sex groups
> are more concerned about interpersonal relations and hence
> conform more than members of same-sex groups, who are
> more concerned with the task at hand. (p. 235)

The practical implications of these findings, however, are not
developed by Shaw and this work remains for the reader. The
conclusion cited could, for example, have significance for
League of Women Voters unit meetings if men were to become
active members. But the what-of-its and how-to-do-its are not
available in this source. And a few of the reported findings are
somewhat obvious and offer little useful information to the
person involved in community efforts. One example would be:

> The high-power person has greater influence upon the group
> than low-power group members. (p. 290)

Most of the findings listed, however, would be of interest to
group participants.

Similar, but much more detailed, information from social
psychological research is available for the interested reader in
the following:

Gardner Lindzey and Elliot Aronson, eds., *The Handbook of Social Psychology*, 2d ed. (Reading, Mass.: Addison-Wesley Publishing Company, 1969), especially Volume IV, *Group Psychology and Phenomena of Interaction*, Chapters 1–4 inclusive.

Marvin E. Shaw, *Group Dynamics*: *The Psychology of Small Group Behavior, 2d ed.,* 1976

Contents

PART ONE INTRODUCTION

PART TWO THE ORIGIN OF GROUPS

PART THREE THE INTERACTION PROCESS

PART FOUR GROUPS IN ACTION

PART FIVE EPILOGUE

10.29 Handbook of Leadership: A Survey of Theory and Research

Author: Ralph M. Stogdill
Publication Data: New York: The Free Press, 1974

> Ralph M. Stogdill is professor of Management Sciences and Psychology at the Ohio State University. He has served as staff psychologist for the Ohio Bureau of Juvenile Research, and was associate director of the Ohio State Leadership Studies from 1946–1954. He has written widely on leadership in business and large organizations.

Handbook of Leadership: A Survey of Theory and Research is an organized inventory of the published research findings on leadership. It is a source book for "the serious reader who wants to know what results have been obtained, who did the research, and what conclusions can be drawn from the accumulated evidence."

Going beyond a mere listing of three thousand individual studies of leadership, Professor Stogdill has provided an organization and synthesis of these findings that make the large body of material comprehensible and useful. Professor Stogdill's practical experience with real groups in field settings has tempered his synthesis so that this book will be useful to other people than researchers on leadership. It would be useful on the shelf of any person who is seriously interested in the functions and operations of leadership in practical settings such as in community and work groups.

Ralph M. Stogdill, *Handbook of Leadership*: *A Survey of Theory and Research*, 1974

Contents

PART ONE   LEADERSHIP THEORY

PART TWO   LEADER PERSONALITY AND BEHAVIOR

PART THREE   LEADERSHIP STABILITY AND CHANGE

INDEX OF NAMES

323

INDEX OF SUBJECTS

Scanning strategy, 24, 54n, 268–269, 296–298
Second solution, 41, 42, 76–77, 251n, 275
Size of dicussion groups, 120–121
Socio-emotional leader, 84–86
Sound thinking, 17–23
Sources, tests of, 18
Spiral movement, 195
Status, problem of, 66–67, 134–135
Storming, 161–162, 197
Substitutability, 232, 234
Summary, 94–95, 217–218, 247
Supportive/defensive climates, 146, 186–188
Supportiveness, 69–72
Symptoms, as used in PMS
  of problem, 27, 28–29, 43–44
  untouched, 27, 41–42, 51
Synectics, 39, 173–174, 269–273, 312–313
Synthesis
  different from summary, 217–218
  first synthesis a test-point, 154
  in coverging phase, 216–221
  of nature and urgency of problem, as used in PMS, 27, 30–31, 46
System 4T, 291–294
Systematic thinking, 23–52

Tangents, 96, 105n, 185
Task-orientation, 93–99
Task work
  conflict management in, 203–204
  converging phase in, 205–225
  diverging phase in, 168–180, 198
  leader's preparation for, 130–132
  sound thinking, 17–23

systematic thinking, 23–52
Teamness, aspects of, 226–234
Team-orientation, 99–103
Team work
  conflict management in, 204–205
  converging phase in, 226–236
  diverging phase in, 180–189, 198
  leader's preparation for, 132–135
  nature of, 12–13
  necessity of shared goal, 56–57
  necessity of shared procedure, 57–58
  risks in, 75–79
Tentativeness, 71, 100, 101, 193, 224–225
Test-points for leader, 150–156
  after first member contribution, 151–153
  after invitation-to-begin, 150–151
  first member challenge, 155
  first synthesis, 154
Thought-line
  building, 96–99
  managing, 94–96
Thought-stoppers, 62
Trigger sessions, 260
Trust, 229

Underlying conditions, as used in PMS, 27, 31–32, 46–47
Untouched symptoms, as used in PMS, 27, 41–42, 51
Utility, as used in PMS, 27, 34, 40, 48, 50

Volunteering, 59–64, 101

We-ness, 71, 102, 226–232